TOO YOUNG

FOR A

FORGETTABLE WAR

Second Edition

WILLIAM EDWARD ALLI

TOO YOUNG FOR A FORGETTABLE WAR

PUBLISHING HISTORY

First Edition

March 3, 2009

Copyright 2009 by William Edward Alli

(Published by Xlibris Corporation)

<>

Second Edition

Copyright 2012 by William Edward Alli

2803 Baker Lane, Bowie Maryland 20715

ISBN-10: 147929280X   ISBN-13: 9781479292806

This book is dedicated

to all who served,

regardless of age,

in any war

however forgettable

. . . and to their families.

INTRODUCTION

Wars are worth reading about, if for no other reason than trying to figure out how to avoid them. War lays bare human evil, making nobler those actions that counter it through bravery, compassion, and endurance.

This book is my memoir of the Korean War; I served 12-and-a-half months on the east-central front, March 1951 to March 1952. It describes my activities before, during, and a little bit after that war.

It is my first literary endeavor and I have been mindful of the ancient ideals of the artist: to write about "the good, the true, and the beautiful." But war is not a pretty business and my basic aim of presenting "truth" (or at least historical accuracy) has led me to also note the bad, the false, and the ugly.

I and my fellow Marines were part of the First Marine Division. That broad context shaped Marine lives, and deaths, in easily demarcated phases: the Pusan Perimeter defense, the Inch'ŏn Landing, the Battle of Seoul, the Chosin Reservoir Campaign, the Pohang Guerilla Hunt, Operations Killer and Ripper, the Punchbowl battles, and the Battles of the Outposts on the western front.

The bulk of my narrative about Korea deals with the phases I personally experienced. However, I have included brief descriptions of the others, out of respect for my fellow Marines.

Along with a goodly portion of my own introspections, the book deals with individuals, their interactions, and the settings in which they operated. With only a few exceptions, I use our real names. One exception is in profiling the experiences of the returned veterans (Chapter 36), where I supplied fictional names to avoid betraying any confidences or embarrassing anyone, including myself. In other chapters you will find fictional names for persons involved in one occurrence of moral turpitude and two probable incidents of war crimes. I employed such names to avoid slandering or stigmatizing the people involved.

Writing a memoir makes us relive the past. I was able to do it, though not without tears. And when I contacted fellow veterans for

4

information and corroboration, I felt the conflict between their desire to be helpful and their instincts to avoid bad memories. A Marine friend of mine wrote:

> "I really do not want to go back in memory to the actual fighting . . . I have found peace and great happiness in where I am right now in life. I don't want to go back to memories and sorrow and the pain of losing comrades whom I loved."

Others had a variety of reactions, most reflecting amazement that they had survived the war. From a few I was delighted to hear their warmer memories – ones that recall youthful days and foolish ways.

Aging and its toll on their memory increasingly hinders too many veterans from delving into their personal history in Korea. So, in a race against time, I have pressed them to share with me some "final" words about the war's impact on their lives.

This undertaking has forced me to explore deep recesses of my own mind, and put words to paper. As I wrote, I felt the fabric of my story becoming more clearly and tightly interwoven with theirs. Before the curtain drops on my life's story, I seem to be bringing a finale to that long journey that began when I was too young a warrior caught up too far away in a forgettable war.

MAP OF KOREA

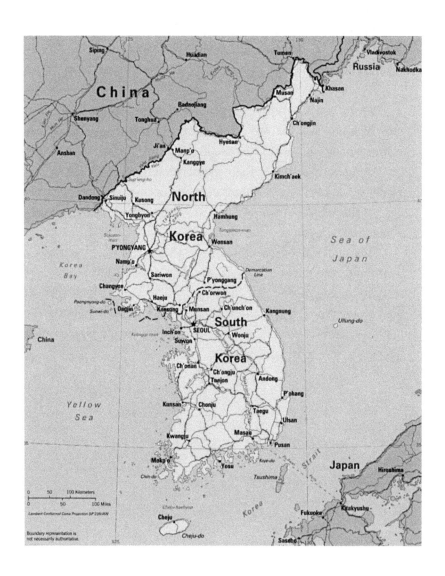

CONTENTS

Title Page 1

Publishing History 2

Dedication 3

Introduction 4

Map of Korea 6

Notes on Language (English, Korean, Turkish) 10

Abbreviations 13

Text Grafix List 16

P o e m 21

BACKMATTER

Notes on Language

English

Marine Lingo: US Air Force General Curtis E. LeMay (1906-1990) allegedly and derisively referred to Marines as a bunch of soldiers in funny uniforms running around trying to talk like sailors. He was wrong about the uniforms but right about the talking. The talking uses "sea service terminology" which grows out of Marine Corps tradition and history.

Marines also use many terms that are the same as those of the U.S. Army. One difference is that the Marine Regiments are called by the designation of "Marines." Thus, the 1st Marine Regiment is called "The 1st Marines," the Fifth is "The 5th Marines," The other two in the 1st Marine Division were "The 7th Marines" and "The 11th Marines." The entire Division was referred to as the "1st MarDiv FMF," identifying it as part of the "Fleet Marine Force."

In all cases I capitalize the noun "Marine," when applied to any member of the United States Marine Corps.

WARNING! This book makes minimal use of modernized spelling. It involves substantially fewer than 1% of the book's 100,000+ words. Now that English has become the world's link language, and we are in an age of widely used electronic devices which feature texting, we may be able to start a process of making English spelling easier for everybody. That's why I have devized INCOMENG: International Combined Modern English.

International Combined Modern English: INCOMENG (or In-CoMEng) is a system for promoting use of English thru-out the world. It is inspired by the reform efforts of Americans Noah Webster and President Theodore Roosevelt, as well as British writer George Bernard Shaw. The idea behind it is to make English easier for our children, foreigners, and maybe even ourselves.

It is composed of words and abbreviations from different Englishes. The criterion is foneticism and simplicity, for example "grey," from British English, "dialog" from American English, and "foto" and "nite," from various commercial sources. My Saxonist leanings have led me to resurrect (or invent) some regularized past tenses - for example, I use "fitted" as the past tense for "fit, " by analogy with "benefitted, outfitted," etc.

Because the old English gutturals (velar fricatives) died centuries ago, there's really no need to keep writing their "gh" symbols in "although, thorough, though, through," or anywhere else. For these I use: altho, thoro, tho, thru.

When Greek words were brought into English, "ph" was used to represent the single Greek "F" (ϕ). INCOMENG uses an "F." An example is "foto."

INCOMENG uses "native" names. Thus, Anatolia, Izmir, and Turkey are rendered as "Anadolu, İzmir, and Turkiye," except for quotations by other authors. For Anatolian, I use "Anadoluan."

In addition to those listed above, this book includes the following INCOMENG terms: alfabet, amfibious, atmosfere, bibliografic, bibliografy, burocracy, dolfin, nefew, nite, Osmanli, semafore, synagog, telegrafic, thru-out, tyfoon,

Other: Dates are shown in the format used by the U.S. Marine Corps, and other departments of the U.S. Navy. The U.S. Postal Service uses a 5-digit basic area code (ZIP) after a 2-letter abbreviation, without the period (full stop) mark, for all States, territories, and the District of Columbia. The USPS also recommends that the comma be omitted between the city (or other locale) name and the 2-digit abbreviation. I follow their rules, hence: Bowie MD 20715 and Washington DC 20036.

While American English often uses "goodby," I use the older form "goodbye," which gives a clearer view of its original form: *God be with ye.* I like the sentiment in that old phrase.

Korean

Romanization: Thru-out the book, I use the McCune-Reischauer (M-R) system of Romanizing Korean words. It is the best system I know of. M-R is used by the U.S. Library of Congress. However, instead of writing one vowel as "ae", I use the ligature "æ" from the International Phonetic Alphabet.

An exception to the M-R spelling is allowed for the capital city of Seoul; M-R would have rendered it as "Sŏul."

Redundancy: The English terms for "mountain, province," and "river" are used when translating Korean names, even when those Korean names embody the equivalent descriptors as suffixes, namely: -san, -do, and -gang. Thus, /soyang-gang/ means the Soyang River, but reading it as Soyanggang River is, literally, the "Soyang-river River." Americans are already familiar with the name *Rio Grande River.* Since "rio" is Spanish for "river," we are saying the equivalent of the "River Grande River."

Turkish

Spelling: Turkish spelling is used for all Turkish words except "lahmacun." That word is Anglicized to *lahmajun*, because the Turkish "c" has the "j" sound in English. In the Index, the diacritical Turkish letters are shown, but alfabetized according to closest English order.

These letters, uppercase/lowercase, are: Ç/ç, Ğ/ğ, I/ı, İ/i, Ö/ö, Ş/ş, Ü/ü.

12

ABBREVIATIONS
Military Terms & Bibliografical References(*)

1stLt - First Lieutenant

1stMARDIV - First Marine Division

2ndLt - Second Lieutenant

AIK - Alexander I. Solzhenitsyn*

AIT - advanced infantry training

AT - anti-tank

AKD - A. K. Dawson*

AM - Andrew Mango*

BAR - Browning Automatic Rifle

BAS - Battalion Aid Station

BFA - Burton F. Anderson*

BGen - Brigadier General

C&L - Charette & Lanham*

C&N - Chenoweth & Nihart*

Capt - Captain

CC - Commemoration Committee

CCF - Chinese Communist Forces

CD - Celal Dora*

Co - Company

Col - Colonel

Cpl - Corporal

CVL - Carl V. Lamb*

D&E - Death & Exile* (JM)

DANFS - Dictionary of American Naval Fighting Ships*

DH - David Halberstam*

DI - Drill Instructor

DLG - Deborah L. Grassman*

DS& - David Satcher & others*

EHG - Ernest H. Giusti*

EHS - Edwin Howard Simmons*

EO - Executive Order

FA - Frank Ahmed*

FAO - Forward Artillery Observer

FBN - F. Brooke Nihart*

FMF - Fleet Marine Force

FPO - Fleet Post Office

Gen - General

GL - Guenter Lewy*

GVS - George Van Sant*

H&S - Headquarters and Services

HHJ - Helen Hunt Jackson*

HMG – heavy machine-gun

13

HQ - headquarters

H&S – Headquarters & Services

HWB - H. W. Brands*

InCoMEng - International Combined Modern English

ID – Infantry Division

Inf - Infantry

ISBN - International Standard Book Number

JHJ - John H. Johnstone*

JM - Justin McCarthy*

JS - John Schneider*

KIA - Killed in Action

KSC - Korean Service Corps

KW - Korean War

KWCC – Korean War Commemoration Committee

KWVA - Korean War Veterans Association

KWVM - Korean War Veterans Monument

LMG - light machine-gun

LN - Louise Nalbandian*

LST - Landing Ship Tank

LtCol - Lieutenant Colonel

LtGen - Lieutenant General

MajGen - Major General

Major – Major

MAW – Marine Aircraft Wing

MBR - Matthew B. Ridgway*

MC - Marty Callaghan*

MCRD - Marine Corps Recruit Depot

MG - Machine-Gun

MKÖ - Mim Kemal Öke*

MLR - Main Line of Resistance

MLS - Mary Lee Settle*

MOS - Military Occupational Specialty

MSR - Main Supply Route

NAS - Naval Air Station

NATO - North Atlantic Treaty Organization

NDS - Nazım Dündar Sayılan*

NKPA - North Korean People's Army

OD - Officer of the Day

OT - Ottoman Turks* (JM)

PFC - Private First Class

PNM - Paul N. McCloskey*

POW - Prisoner of War

PUC - Presidential Unit Citation

Pvt - Private

PX - Post Exchange

RCT - Regimental Combat Team

Regt - Regiment

ROK - Republic of Korea

ROTC - Reserve Officer Training Corps

S&K - Stanford J. Shaw & Ezel Kural*

Sgt - Sergeant SSgt - Staff Sergeant

TIA - Turk in America* (JM)

TSgt - Technical Sergeant; "Gunny" in the Marines

UNMCK - United Nations Memorial Cemetery Korea

USMCR - U.S. Marine Corps Reserve USO - United Services Organization

USMKW - U.S. Marines in the Korean War*

USMOK - U.S. Marine Operations in Korea*

USNS - U.S. Naval Ship

VADM – Vice-Admiral

VAN - Van* (JM)

VD - venereal disease

VMO - Marine Observation Squadron

WEA - William Edward Alli*

WHD - William H. Dabney*

WSB - Wilburt S. Brown

ZE - Zeki Ehlioğlu*

TEXT GRAFIX LIST

2-1: *USS Missouri* firing main guns. A salvo of 16-inch shells from turret # 2 bombarding Chongjin, North Korea, October 1950. The foto is a color-tinted version of a black & white original. The original photograph is Photo #: 80-G-421049. Official U.S. Navy Photograph, U.S. National Archives.

3-1: Corsairs preparing to launch from carrier. Vought F4U-4B "Corsair" Fighters, of Fighter Squadrons 113 and 114 (VF-113 & VF-114) prepare for launching aboard USS Philippine Sea (CV-47), during strikes on North Korean targets, October 1950. Official U.S. Navy Photograph, National Archives.

4-1: Brodhead Naval Armory entrance. The R. Thornton Brodhead Naval Armory is located at 7600 E. Jefferson Ave., Detroit, at the Northwest boundary of Gabriel Richard Park, just east of the MacArthur Bridge (usually called the Belle Isle Bridge). Construction completed in 1930. Added to National Register of Historic Places in 1994 (Bldg. No. 94000662). It served as an armory for the USMCR until 2005, when the Marines relocated to Selfridge AFB in Mt. Clemens. It was turned over to the Government of the City of Detroit and has been reportedly described as in "deplorable condition," as is most of the city of Detroit.

4-2: Naval Armory drill deck

5-1: WEA at Camp Pendleton 6SEP1950

8-1: Boot Camp Graduation, December 1950. WEA (center). Searles (top left) .(See Appendix B-1 for full platoon foto)

8-2: A studio portrait in Detroit

8-3: With Baba, homeleave December 1950

10-1: Col. Lewis B. Puller

11-1: USNS General G. M. Randall

11-2: Inchŏn: Lt Baldomero Lopez leads his Marines over the seawall. Soon, while wounded, he sacrifices his life on an enemy grenade to protect his men.

12-1: At Inchŏn: (L to R), Gen. MacArthur, driver, Gen. Almond, Marine Gen. O.P. Smith, VAdm Struble.

12-2: Smoke from Corsairs bombing in support of Marines at Chosin

12-3: Chinese prisoners near Chosin

12-4: Marines on the Funchinlin Road near the Chosin Reservoir

12-5: Marine dead at Kot'o-ri

12-6: Marines boarding evacuation ship at Hŭngnam. The USS Bayfield (APA-33) transported then to Pusan. Marine at left is carrying a Soviet Mosin-Nagant carbine in addition to his M1. Official U.S. Navy Photograph, from the collections of the Naval Historical Center.

12-7: Refugees aboard ship. Some of the 14,000 Korean refugees crowded on board the SS Meredith Victory in December 1950, as she transported them from Hŭngnam to South Korea. U.S. Naval History & Heritage Command Photograph.

14-1: Chief

14-2: Jackman

16-1: Gen Matthew B. Ridgway

16-2: Insignia of the First Marine Aircraft Wing

17-1: Whitten, Lohr and WEA on a battle-scarred hill

18-1: US Army 155 mm gun firing at nite

19-1: Charles Lundeen

19-2: Bob Davis

19-3: My trophy NKPA leather belt

19-4: "Burp Gun" Bill (WEA)

20-1: Medical Aid Station with helicopter landing pad. A Bell evacuation helicopter of Marine Observation Squadron 6, carrying casualties from the front lines, lands at "A" Medical Company of the First Marine Division in 1950. Naval corpsmen stand by with stretcher to unload the wounded men from helicopter "pods" and rush them to the operating and hospital tents in the background. (U.S. Department of Defense)

22-1: Randy & WEA carrying hot food

22-2: Bourassa, WEA, and Mancha swimming

22-3: WEA and "Sam"

22-4: WEA ready to go on a training exercize

22-5: Our MG Section

22-6: Cleaning my rifle

22-7: Official Division patch

22-8: Unauthorized patch

22-9: Detroiters Charlie Ford and Manert Kennedy

23-1: Tex in an amphibious truck

24-1: 25TH Inf. Div. "Tropic Lightning" shoulder patch

24-2: USMC 1912 cavalry holster

24-3: NATO Supreme Commander Gen. Eisenhower visiting Istanbul.

24-4: Turks sailing to Korea from İzmir 1952

24-5: Gen. Walker awarding medals to Turks

24-6: Mortar training of Turks

24-7: Turkish Army national patch

24-8: Turkish North Star Brigade shoulder patch

25.1: WEA practicing haircutting

26-1: 2dLt Ernest Brydon

27-1: Lt Col Nihart's forward command post just behind the summit of Hill 749 soon after its seizure. Handwriting at top: "My base"

27-2: At right, LtCol Nihart in his HQ.

28-1: Before Hill 749

28-2: After Hill 749

28-3: In reserve soon after 749, left to right: LtCol Nihart, Maj Jack

Lanigan (Exec. Officer), Maj Carl Walker (Supply Officer)

28-4: Dog Co., 3rd Platoon men after 749, left to rt.: Sgt Bill Rogers, PFC Jack Underwood, 2dLt John Gearhart

28-5: WEA and Vic Knabel in H&S Company

29-1: WEA with Lt Dong

29-2: WEA with KSC officers

30-1: WEA with Sgt Farquhar and a KSC worker

31-1: Leaving Korea with two buddies

31-2: George Coyle

32-1: United Nations flag

32-2: Ceremony for fallen Americans and Turks at future UNMCK

32-3: USNS Gen. W.H. Gordon

32-4: USS Gordon docking at San Francisco wharf

34-1: Grosse Ile NAS Marines; Sgt Tanner at right

34-2: Grosse Ile Naval Air Station; WEA front row, center

34-3: WEA in Argentia Newfoundland on return from trip to Turkiye

34-4: SSgt WEA & TSgt plus Major at Selfridge AFB

34-5: Memphis TN - USAFR 2dLt WEA, Officer-of-the-Day during annual encampment

35-1: Manert Kennedy and WEA, Seoul Korea June 2000

35-2: WEA with General Bowser

37-1: John Alli, 28 February 1996.

38-1: KWVM 1995 Dedication patch.

38-2: KWVA circular patch.

38-3: 2/1's logo

38-4:: MG-Unit, right side.

38-5: MG-Unit, left side.

39-1: Logo, DOD 50th Anniversary of the KWCC. The circular object is a 3-lobe Tæguk. The Tæguk is a traditional symbol used (with two lobes) on the flag of the Republic of South Korea (ROK). The KW50 Tæguk's red and white striped lobe represents the United States; the dark blue lobe represents South Korea; the light blue lobe with 22 gold stars represents these UN countries involved in defending South Korea: Australia, Belgium, Canada, Colombia, Denmark*, Ethiopia, France, Greece, India*, Italy* (UN membership - 1955), Luxembourg, Netherlands, New Zealand, Norway*, Philippines, South Africa, South Korea (UN membership - 1991), Sweden*, Thailand, Turkiye, United Kingdom, United States.

Note: An asterisk (*) indicates medical personnel only; no combat forces were provided.

39-2: American & Turkish Veterans Association patch.

39-3: U.S. postage stamp issued 27 July 2003, 50TH Anniversary of Korean War Armistice. The stamp features the foto "Real Life" by John W Alli. "This issue honors the Korean War Veterans Memorial, which recognizes the sacrifices of those who served during that conflict. Authorized by law in 1986, the Memorial was dedicated by Pres.Clinton and ROK Pres. Kim Young Sam in 1995. The stamp features John W. Alli's photograph of the memorial's 19 stainless-steel statues. Its issuance coincides with the 50th anniversary of the armistice that ended the hostilities." Source: USA PHILATELIC, The Official Source For Stamp Enthusiasts; USPS; Spring 2004, Vol. 9, No. 1, page 14.

39-4. John Alli autografing stamps for former 2/1 Marine Ray Gramkow, 27 July 2003.

39-5: Turkish Brigade veterans with BGen. Orhan Uğurluoğlu; 27 July 2003.

40-1: President Franklin Delano Roosevelt.

40-2: USMC Eagle, Globe, & Anchor.

The Mountain

The mountain may be high,

but it is still below Heaven.

Climb and climb again.

Everyone can reach the summit.

Only the man who never tried

Insists the mountain is high.

Yang Sa-Ŏn (1517-84)

Chapter 1
PILGRIMAGE TO THE STEEL TEMPLE

AT LAST, MY PILGRIMAGE to the Temple was reaching its climactic moment. I would soon be entering it.

The Temple projected superhuman strength. Thirty years earlier I had witnessed its fearful power to bring death to enemies. It also brought hope to its people.

On this day in September 1981 the scene was emerging from morning fog and overcast. Now the details of its lethal architecture were unmistakable; it was a temple of steel. It was America's mighty battleship, the USS *Missouri*, peacefully docked at Naval Station Bremerton in Washington State.

I would not be boarding her as a crewmember, because neither the *Missouri* nor I were on active duty. Rather, she was open to visitors as a floating museum. But I was more than a mere visitor; I was a pilgrim seeking to relive a memory anchored in 1951, when I was in a soon-to-be-forgotten war, and too young to understand much about what was going on around me.

My thoughts and actions would be appropriate – a feeling of awe and respect, and an awareness that in some way my life had been affected, for the good, and I needed to offer up my thankfulness to something far more powerful than I.

Reverence cannot be rushed. So, before going up her gangplank, I needed to behold the *Missouri*'s towering presence, from bow to stern, from waterline to top of the main mast. But most of my attention was on her huge gun turrets, because these had displayed her awesome power, when I looked down at her from my foxhole, high in the North Korean mountains that overlook the shores of the Sea of Japan.

An obeisance was in order. It required that I go to the main deck portside, amidship. There I stood, facing the bow, with my legs spread out slightly, as one does for stability at sea – part of having

22

"sea legs."

Then I slowly tilted my head up about 45 degrees as I turned it to look over my left shoulder. In a worshipful mood, I thought, *If a crew member had been doing this, one brightening morning in May 1951, he would be looking up at the mountains where I was looking down.*

That act closed a ring of memory and I could depart, thankful to have survived the war and make this pilgrimage.

Chapter 2
DESTRUCTION FROM OFFSHORE

AT THE END OF ANOTHER GRUELING DAY of climbing up and down the hills and mountains of Kangwŏndo province on Korea's east-central front, Dog Company, 2nd Battalion, 1st Marines stopped its advance and got ready to dig foxholes for the night. It was the end of just another day for us in late May 1951. We'd had no contact with the North Koreans or Chinese since Ch'unch'ŏn, during their violent April offensive.

We were a little closer to twilight than usual and exhausted as usual as my buddy Randy and I took turns hacking away the soil until we got a hole deep enough to hold us for the night. During this strenuous effort, I paid no attention to my dimming surroundings, other than to note that we were amid mountains. I didn't turn my gaze toward any distant horizon; after all, nearly every gaze those days took in just more mountainous terrain. Besides, it was getting dark and all I wanted to do was sleep.

Ah, restful sleep, blissful sleep, nature's heavenly gift to its creatures to compensate for their toils, a wonderful part of life. Sleep is something that really shouldn't be confused with death which, paired with life, is a totality, I believe.

But on the front line, a night's sleep is cruelly invaded when you are woken up to crawl out of your sleeping bag and take your turn on watch, usually peering into the darkness, ready to shoot at anything coming at you – or looking like it is coming at you. A 50-percent watch means you will go thru the night, alternating with one other person, usually for one or two hours at a time. Because each Marine was paired with a buddy, every foxhole had at least one person on guard at all times during the night. A 25-percent watch means that the four men in two adjacent foxholes take turns of one hour on watch and three hours sleeping. A 100-percent watch means no one sleeps.

24

I was at the end of the final watch, the one that would end around sunrise. I could see nothing as the blackness gave way to a wall of grey fog. I strained my ears to catch any possible sound, but there was none. Slowly, dark spots appeared, suspended in the air in front of me, but I could not determine what they were or how far away.

The spots were changing shape from some kind of fuzzy circles into some kind of fuzzy triangles. Gradually the triangles got darker and bigger, expanding downward. Soon, I recognized these triangles as mountaintops; they looked like islands in a sea of clouds. These "islands" got bigger; it seemed as if they were growing out of the still sea of clouds. Then I realized that the clouds were dropping and gradually becoming confined to covering valleys below, before disappearing completely.

I looked to my right, eastward, hoping to see a sunrise but could not see much light. Then at a slight downward angle, I saw an expanse of water stretching to the horizon. It was the Sea of Japan. I gaped at it; I had not seen the ocean since arriving in Pusan two months ago as part of the 6th Replacement Draft of the 1st Marine Division.

I had never been at such a high altitude on land. It was exciting, and a little scary.

Then I noticed something small: a grey, narrow oval on the sea's surface, its axis parallel to the coast. I strained to identify it and suddenly a bright yellow circular flash blotted it out of sight. Right after the flash, the grey object reappeared. Then at about forty-five degrees to the left of the grey object, but higher up on the mountain tops along the seacoast, a black cloud suddenly appeared, then soon dissipated, revealing part of the mountaintop gone. The yellow flash and the eruption had been silent.

Next I heard the distant explosion, followed by a prolonged whine and then another explosion that ended the whine. I had just witnessed the USS *Missouri* firing a one-ton, sixteen-inch shell at North Korean positions on the Tæbæk coastal range. And because I was so far away, I had not heard the sound of the gunfire, the shell's travel, nor the exploding target, until after I had witnessed the sight.

¶After that spectacle, I felt that neither my rifle, my grenades,

Fig. 2-1: USS Missouri firing main guns

nor even the two cans of machine-gun ammunition that I carried for our unit's .30 caliber Browning M1919A4, air-cooled, light machine-gun, were of much significance. They were for small-scale warfare; the *Missouri* had just shown me what a *big* weapon could do.

Randy was beginning to stir from his deep sleep. *Had he heard the bombardment?*

I said, "Randy, look at that!"

"What is it?" he asked.

"You gotta see this, Randy. Look over there!" And I pointed. "It looks like a battleship, or at least it's big enough to be one, I think. And look, it's firing again, and you can't hear the noise, but just wait and the sound'll come."

Sure enough, it was the same thing; without sound the big gun had fired with a bright flash and after several seconds, the top of a mountain blew up. Next came the sound of the firing, that rising and then falling whine, and another explosion. I was exhilarated and had no pity for the people getting bombarded; they were the Communist enemy. Years later, as I became more aware of the pitilessness of war and the helplessness of humanity caught up in the control (and maybe deceptive allure) of Communism, my feelings would change and my heart would soften.

Up and down the line of foxholes the guys were all awake now, looking at the naval bombardment. Some were talking excitedly; some were gaping. I wondered how many of us would ever get up close to a battleship, assuming we survived this war.

Chapter 3
DEATH IN THE VALLEY

WE GOT WORD that we would be staying here one more night, one day of relief from climbing up and down hills and having to dig another foxhole. We had a saying that Korea was the only place in the world where the slopes went uphill both ways. Now we would have time to write letters, maybe read some book or other, and walk around the area, staying on the back slope, below the ridge line, and not straying beyond some fifty yards or so from our holes. A few of us took naps to catch up on what sleep we had lost from being on watch during the night.

Naturally, the first thing was to have some breakfast. This meant heating up a can of food from our C-rations. We used jellied fuel (Sterno) in stoves that we had made out of the tin cans that had held the crackers, powdered coffee, and other dry foods from our daily box of rations. We heated water in our aluminum canteen cups and added the powdered coffee to it, always taking the first sip carefully; it was too easy to get our lips burned on the metal rim.

Some guys removed the liner and heated water in their helmets, in order to have a sponge bath, or maybe wash some socks or underwear. Nobody could take a full shower until a month or two later, when we were pulled back off the front line into a reserve area that had access to shower tents set up by the supply people.

About midmorning, somebody called out, "Hey! What's that?" We looked where he was pointing, north, toward enemy territory. There was a road in the valley paralleling the coastal range that we had just seen getting pounded by the USS *Missouri*.

At first we saw nothing odd. Then we saw two lines of enemy troops heading south, toward our lines. They were hardly more than specks, marching in two parallel columns, each close to a side of the road. It was in broad daylight, something the Communist forces never did, we thought, because our planes would be able to hit them.

28

A few of us instinctively crouched down, so we would not be seen by the enemy. Then it occurred to me that it was not likely that we could be seen by them, unless they had powerful binoculars and were assiduously looking for us to be around here. But then they wouldn't be on the open road either.

Soon the Forward Artillery Observer (FAO) team came run-

Fig. 3-1: Corsairs preparing to launch from carrier

ning up. The lieutenant had some binoculars with him. His assistant, a noncom, was saddled with a big, heavy radio, the antenna sticking up about three feet and swaying each time he moved.

The officer pulled a folded map out of his jacket pocket and quickly studied it, alternating with peering at the target thru his binoculars. Then he took the phone from the radioman and began giving information to the artillery batteries a couple of miles behind us. Meanwhile, the enemy troops continued their march toward our lines, oblivious to their impending rendezvous with explosive death.

After a few minutes, we heard a barrage from our artillery and the whoosh of artillery shells flying over us, toward the enemy. Then we saw – and quickly heard – the explosive impact of shells raining down on the enemy, blanketing the road and terrain on each side of it. The enemy columns scattered, fleeing up toward the slopes on both sides of the valley where there were draws that might provide some protection. More shells were fired after the lieutenant radioed info about where the first shells had struck and where the enemy had fled.

The Forward Air Controller arrived, consulted with the FAO, and began talking on his radioman's phone while referring to a map. Twenty or thirty minutes later, a couple of Marine Corsairs arrived over the valley. They sounded like they were strafing as they crisscrossed the area on each side of the road and then flew back to their aircraft carrier.

I wonder what my fellow Marines carry in their memory about that day. We had been merely spectators, watching mass destruction from a safe and lofty perch. *And what about memories in the minds of the surviving enemy soldiers? How would they remember any part of this?*

I could not be sure of the sentiments of the "enemy," even when I visited Beijing's Military Museum, nearly fifty years later. I walked thru the galleries, with their unpleasant fotos of captured or dead Americans, Turks, and other fighting men of our United Nations forces. Patriotism and triumphalism were the themes of the displays. However, by then, I had no enmity in my heart. My own sons had already been in a war and, perhaps, I had evolved enough to understand, if not accept, the ways of our violent species: Man.

I cannot believe that all Chinese war veterans, especially those who went on to raise sons, are devoid of sentiments like mine.

Chapter 4
OUT OF THE ARMORY

HOW DID I GET INVOLVED in this war? I guess it all started on 12 January 1950, less than two weeks after I turned eighteen, when I joined the United States Marine Corps Reserve (USMCR), the 17th Infantry Battalion, stationed at Detroit's Brodhead Naval Armory. I signed enlistment papers for four years' service.

Fig. 4-1: Brodhead Naval Armory entrance

It seemed almost inconsequential at the time. At Cass Technical High School a fellow student who had already joined the Reserves told me the advantages: we would get uniforms and be paid money to go to the armory each Thursday evening for two hours. Also with pay, we would have sort of a vacation, two weeks training at an annual summer encampment on some Marine Corps base, either in California or North Carolina. I never heard mention of the likelihood of being quickly called up for full-time duty in a national emergency, such as a war. I don't recall any God-talk, nor spiels about the country, freedom, democracy, etc.

Nevertheless, patriotism resided inside us, a product of World War II, when we knew all the Armed Forces' official songs and helped out in neighborhood collections of scrap metal, newspapers, and used cooking oil. We bought ten-cent savings stamps and pasted them into little grid books until they accumulated to $18.75 and were traded in for a war bond redeemable for $25.00 in ten years. We had been propagandized by the media to hate "the Japs" and the Nazis but pay little or no attention to the Italians.

I may have been tilted in favor of the Marines by some reading I had done in high school. It was a library book about the battles of Marines in World War II.

When I signed up and took the oath, I still had five months left before high-school graduation. The Cold War was the current war and I guessed that my only involvement in the military would be if I were drafted, which might be a year after my graduation.

I actually enjoyed going to the armory for training in my uniform and marching in close-order drill, something I had done in my Boy Scout troop and later in high school ROTC. I learned a little bit about U.S. Marine Corps history and even something about the armory's history; it still had wall frescoes from the Depression, when President Franklin Delano Roosevelt's WPA hired unemployed painters to decorate public buildings.

In peacetime the armory was used for auto shows, exhibits and political events, as well as dances and boxing matches, tho not necessarily all at the same time. Also, it was the facility for training Marine Reservists living in the metropolitan Detroit area.

As to war, the armory was a site for training active-duty person-nel and facilitating the send-off of sailors and Marines of "the greatest generation," the ones who had come thru the Great Depres-sion and went out to battle in the Atlantic and Pacific theaters during World War II, America's biggest war, a just war, a war worthy of remembering.

When I joined the unit, some of the reservists were World War II veterans. Each of these sur-vivors had a bundle of experiences they could tell, but I

Fig. 4-2: Naval Armory drill deck

32

never got a chance to talk to any of them about "the War." At the time I was unaware that too many of America's veterans could not break thru an inner wall of anguish, fear, or anger to talk to anybody about their war. It was not the scope of that big war that had shaped their lives, as much as what happened directly to each of them. Because all experiences are local, the vastness of the war was hardly relevant to them, except to provide great variety in the geographical settings for their particular journeys thru hell.

¶On 31 August 1950, the armory witnessed another send-off to war. This time those being sent off included both members of the greatest generation and their younger brothers. The war was in Korea, much smaller than WWII. But it met the test of violence and death that could provide veterans with enough experiences to affect them for the rest of their lives, even if they went too young, like me, and the war would soon be forgotten by most Americans.

I looked good, like the rest of the 17th Infantry Battalion, dressed in starched-cotton khaki uniforms, arrayed in neat formation on the indoor drill deck. At eighteen-and-a-half years old, just out of high school, I was most certainly the kind of young man who was eligible for going off to war.

Buses were parked outside to take us and our stuffed seabags to the train station. Also outside were our friends and kinfolk, waiting to see us, embrace us, and embarrass us with their unnecessary emotionalism, all in front of our fellow Marines and too many other people.

"We are giving you men one hour to visit with your folks, before boarding your assigned buses," said the sergeant. So we broke formation and streamed out of the building to the adjacent grassy field that slopes gently down to the Detroit River. There's where the Battalion's 25 officers, 459 Marine enlisted, and 10 Naval enlisted (medical corpsmen), in four companies (Headquarters, Able, Baker, and Charlie, my company) would say our farewells.

It's nice outdoors, not too hot for comfort, and the place is

33

swarming. Where's my family? I don't seem to recognize anybody, just the other guys in uniform, it seems. Gosh! There's a lot of unhappy faces, especially on the older women, the mothers. But where are my folks?

Finally, I see them. My dear mom is easier to see in a crowd because she is tall, five-foot nine, not all that rare for a woman from the hills of eastern Tennessee. Standing next to her is my dad, at five-foot six or seven, and there's my sister Geri, only fifteen years old, standing next to my mother's sister, Rose, who is about my dad's height.

As I reach them, my mother, Aunt Rose, and sister Geri, embrace me and, surprisingly, so does my dad. They have forced-smiles on their faces. I don't understand why they can't just be upbeat. Our outfit is only going to California, and they'll see me again in a few months.

They ask me some questions, but I don't have much information to give them. "We're going to take the train to Camp Pendleton in California and get trained," I say. "After that I'll come back on leave before reporting for duty at my next assignment."

I don't mention Korea, wherever that is. "And after I'm all done with my Marine Corps service, I'll come back home and get a part-time job, so I can go to college and get a good job, as an engineer, like you want, Dad." That was the kind of job my father had in mind each time he warned me to be sure to get a college education and not be an unskilled worker on some factory's assembly line, like him and too many of his fellow Turkish immigrants.

Soon it's time to get on the bus. A final hug, and I hear them utter a few words like, "be sure to write home." Mom is teary-eyed and, to my amazement, so is my father. I don't think I've ever seen my father with tears in his eyes (this man who was usually so stoic most of the times I'd seen him). Aunt Rose and Geri are no longer trying to look cheerful.

Because boys pattern themselves so much after their fathers, I find it difficult, maybe tabu, to admit how negative an image so

34

many people had of him. Harshness and sternness seemed more natural to him, along with a temper, frequently short and occasionally uncontrollable. He was not totally without humor, but he didn't do any joking himself. He was the opposite of my mother and sometimes mocked her joviality. Maybe it was because of the hard life he faced in a factory city like Detroit, frustrated by his illiteracy, paltry English, heavy foreign accent and lack of any technical skills (or satisfactory social skills). It's easy to understand why Mom had divorced him when I was eight years old.

My mother had also had a hard life as a girl in Tennessee with a father abandoning the family, and the children being farmed out to live as overworked servants with other farm families. But her temperament was far more loving and generous; I benefited from her good nature and conscientious efforts to be a single parent breadwinner for me and my sister.

But teary-eyed? That I had never seen. Was he thinking of his older brother, Bekir Çavuş (Sergeant Bekir), who had died in the first World War, God knows where, as the Osmanli (Ottoman) Empire's armies were bled to death in Caucasia, Palestine, Suriya, Iraq, Gelibolu, etc.? Some of these soldiers had even been "lent" by the Osmanli dictators to their German allies for fighting against the Russians in Poland! The actions of the Osmanli rulers bear out the wisdom of the ancient saying that "those whom the gods would destroy they first make insane."

Years later I learned that in the spring of 1913 my father had been in uniform, with the other young Osmanli soldiers, saying goodbye to their families in Harput Turkiye, a town just a few miles east of the Fırat (Euphrates) River in eastern Anadolu. They marched off to replace a garrison in Yemen, wherever that was. They couldn't know they would be annihilated in World War I.

I did not know what fate awaited me. If I died, would Detroiters lament me saying "Billy, we hardly knew you?"

After I came back from Korea, Dad would come around to telling me how he and his army buddy, Veysi Kaplan, avoided going to

35

Yemen by deserting their military unit, switching to civilian clothes, buying passage on a ship in İstanbul, and coming to America in April 1913. Naturally, the survival of these two soldiers could not diminish the grief of Harput's families for all their other lost sons. To this day, they sing a sad folk song that can bring tears to my eyes:

> There is no cloud in the air. What is that smoke? There is no corpse in the neighborhood. What is that wailing? Those Yemen regions are so forbidding. Ah, over there is Yemen; its 'flower' is fenugreek. Those who go never return. Why? That place is *Housh;* its roads are arduous. Those who go never return. What's happening? [ZE 17; WEA translation]

If I were a father and had a son ordered to war, how emotional would I be? Forty years later, during America's first Gulf war, I would be distressed to find out. As a young man in Korea, I could often shut down my feelings about my precarious existence. As a middle-aged father, I could not shut down my mind to the dangerous conditions for my Marine sons, John and Rob, in the Persian Gulf.

I suffered nine months of unrelievable anxiety, a middle-aged man, crying at times with my wife (at home) or weeping alone in my office at work, constantly remembering them by looking over my desk and seeing the Marine Corps flag that I had deliberately hung on the partition wall straight ahead.

The man who cannot cry is not fully human and not fit to be a parent!

Chapter 5
CALIFORNIA, HERE I COME

THE BUSES ARE FULL now and we pull away from the armory parking area, waving goodbye. Soon we are passing by the end of the bridge that connects the mainland to Belle Isle. But we are not going to that pleasant island in the Detroit River between the United States and Canada.

The bridge reminds me of the happiest single day of my unhappy teenage years. I went swimming at the Belle Isle Beach with my father and Uncle Ahmet Ali. Good-natured Uncle Ahmet was not a blood relative. He was from İzmir in western Turkiye; nearly all the other pre-World War I Turkish immigrants were from around Harput in eastern Anadolu, like my dad.

What a nice day it was, interacting with them, having their attention, feeling their affection, plus even picking up a little bit of Turkish and, of course, splashing about on the shore of the Detroit River on a warm summer day. It's so important for a boy to have a father spend time with him, and learn to be a man. Because of my parents' divorce in 1940, he was not around me much. Usually I had to go to the Turkish coffeehouses to visit with him, and maybe eat together at one of the nearby Turkish or Greek restaurants.

Naturally, I had already decided that when I grew up I was not going to be poor, uneducated, quick-tempered, or crude like my dad. And when I married I would never divorce; and as a father I would love my children, as I definitely knew he loved me.

We board the buses and head westward on Jefferson Avenue, passing neighborhoods I had known most of my life. I try hard to avoid thinking too much about those younger years.

When the buses arrive at the Fort Wayne Railroad Station on Detroit's lower west side, we get off and go thru the lobby, onto the platforms, and board the trains. Some of the families have managed to come to the lobby and wave goodbye to their Marines. My folks are not there. Even tho Aunt Rose could have driven them there, they may have felt that one goodbye was enough. Why start the tears again?

It was just like a scene from a Hollywood movie about World War II, but there was no background music and I was not a spectator; I was part of it: lots of guys in uniform, getting on trains, and a few civilians waving goodbye. I knew that those movies also contained scenes showing people engaged in military combat. And I realized that I was no longer too young to be in such a setting; I would not be safely observing but instead dangerously participating, as did generations before me, like generations after me, maybe including my own sons, if I survive this war and have any.

How many eighteen-year-old sons of poor families could expect to travel in style, as I was now doing, with waiters serving me fine meals in the dining car of the train and porters preparing a pull-down bed for me in the Pullman car each night. I was certainly going off to war in style.

What goes thru the mind of an eighteen-year-old who is "going off to war"? Not much, at least not much in the case of my immature mind.

I had been clueless about what was happening to the Marines deployed to a seemingly doomed southeastern corner of Korea while I was nonchalantly experiencing August in Detroit. I was going to join them, yet I made no effort to read the newspapers or otherwise find out what was happening in Korea. Did I believe that "what you don't know can't hurt you"?

And what good would it have been to my morale if I knew any of the details of the desperate fighting by our 1st Provisional Marine Brigade in the Pusan Perimeter? What combination of fear and misconception would swirl around in my brain and ruin my final weeks of summer?

¶Our combatants in Korea now included 6,534 Marines – infantry (the 5th Marines), artillery (the 11th Marines), aviation, and support units – thrown into that sixty-mile wide and 90-mile long strip of land called the Pusan Perimeter – a place that seemed like a Dunkirk-in-waiting. Our men had been stripped from the 1st Marine Division at Camp Pendleton, which was my next destination.

Their arrival brought the total strength of the U.S. 8th Army to 92,000 men facing the North Korean People's Army (NKPA) of 70,000. But the numbers were deceptive; the 8th Army had to man the entire perimeter, while the NKPA had the option of concentrating its forces for a breakthru at any selected point.

The Marine Commander, BGen Edward A. Craig, had quickly assessed the situation:

> The Pusan perimeter is like a weakened dike and we will be used to plug holes in it as they open. We are a brigade, a fire brigade. It will be costly fighting against a numerically superior enemy. [USMKW 8]

During its one-month of furious combat, the "fire brigade" traveled some 380 miles and mounted three difficult operations, much of it in debilitating summer heat and humidity. New to the NKPA were the swift, low-altitude air attacks by carrier-based Marine planes. The strikes caused havoc among the Communists, whether they were attacking UN forces or trying to defend themselves. Our Marines had prevented the potential catastrophe of an enemy breakthru. Our men had their casualties but the NKPA had suffered five times as many.

For that heroic service the Brigade received the Distinguished Unit Citation. The award is now named the Presidential Unit Citation.

¶As our train rolled westward I was blessedly unaware of the "big picture." The Department of Defense (DOD) was cranking up America's war machine. A giant race was under way and I didn't know about it. South Korea was the prize and the issue at stake was whether the NKPA could conquer it before the United States could marshal enough military strength to stop them. If South Korea fell,

39

Japan might become neutralist and become unstable. It could affect our occupation status and jeopardize our military bases there. Sending the Brigade, all of them "regulars" on active duty, was just a desperate emergency response.

From all around the United States, Marine Corps Reservists like me had been converging on Camp Pendleton. From 20 July to 11 September, nearly 32,000 enlisted and almost 2,000 officers were activated. Our 17th Infantry Battalion was among the last to report for duty. [EHG 27-40]

About two weeks before our 17th infantry Battalion arrived at camp Pendleton, the last ships had left from San Diego with the troops that were going to land at Inch'ŏn:

> The final assembled division steaming out of San Diego consisted of 6,831 men from the 2nd Marine Division, 812 from the 1st Replacement Draft, 3,630 regulars from posts and stations and more than 10,000 from the Organize Reserves. [RMW 156]

Our whole military situation in the Pusan perimeter would be at great risk in the final days before this newly assembled force was to actually go ashore at Inch'ŏn. The danger was in withdrawing the First Provisional Marine Brigade from the front line fighting at the Perimeter and putting them on ships bound for a rendezvous near Inch'ŏn with the forces coming from San Diego.

When the First Marine Division, now at full strength, invaded at Inch'ŏn on 15 September, seventeen percent of the troops were Reservists. When the Division launched the September 1951 battles at the Punchbowl, 60 percent of the officers and 46 percent of the enlisted were Reservists.

How was I to be fitted into that growing war machine? Would I be just a minor operating part? Was I to be a blood lubricant? No, I would be part of the fuel and hope that I didn't become totally consumed.

¶On the morning of 4 September our train arrived at Camp Pendleton California and we took buses to our brick barracks. In the evening I wrote a postcard to my mother:

Dear Mom, I just got out of the theater and I thought I'd write you. The P.X. is closed [Labor Day] but tomorrow I think I'll be able to purchase some stationery, and I'll write you a letter. I had a good trip. We arrived this morning and I saw my first palm trees. This camp is really nice. It's *60 square miles* in the hills. And I mean *hills*. The show costs 10 cents and they have the latest pictures. Tell Dad I might have a chance to be an engineer for the Marines. Will write more tomorrow. Love, Bill

The next day we went thru an administrative triage. The idea was to separate us into three groups, according to our training and military experience. The prime group they were looking for were the "combat ready," who were to be given two weeks of refresher training and shipped to Korea. They would reach the combat zone soon after the Inch'ŏn Invasion. But they would arrive in time to suffer and, God willing, survive the winter weather and battles of the Chosin Reservoir Campaign.

The non-combat-ready were divided into two groups: the recruit class and nonrecruits. Persons who had less than one-year service in the Organized Reserve or poor drill attendance records were classified as recruits. The remainder were to receive about four-weeks training, and then be sent to Korea.

We queued up to fill out questionnaires and be interviewed. When I got to the clerk's table, he asked me how long I had been in the reserve unit; I told him eight months. He asked me whether I had been at a summer encampment; I told him no. Did I have any previous military service? No. Had I received any weapons training? I said No.

The clerk turned to a sergeant standing nearby and said, "We better send this guy thru boot camp and the whole bit. Otherwise, he doesn't stand a chance." I couldn't be sure of what that meant. It didn't sound good. But would it lead to good fortune?

It might not be training that would determine my chances of sur-

41

vival. Our forces in Korea were getting badly mauled by the North Koreans. Maybe we would be driven out of Korea and the war would be over. Maybe our side would get stronger and defeat them. At any rate, I thought my chances of survival would be improved merely by arriving in Korea later, the later the better.

On 6 September 1950 the 17th Infantry Battalion performed its last official duty, posing for an official portrait. (See Appendix A-3) Then we would all be scattered to the winds.

After a few days, I found out that I was going to go "thru boot camp and the whole bit." My group would start with the next cycle of training, in three weeks.

For another processing step we went into a large classroom and

were given examination forms. The instructor gave us the Morse telegrafic code for a few letters and told us to memorize them. I already knew Morse code, having learned it as a Boy Scout. A recording of those codes was played and we tried to write down the letters

Fig. 5-1: WEA at Camp Pendleton 6SEP1950

in the sequence that we heard them.

It was all very fast and I had never had that experience before. I don't know whether anybody passed the exam; I didn't. If I had been given some time to practice, I'm sure I would've passed it. Because I failed the exam, I knew I would not be a radio transmitter operator for the Marines.

I received a letter from my mother who told me that she needed money, since she was unable to get a job and was not getting alimony payments from my father who was unemployed. After high-school graduation, I had earned good wages working on the assembly line at the Hudson Motor Car Co. (because it was unionized) and been able to help her. But that lasted only eight weeks. Now that I was getting only a private's salary I couldn't help her as much. She asked me to see if I could be released from active duty.

I asked the personnel officer what could be done. He said, "You cannot be released, but you can pay her an allotment out of your paycheck and apply for a hardship discharge."

The process would take a lot of investigating and require affidavits from professional people (attorneys, religious officials, etc.). She would have to submit an itemized list of living expenses: rent, food, clothing, and so forth. The whole bureaucratic process dragged on until I was notified in April 1951 that it had been rejected. By then I was in Korea.

So she got $45.00 each month while I was in boot camp. After I graduated, and became a PFC, it was raised to $85.00 a month. If I died, she would get my government insurance: $10,000.00.

Chapter 6

BOOT CAMP

THE SETTING FOR MY BOOT CAMP TRAINING was semi-tropical; it was the San Diego Marine Corps Recruit Depot (MCRD), with its attractive Spanish colonial architecture.   But the only connection with Spanish colonial history that I saw or, rather, felt was a lot of stress, maybe akin to the hard life that early settlers had under Spanish rule.

I don't think anybody is really prepared for boot camp training, except people who have gone thru prolonged periods of hazing at universities or living with an abusive parent.   Perhaps being a member of an urban gang and fighting with other gangs would ease the preparation.   Being patriotic probably helps in mentally adjusting or just tolerating the boot camp experience.   Having a sense of humor also helps, as long as one does not reveal it in the presence of the stern drill instructors.   My high school ROTC experience and eight months in the Marine Reserve unit helped somewhat.

I never got used to all the hollering and yelling by the Drill Instructor (DI) and the corporals who helped him (the Assistant DIs). They told us, "Your soul belongs to God, but your ass belongs to the Marine Corps!"   It was just part of the process of disciplining us, frustrating us, challenging us, angering us, and whatever else it takes to get us ready for the rigor of combat training.

It was frustration with military training that we heard in a humorous song that came out of the experiences of U.S. troops in World War II. The troops preferred its raunchy version, which uses a well-known, time-honored, vulgar Anglo-Saxon four-letter verb. Its polite version uses "bless" instead:

> Bless them all, bless them all, bless them all,
> The long, the short, and the tall,
> Bless all the corporals who drilled us all day,

Bless all the sergeants who showed them the way,
For we're saying goodbye to them all,
As back to the barracks we fall,
There'll be no promotion, this side of the ocean,
So cheer up my lads, bless them all.

The first day, I had to turn over my new utility pocketknife "for safekeeping until completion of training." After graduation from boot camp, when I asked for it back, the supply people had no idea where it was. Now I would get a new understanding of the term "safekeeping." Neither the Marine Corps nor I could locate it. Believing that it had *not* been stolen by communist spies, I contented myself with the thought that the knife was still in America, "safe" somewhere. I just never found out who was doing the "keeping."

At the barbershop we lined up to get scalped. Around me were some handsome guys with rich, thick hair that would be the envy of aspiring Hollywood actors; one of them was Ted Bergren. The barbers were masters of electric hair clippers. They removed nearly all of his and everybody else's hair in three or four passes of the clippers, revealing a downside to humanity's use of electricity. Since heads are rounded and clippers have a flat cutting surface, the mowing of each swipe of the clippers left the equivalent of hedge borders between newly formed front-to-back swaths of whisker-length hair. I don't believe any of us spent more than three minutes getting shorn in the barber chair.

After the hair butchery, we were a pitiful sight; no one had been left with a decent-looking head of hair. In fact our heads resembled those of prisoners freed from Nazi concentration camps at the end of World War II.

They issued us a new set of clothing and our rifle. In handing out the weapon, they told us, "This is a rifle; it is *not* a gun!" And at some point you learn that your rifle may also be called "the piece." At first the piece feels quite heavy. It weighs nine-and-one-half pounds; but each week, it seemed to get lighter.

45

Now I looked like a "boot," one of the sixty-five men in Platoon Number 2-33, part of the 2nd Recruit Training Battalion, ready for eight weeks of military training. But the Marine Corps had something else in store for me first: ten days of restaurant training, called mess duty.

¶Mess duty meant working in one of the dining facilities (called "mess halls"; the kitchens were called "galleys"). When our platoon first reported for mess duty, the mess-hall sergeant was amused by my last name since I was pronouncing it then to rhyme with "alley." The sergeant pronounced my name and then made up a ditty that he recited a few times: "Alli in the galley. Alli in the galley." Naturally I was assigned to be "galley boy," which meant an all-purpose kitchen assistant. The experience would give me a different perspective on the ancient naval term "galley slave."

I cooked countless hamburgers, pancakes, and sausage patties over a hot grill. At other times I sat near a wall of 75 egg cartons and cracked open all 900 eggs, using both hands, one egg in each hand, and dumping the innards into a large pot for the cook to make scrambled eggs for morning chow. Peeling countless potatoes and onions was a skill I developed and hoped I would never need in the future.

No description of food in the U.S. military is complete without mention of SOS. It is a breakfast food: creamed chipped beef on toast. A logical abbreviation might be CCBOT, but that fails to capture the intensity of feelings that so many people have about this food; it's also a bit too long. The full (and unofficial) name is: "shit on a shingle."

SOS is the answer to a military cook's fondest wish, something easy to make in large quantities: a vat of cream sauce (actually a gravy) into which is dumped canned chipped beef. The stuff is ladled out onto a slice of bread, usually toasted, lying in a serving tray or dish or even mess kit.

The cook doesn't have to use only chipped beef. I've seen it with hamburger instead. Also, I've even seen it with tomato sauce. I guess it all depends on what the cook has on hand.

For veterans who detest SOS, their return to civilian life was accompanied by a vow that they would never eat it again. I like it, even tho I had never had it before going into the Marines. It is served in Pennsylvania Dutch restaurants and can be an interesting topic of conversation whenever a veteran sees it and decides to make a comment to a nearby diner.

I am puzzled as to why SOS has not made its way into song, as have other foods. One tune carried over from World War II tells us this:

> The coffee they give us,
> They say is mighty fine.
> It's good for cuts and bruises,
> And tastes like iodine.
> We don't want no more coffee;
> We just want to go home.

> The biscuits they give us,
> They say are mighty fine.
> One rolled off the table,
> And killed a friend of mine.
> We don't want no more biscuits;
> We just want to go home.

An onerous galley chore was washing large and numerous pots and pans. I used a hot-water hose to rinse them. Because of the galley's poor ventilation, each day gave me an extended steam bath; my clothes were drenched with sweat. The only good part of this was getting every pore of my skin, head to toe, immaculately clean. After mess duty, I thought I would never again have such clean skin.

Unfortunately, as galley boy I hardly got a chance to take a rest break, the way some of my fellow "boots" did. The cook always had something for me to do. So I was constantly tired that week.

Whenever I was out of the galley and the cook wanted to summon me, he used the ditty: "Alli, in the galley!" loudly and with considerable delight.

Those ten days of travail started each morning at 0345 (3:45 a.m.), when we crawled out of our bunk beds to shower, dress, make the beds and march to breakfast at the mess hall. There, we gobbled our food down and then started our work by 0500. My day ended back at the barracks when I crawled into the sack, just before lights out at 2145 (9:45 p.m.). By the time the camp's loudspeakers played the bugle call for "Taps" the time was 2200. By the final note of "Taps" all lights are to be extinguished, Marines bedded down, and all loud talking is to cease. I was then sound asleep.

Thru each exhausting today, I focused on the thought that after mess duty Marine life would be easier. Little did I know that in Korea I would be faced with even greater exhaustion. But at least in Korea, I wouldn't have someone like the mess sergeant in charge of me, using ridiculous rhyming ditties to determine what I should be doing. Can you imagine being on the front line and getting orders like: "Alli, take the valley!" or "Alli, sally forth!" I would never have survived the war.

Before boot-camp training began I was complaining about moving around. In my 24 September letter I wrote to my mother:

> All we do is move, first from Detroit to Pendleton, then from Pendleton to Diego. Then from one end of the parade ground to the other. Tomorrow we go back to the other end. And every time we move we have to pack and then unpack. I'm starting to feel like a ping-pong ball.

¶Finally, on 2 October, nearly a month after arriving in California, my boot camp military training began. My 11 October letter to home mentions some activities:

> Sorry about not writing but this is the first time I've had to do [so] this week. Usually when we have spare time we clean our rifle or shine our shoes. Believe me. They really keep us going.
>
> We go to bed promptly at nine o'clock and get up at 5:00 a.m.

Then we spend the rest of the day training. We see training films, go to classes, and drill. The food isn't bad. Sometimes it's really good but then there's times you don't know what you are eating. They used to make us eat everything on our tray but they changed that a few weeks ago. They give us some kind of beans at least once a day. The food might not be the best but boy does it make your bowels move! After each chow the guy's head straight for the "head" (lavatory).

We went to a football game Saturday night. Our team beat the San Diego College "Aztecs" 28 to 14. It was the first time we were off the base since we arrived here.

Vice President Alben Barkley was here Monday. We didn't get to see him though.

We went swimming Monday. They told some of us to jump in and swim so I jumped in. Well I can't swim very well on top of the water so I swam underwater. When I came up on the other side, this teacher was looking right down in my face. He said, "What do you think you're doing? Playing submarine?"

Last night we went to the show for the first time here at Diego. The pictures weren't too good but the organist who played before they started was good. He played requests from the Marines in the audience.

So far I've taken four tests. I got hundreds on three of them and 96 on the other. The only reason I didn't get a hundred was because I misunderstood the question. However, my average is 99 percent.

Most of our close-order drill was on the parade ground, referred to as the "parade deck," and sometimes "the grinder." At that time the deck had remnants of World War II paint used to make camouflage patterns. The patterns resembled the tops of buildings. The intention was to deceive Japanese pilots into thinking that the parade deck was just another group of building in San Diego. Naturally, the paint was well-weathered by 1950, but it had a quirky attraction to it. In looking back, I think it had some historical value, which was lost when the deck was resurfaced a few years later.

Actually, I enjoyed close-order drill. There's some satisfaction in seeing a group of men with rifles, moving smoothly, robotically and orderly, in response to the commands of the DI. But the San Diego sunshine was sometimes uncomfortable; we northerners just weren't used to such mild weather in autumn.

Cooler weather was in store for us in our next location, rifle camp. Finally we would be using our rifles for a more lethal purpose.

Chapter 7
BECOMING A STRAIGHT SHOOTER

ON 21 OCTOBER OUR PLATOON WENT BY BUS to Camp Matthews, near picturesque La Jolla, about twenty miles from Camp Pendleton. There we would be involved in three weeks of M1 rifle training and some brief acquaintance with the .45 caliber Colt pistol, the M1 carbine, and the Browning Automatic Rifle (BAR). That's where I would learn how to use my M1, probably the best infantry rifle (*not* a gun) of World War II.

I wrote my mom on 29 October:

> Right now we're at Camp Matthews. This is where the rifle range is located . . . The terrain around here is mountainous. Early in the morning one can see the sun come up over a huge ridge of mountains. At night it gets so cold that we have to sleep with two blankets, a sheet, and a poncho. However during the day we can go around in a tee-shirt . . . There's only four more weeks before we graduate.

Our part of the camp was laid out in about five rows of tents, each having around eight pyramidal tents. The rows of tents were separated by narrow asphalt roads and there was a road that bordered the whole tent area. The middle row, which had a few tents at each end, also had several heads in shed-type structures.

The wooden-floored pyramidal tents each held six men. The floors resembled palettes that forklifts move around in freight yards, but much bigger. Sleeping cots were placed against the low walls of the tent and a tall pole in the middle held up the peak. Each corner had a short pole to support the tent.

Outside, ropes were connected from the top of the tent walls, about four feet up from the ground, to some horizontal posts (like hitching posts) that were all around the sides except for a gap at the front, as an entryway. The horizontal posts were supported by vertical posts stuck into the ground.

The heads had open doorways facing the streets. This allowed

51

large numbers of men to run in and out quickly. The commodes were in a long line against one wall with no partitions to separate them. Unlike the heads in the brick barracks back at Pendleton, these did not have two commodes at the far end under a wall sign designating them as "VD only." Along the opposite wall were sinks. Showers were near the end of the building.

During a two-day period I learned the value of having heads with open doorways. It started after lunch, when most of our platoon suddenly developed diarrhea as we were marching. We had started at one end of our street, sixty-five men. As we continued along, one by one men sped out of formation and raced for the heads. The platoon continued marching with fewer and fewer men, quickly closing up the gaps as men ran out of formation and raced to the head. The remnants of the platoon arrived at the end of the street, far fewer in number, no more than about twelve.

I'm not exactly sure what was going on, except I knew it had to be a sanitation problem at the mess hall. After it was taken care of, I wondered whether any galley boy or other low-ranking person on mess duty was punished, regardless of culpability.

Rifle marksmanship is one of the most important skills that Marines are taught. Even before we fired live rounds, we were given practice in how to hold the weapon in various positions: prone, kneeling, sitting, squatting, and standing. We also practiced lining up the sights with the target, and even how to squeeze (not pull) the trigger of our unloaded rifles.

The idea is to squeeze the trigger so as to be unsure of when the weapon is going to fire. That way, you can avoid flinching. And in the process, one learns something very subtle. You can be sighting in on a target, squeezing the trigger, and realizing that there is a split second when the weapon has not yet fired, but it's too late to release the trigger in time to prevent the firing. And when I first experienced this on the rifle range, an old memory was triggered in my mind; I had almost killed somebody in Detroit by my stupidity in shooting a rifle in a residential area.

Several of us boys, about twelve or thirteen years old, had gotten together early one evening in our lower east-side neighborhood and one of my friends had brought a .22 caliber rifle. A few of us wanted to fire it, then and there. So we went into the alley behind some homes and found an old tin can that we set up in the middle of the pavement at the end of the alley. That's where the alley dead-ended perpendicular to a cross street. Nobody was tasked with being a lookout near the end of the alley to signal if anybody was coming toward the line of fire. Dumb boys!

I remember squeezing the trigger and then seeing beyond the tin can a girl riding her bicycle on the cross street. But it was too late to release the trigger pressure. We were in shock as the rifle fired at the same time that she rode by. In near panic, we ran down to the street and looked to see where she had gone. She was nowhere in sight.

Our anxiety was mounting. Soon she was bicycling back. We asked her whether she had heard anything and she said she thought she heard a loud noise and a whistling sound, like something flying past her ear. She had almost been killed by my youthful stupidity.

Detroit has come a long way since my shooting caper. It is now the "murder capital" of the United States. The best part of the current situation is that you are less restricted in your options for getting killed. You don't need to be riding a bicycle or relying on untrained young teenage shooters in order to get shot.

Our rifle training ended with the qualification exercise. As I was going thru it, I was distracted by the spotter next to me, telling me the results of each shot. He kept trying to be positive, saying "That's the way" or "keep it up." Unfortunately it detracted from my concentration and I did not score high enough to qualify as an Expert rifleman; I did qualify as a Sharpshooter.

The sharpshooter medal looks like the Iron Cross, a famous German military medal awarded for valor. Seeing photographs of me in uniform, civilians have raised their eyebrows and asked whether I was some kind of a hero. I would smile and explain that the medal was only for skill in shooting the rifle.

53

My 13 November letter states:

I qualified last Thursday on the rifle range. I shot 212 out of a possible 250. That makes me a "sharpshooter." I got a medal for it. The medal looks about like this.

I've got only 11 days more to go. This week we're doing police duty. Don't let the name fool you. Our job is to keep this tent area clean. We picked up papers and all that stuff. Then we get our big brooms and sweep the street. After that we work on whatever needs it. For instance, today they had us moving lumber and piling it up.

Of course we still had time for some marching and close-order drill. But we didn't spend as much time doing it as we had back at the MCRD.

One DI (not ours) had a reputation for being the meanest DI in boot camp. For whatever reason, one night he had his platoon put on their full packs and march in formation along the side of the Olympic-sized swimming pool. Then he gave them the command "right flank march" and they all marched into the pool. The men struggled to avoid drowning and managed to reach the sides of the pool to climb out.

A member of his platoon told me of an incident that started out as a prank. In one of the tents a Marine climbed up the eight-foot center pole with the intention of dropping down to scare the next person entering the tent. The idea was to land on the floor like some kind of a big bird, or maybe a fictional character, like Superman. For best effect, the deed was to be done during the darkness at night since anybody entering would not quickly notice the man on the pole.

54

When the Marine heard the sound of approaching footsteps, he rapidly climbed to the top of the pole and waited. As the person on the outside pushed open the door flap and came in, the Marine dropped down, landing on the floor with a loud thud and screeching, while flapping his arms like they were big bird wings.

The person who had entered was the DI. The jumper and the DI were face-to-face and both in shock. The other guys in the tent were in shock; they were probably thinking "Oh, my God. What kind of punishment is he going to give to all of us for this?"

The DI stared at the Marine for a few seconds and said nothing. Then he shook his head out of disgust, and maybe consternation. He could have been wondering whether the boot was having a nervous breakdown. At any rate, he turned around, still shaking his head, and walked out. The platoon was not punished for that stunt. Perhaps the DI realized that he needed to ease up the pressure he was putting on his men. For days the Marine's antic was the talk of the camp while anticipation of any retribution from the DI gradually dissipated.

The pool was used to punish a small-sized member of our platoon who was caught with "pogey bait" (candy or other junk food). His teeth were in terrible condition; they looked like they were rotting. All of us presumed it was from years of eating too much candy. He was ordered to climb up the tall ladder to the diving board, about one hundred feet above, and then to jump into the pool. He was afraid because he did not know how to swim. Even if a person did know how to swim, that was a high spot to jump from.

He showed his fear, trying to go back down the ladder, but getting yelled at by the drill instructor. After a few approaches to the edge of the diving board, he backed off. Meanwhile, the DI was yelling for him to jump. The boot went back to the end of the diving board and stood there. We were all looking up at him, wondering what would happen. Then he stepped off the board and plummeted, practically fluttering as he fell.

He hit the pool, almost vertically and disappeared below the surface. He popped up once, sank again, and after a short period of time, but not short enough I thought, he was rescued by the lifeguard.

I prayed that I would never have to do that because I could barely swim. And I was really afraid of water, based on an incident in summer camp at Lake St. Clair, when I was eight years old. I was asked by another kid on the pier whether I knew how to swim. I said no and the kid said, "Let's see" and pushed me off the pier. I slipped underneath the water, vainly struggling and would've drowned if it hadn't been for the lifeguard. Even tho I learned to swim after my Marine service, I've never felt completely at ease in the water.

I used to notice one of the guys in a tent behind ours, in another platoon. He had a rather odd look to him; his eyes were oversized and bulged out. Also, he often seemed depressed or confused. He showed no spontaneity and habitually stared blankly. One day I didn't see him anymore and I heard that he had committed suicide. I was shocked. Why would somebody training to go to war kill himself? There is at least a chance of surviving a war but usually not a suicide attempt. I could not conceive of what inner torment must have driven him to it.

During one of our last evenings at Camp Matthews we were allowed to see a movie, an outdoor showing of *All About Eve*. While we were watching it, somebody called "Hey! Look up in the sky." We looked at the dark sky above the screen and saw a bright shining object with a pointed tail hurtling our way. As it got closer we saw that it was a comet. I was mesmerized by its beauty but soon startled to see it break into three pieces which fell in a fiery burnout. The next day the comet was reported in a San Diego newspaper. Was it an omen? What could it portend? And for whom?

¶I have another memory of the dark skies above Camp Matthews. We were on a short march one night, maybe just a part of the Marine Corps practice of keeping us busy so that we would have less time for dwelling on negative thoughts. I looked up at the stars, there seemed to be so many of them, unlike the few that Detroiters

56

see because of the competing glare of city streetlights. I immediately looked for the Big Dipper as I had been trained to do as a Boy Scout. From that I visualized a line connecting the two stars farthest from the handle of the Dipper and extended that line till it took me about seven lengths away, where I would find the North Star, in a field by itself.

As I beheld the vast skyscape, I started feeling small and sad. All human life is insignificant to them. I believe that the Old Testament writer must have been gazing at the heavens when he posed the question, "Oh God, what is man that thou art mindful of him?" Like us puny humans, the stars have their place in our matrix of time and space. Light and darkness have their place, as do good and evil, pain and pleasure, war and peace.

And in the next year, in a time and place of war, I would have opportunities to refer to stars again. Then it would be the Southern Cross and the North Star, but I would not feel overwhelmed by the vastness of space, only intent on surviving, one day at a time, God willing.

Chapter 8
BOUND FOR COMBAT TRAINING

IT WAS THE FIRST WEEK OF DECEMBER when we returned to the MCRD with our shooters' medals for our final week. It was a week of close-order drill, the usual frustration, DIs hollering at us, but not as much or as loud, and getting ready for graduation.

We cleaned everything in sight, our clothes, our rifles, and our barracks. On the last night before our final inspection, my squad leader, Gaylen E. Searles, showed me a jar of something he had gotten in a package from home and asked me whether I liked pickled prawns.

I looked at it; the things inside appeared to be large, skinless, and legless caterpillars, in some kind of liquid. I said I had never eaten them. So he offered me one and I bravely ate it. That night the consequences were severe; I leapt out of my bunk and raced to the head to vomit my guts out.

By the time reveille rolled around I was in no condition to get up and get ready for our formation.

Fig. 8-1: Boot Camp Graduation, December 1950. WEA (center). Searles (top left)

Gradually I got better during the day. When the guys came back from their formation, they told me that we had passed platoon inspection. That meant we would all be promoted from Private to PFC.

The next day we marched in review with all the other platoons. We felt a great sense of accomplishment and relief that the tension and stress of boot camp were finally over. We weren't thinking about Korea.

As a reward, we were given our first weekend liberty. I felt like a released prisoner. Except for that October football game, I had not been off the base since my arrival ten weeks earlier.

I spent most of my time just walking around downtown San Diego. The only member of our platoon who had previously been off the base legally was a Jewish guy from Texas; he was allowed to go to religious services at a synagog in the city. It showed me one advantage of being Jewish.

I was astonished to see how many of the guys bought liquor and took it up to a hotel room they had rented downtown. And of course, a few Marines had to get the obligatory tattu. I guess for them it was some kind of male rite of initiation. Personally, I thought it was stupid.

¶My feelings against alcohol were quite strong, mainly because of how much my dad opposed it. One day I learned why. Alcohol was forbidden to the Muslims of his hometown, Harput (the Christians did not have such a prohibition). Of course that meant that alcohol was a challenge to the young Turks and Kurds as part of their coming of age. The challenge was how to find it. Dad did and proceeded to drink too much.

Unfortunately, alcohol does not mix well with a volatile temper and, for whatever reason, he got enraged, pulled out a dagger, stabbed a man repeatedly, and then fled. By the time he sobered up, he realized that he was in serious trouble. He was worse than a sinner; he was a criminal. He vowed that he would never again drink alcohol but realized that he had to do something right away to escape quick retribution. He joined the army immediately and hoped that he would not be caught.

A few weeks later he was summoned to the commander's office. As he entered and approached the commander's desk, he saw a *jandarma* (constable) standing off in a corner. My father saluted and the commander said to him, "I have here a warrant for your arrest brought to me by this *jandarma*. And I have some questions. Do you know what it is about?"

"Yes, my commander," Baba admitted.

The commander said, "I'm going to let you decide whether I should hand you over to him. But first I have to tell you that we have orders from İstanbul. Our unit has been assigned to garrison duty in Yemen. In two weeks, we leave. We will march to the Black Sea and board a ship at Trabzon. The ship will stop in İstanbul for a few days before departing for Yemen. What is your decision?"

My father said, "I want to stay with our unit." Since the *jandarmas* were subordinate to army officers, the commander signed the arrest warrant as "rejected." Of course Baba stayed with his unit – until İstanbul. That's when he decided that his future would probably be better if he left the army and joined his older brother in America, rather than go to Yemen.

On 18 April 1913 Baba and Veysi Kaplan disembarked from the SS *Germania* at Providence Rhode Island, wearing civilian clothes. And to think, his path to America all started with his first (and only) alcoholic drinking.

¶At the MCRD I received orders that gave me permission for home leave (1 thru 10 December) and then directed me to report for Advanced Infantry Training (AIT) at Camp Pendleton, a week before Christmas 1950. My entire home leave would be ten days. I would be back in California after it and spend my Christmas at Camp Pendleton.

Now I would have my first airplane ride, with the Marine Corps paying for it. It would be an adventure riding in a big Lockheed Constellation, refueling in Amarillo, landing in Detroit. In Amarillo I marveled at how flat the terrain was. The Marine Corps certainly was introducing me to a lot of different places. It never occurred to me that some guys go on leave and never come back; they may even leave their country, like some Turks before World War I, or Americans during the Vietnam war. And they don't have to get drunk to set the process in motion.

Fig. 8-2: A studio portrait in Detroit

¶Shouldn't home leave after boot camp be a pleasant, even a merry time for a Marine? Well, after being in southern California I found Detroit's weather colder than I remembered. But my leave was dampened down mostly because I was carrying orders to report for advanced infantry training at Camp Pendleton. A war was being fought in Korea and the First Marine Division was desperately fighting for survival in northeastern Korea, near a frozen reservoir named Chosin. I deliberately avoided reading any news reports or watching any movie news coverage of the ordeal. I would continue being fatalistic about my future.

Fig. 8-3: With Baba, home-leave December 1950

The time went by quickly. I spent time with family and friends. I even went out on a date with a gal whom I had met about a year or so earlier.

There was not much talk about the war in Korea but I'm sure that my folks had a nagging awareness of what was going on there, even tho they had no television set nor listened much to news on the radio. My mother was starting to read newspapers more and my illiterate dad went at least once a week to the Telenews, a downtown movie theater that showed newsreels only. I didn't think about what was in store for me nor try to find out what was happening in Korea.

I still remember being invited out to a pizza restaurant by Eddie Tazzia and his wife Angie. He was an older brother of my close friend, Henry Tazzia, and a US Air Force veteran of World War II. His experience, including being a POW of the Germans, probably made him savvier about what a young person like me might expect in the war that I was headed for. I will not forget their kindness and even introducing me to pizza for the first time.

¶Ignorance provides no protection from the future. It can abet a sense of dread about things unlikely to happen in the future. Mark Twain once spoke about his many bad experiences, "most of which," he admitted, "hadn't really happened."

Christians and Muslims, especially clerics, have spoken about horrible burnings in hell for sinners. They have described torments of fire with pain that is unimaginably excruciating, and yet continues forever, because it is the soul rather than the body that is suffering.

I remember being a sixteen-year-old visiting some of my mother's kinfolk in the hills of eastern Tennessee and going to a Baptist revival meeting. The preacher was all worked up and so was the congregation, as he talked about fire and brimstone and the terrible fate that awaited the souls of unrepentant sinners in the afterlife.

Finally he invited people to come up to the altar and declare that they were sinners and ask Jesus to forgive them. I was so scared of the prospect of the hell that he was talking about, that I eagerly went up and was saved then and there. Unfortunately, being saved, in 1948 didn't offer me any protection from going thru hell in this life, and in 1950 the most likely place for me to encounter it would be Korea.

In three wars of the 20th century, Christians and Muslims have had experiences of earthly Hell that were much cooler than what preachers and mullahs could conjure up. In those wars the flames of hell might be an actual relief from cold. The conflicts were in Caucasia (Sarıkamış, World War I), Russia (Stalingrad, World War II), and North Korea (the Chosin Reservoir, 1950).

On 22 December 1914, the impetuous Osmanli dictator, Enver Pasha, launched his 95,000 troops against the Russians at Sarıkamış, sending them thru heavy snows in mountainous terrain, with inadequate equipment and clothing. By 17 January 1915, some 75,000 Osmanli soldiers had been lost, many having frozen to death. The body of my Uncle Bekir may have been among those dead.

In August 1942 Adolf Hitler sent his Sixth Army against Stalingrad, where urban fighting negated much of the technical advantages of the Germans. He refused to allow his troops to retreat, even as Soviet troops encircled them and winter closed in. When the Germans and their allies surrendered in February 1943, they had experienced 1.5 million casualties. mostly from starvation and freezing. The surrendering troops faced further suffering in labor camps. Ten years later only five percent returned home.

In autumn 1950, while I was in boot camp, General Douglas A. MacArthur, an American hero, directed another winter catastrophe. This one was fresh on the heels of his brilliant success, the Inch'ŏn Invasion and liberation of South Korea's capital, Seoul.

He ordered all United Nations forces to race north to the Yalu River border with China, in disregard of China's repeated warnings that it would not tolerate any enemy presence on its border. China's massive invasion secretly began in October and by November it was smashing UN forces, driving them back, halfway down the length of South Korea. Some 8,000 UN troops, mainly from the United States, are still listed as missing.

¶Leaving Detroit was tough on my family. Mom cried; Aunt Rose, Sister Geri and Dad looked mournful. I was sad because I had to report to Pendleton just before Christmas, missing the whole holiday season at home. I was vaguely aware that our Marines were having a rough time in Korea.

In fact, by the time I was scheduled to begin AIT at Pendleton, the 1st Marine Division had survived the agony of fighting the Chinese, and the winter, to reach the North Korean port of Hŭngnam on the Sea of Japan. The U.S. Navy's masterful evacuation brought them to the port of Pusan in South Korea.

When the 6th Replacement Draft of fresh Marines arrived in South Korea, early in March 1951, I would be among them. By then the Division would have cut short its recuperation near Masan and been fighting the enemy again for almost two months. It would be driving northward, but still be south of the Thirty-eighth Parallel, that partition line between North and South Korea, drawn by the U.S. and the USSR at the end of World War II (1945).

My next experience would give me combat training. Then I would complete going "thru boot camp and the whole bit" as the evaluation clerk recommended in September as necessary for me to "stand a chance." Would it be chance itself, or was it fate that would decide whether I was to survive?

Chapter 9
A TENTLESS TENT CAMP

CAMP PENDLETON IS A BIG BASE. It occupies more than 125,000 acres of hilly terrain, including seventeen miles of Pacific shoreline. Back in September, before boot camp, I really didn't grasp its size. This time I would see more of it, on foot.

I arrived at the main gate with my official orders to report for training. The guards had me wait for the bus to go to Tent Camp Number One. On the bus I naively visualized a bunch of tents, laid out in rows, about like Camp Matthews.

I got off the bus at a small base of Quonset huts; I saw no tents. Maybe the tents were hidden. Or they might be part of a disinformation system to protect national security. It's possible that there used to be tents there and after they were taken down, somebody in the Marine Corps burocracy forgot to change the name. Years later I heard the place was named Camp Las Pulgas (the Fleas). I don't remember any fleas, either.

Our training platoon was part of Able Company, 1st Infantry Training Battalion, Training and Replacement Command. It was a hodge-podge of men from different boot camp platoons. Most of them had been in those Marine Corps Reserve units that were activated, as was my 17th Infantry Battalion. Strangely, most of the last names started with A, B, or C; we had Abney, Adamy, Alli, Anderson, Buchanan (two of them), etc.

And what a mixture they were. They spoke some strange dialects. Several were from New Jersey and spoke almost like some actors I had heard in the movies. But maybe I was confusing them with New Yorkers. Experts claim that there is a difference.

The really weird sounds came out of the mouths of Marines from Louisiana. They told me they were Cajuns. I didn't ask how it was spelled, but it sounded like "caged ones." Had their ancestors been oppressed? Maybe imprisonment in cages had permanently affected their speech. I really had trouble understanding anything they said. It made me think I was at the outer limits of what could be done in, or rather, *to* the English language.

There were communication frictions between the Cajuns and the New Jerseyites. Sometimes tempers flared between them and they would angrily turn to one of us Midwesterners or to somebody from the West Coast, and demand to know what had been said. Somehow those of us who were neither Cajun nor New Jerseyite were considered natural translators.

I avoided refereeing any disputes, even tho I was from southeastern Michigan and did not speak with a dialect. I sympathize with people who migrate as adults to different regions and have communications problems. My mother was never completely cured of her Tennessee dialect, despite living nearly forty-two years in Detroit.

A conflict in the Quonset huts could be revealed the next morning by a swollen and discolored eye, which I saw on one guy. I asked him what had happened and he didn't want to talk about it. Somebody else told me that during the night the guy had gotten into a quarrel with, unfortunately, Abney, who had been a professional boxer, and both of them stepped outside to settle the matter. I prefer mediation for settling disputes; it's less painful, especially if a professional boxer is involved.

¶I never thought about who in our training platoon would survive the war. It just wasn't worth speculating about. In Korea, I can say I felt shock, sadness, and numbness when hearing a familiar name of someone who'd gotten killed or wounded. Yet all of us were vulnerable. Had we known during training who was doomed, we might have interacted more with them. But such speculation is just an attempt to anchor something in time before it happens and relate it to a time later on. It's all beyond our control, and a fertile soil for superstition, fatalism, and fear.

The two men in our platoon named Buchanan were both from Nebraska. The bigger man was more than six-foot tall and husky, we nicknamed Big Buck. He was probably from Omaha. The other man, about 5'7" and stocky, we called Little Buck; his full name was Edgar Buchanan and he was from Alliance Nebraska. There was also Hollywood actor named Edgar Buchanan; he appeared in minor roles in movies and later in television. Little Buck was handsomer than the actor and was rather quiet and likable.

On a nice June day in Korea when our unit was on the trail, we passed another group and I saw one of my Oregonian friends from Camp Pendleton, Galen P. Anderson. There was no time to chat with him, but I asked, "How's it going?" He barely had time to stop and grimly said, "Not good. Little Buck was killed. A mortar shell landed on his back. Big Buck got blinded by an explosion."

Our columns moved on. I tried to process the bad news, but all my mind could picture was a mortar shell landing on Little Buck, without any accompanying sound, just a horrible thought. On open ground there's no way you can protect yourself from a mortar shell.

In a partial daze, I kept putting one foot in front of the other along the trail; my mind was shutting down. There would be no crying; that would have to wait till after the war.

Later I remembered Little Buck and realized how little I actually knew him. I found out that his middle name was LeRoy and that he had been born in Alliance NE on April 2, 1931; he was just nine months older than me. He had been in Korea barely three months.

The main thing I remember is something unexpected that he did during our final live-fire exercise at Tent Camp One. Each man had to run across a small field which had pop-up targets. Nearly everybody dropped to the ground, to the prone position, to fire his rifle. I was surprised when Edgar's turn came and he dropped down to the kneeling position and fired. Then I realized that his shooting time was quicker than if he had first dropped down to the prone position. Just a second or less difference in shooting time might save one's life. But with a mortar shell coming at you, no shooting technique will save you.

¶On 4 January 1951, I wrote my mother saying the following:

The training is quite rough. Sometimes when we're climbing the hills I feel like I'm never going to make it. We usually get to the top puffing like steam engines. Our legs feel like they're going to give with each step. Despite this I've been feeling very good. I'm about tops in physical condition.

I was learning to function in the Marine Corps' basic organization for infantry combat, the fireteam. It was developed in World War II to fight the Japanese on Pacific islands. Much different from the U.S. Army's basic unit (the twelve-man squad), the Marine fire team comprised four men: a Fire Team Leader, a Browning Automatic Rifleman (the BARman), an Assistant BARman, and the Scout. Thus, the fire team leader had to be concerned with managing only himself and three other persons.

Three fire teams comprised one Marine squad. Therefore, the squad leader focused on commanding the three fire team leaders.

The system worked very well for the Marines in jungle warfare, where rapid movement and unit isolation were constant factors. But the Korean War was different in terrain, weather, and attainable objectives. Halfway thru its thirty-seven-month duration, the war came to resemble World War I on the Western front, in France, where troops were in fixed positions on a front line of trenches and bunkers.

A new element in the Marine Corps' advanced infantry training program was cold weather training, drawing upon experiences in North Korea. On 6 February buses took us up to Idyllwild in the San Jacinto Mountains. Here in a majestic wilderness at an elevation of about 6,000 feet above sea level, experts were going to teach us how to survive in cold weather. That meant learning everything from the importance of wearing multiple layers of thin clothing (rather than fewer layers of thick clothing), to rappelling down steep hills or cliffs and, above all, keeping ourselves warm and dry. The rappelling was fun but we would never need it in Korea.

68

There was no training in what to do about weapons that are not designed to function in freezing weather. We could not fire the M1 Garand rifle while wearing thick winter gloves, because the trigger guard wasn't big enough to get a gloved finger onto the trigger. Soviet burp guns, like those used by the enemy in Korea, did not have such a limitation. A special device was finally manufactured for the M-1, but very few of us ever saw it in Korea.

The worst piece of equipment was an accessory for the M1 rifle: the M7 grenade launcher. I had only one encounter with it. It made a bad impression on me, mentally and physically.

An instructor told us that the M7 is a "close support weapon for infantry." He did not tell us its range, other than "somewhere beyond the maximum you can throw a hand grenade." Nobody had told me what that is but it didn't sound very far. Before I could use it, I had to make sure that my rifle was empty of bullets. Then I attached the M7.

It was easy; it looked like a handle for bicycle handlebars. The device had a hinged clamp designed to be attached to my rifle's bayonet lug. It also had a "stud" that fitted into the M1's gas cylinder valve screw to hold it open and vent the excess gas that came from the firing of the special grenade cartridge. That cartridge was like the standard and lethal .30 caliber cartridges that the M1 was made to shoot, but the grenade cartridge had no bullet in it. It was a blank cartridge like what is used to produce the sound of a gunshot in movies or on stage plays.

With the grenade attached to the M7, we were told not to hold our rifle like we do when we shoot bullets; the recoil would knock our shoulder out of joint. Also, "Don't hold it at your side. The recoil will spin you around like a ballet dancer." What's next? You keep your head facing the target while you turn your body ninety degrees to the right. Then you place your right knee against the ground and set the butt end of the stock against the ground. Tilting the barrel up about forty-five degrees in the direction of the target, you use your left foot to step on the much-loosened leather sling, pushing that strap against the ground. Then you turn your head to the left, facing the direction in which the grenade is aimed. And with both hands in the usual position of holding a rifle during "port arms," use your right hand to pull the trigger.

The roar of the firing hurt my right ear. I don't recall being told to tilt my head back away from the rifle before shooting. Right away I noticed that voices around me sounded like they were passing thru a filter made of very thin sheet metal. People sounded like they were talking thru a kazoo. I did not go to the sick bay and after a few weeks the ringing sound had died away. My hearing seemed to be back to normal. Only decades later did a civilian physician notice during an ear exam that I had a scar on my right eardrum.

That was a high price to pay for a weapon that couldn't hit the side of a barn and left me with an unloaded rifle until I could detach the launcher and reload my M1 with real bullets. In the confusion of battle, the time needed to attach it or remove it might cost the user his life. The inventor of the M7 should have been shot!

One day at Tent Camp Number One we saw a demonstration firing of two weapons. One was a recoilless rifle (a cannon that fires a high velocity shell in a flat trajectory); it was mounted on a tripod. The other was a heavy machine-gun (water-cooled .30 caliber). The target area was a draw, coming down from a range of hills south of us. The cannon shell landed in the draw, almost a mile away from us. Next, the machine-gun began firing into the same area.

Soon, one of the trainers looking thru binoculars yelled out to the machine-gunners, "Stop firing. There are people out there!" Everyone was horrified to see human figures coming down the draw. What the hell were they doing there? A couple of Marines ran in their direction and brought them back to our positions.

We had apprehended some "wetbacks," Mexican migrants who had crossed the U.S. border illegally. They seemed in shock at their violent reception, an exploding cannon shell and machine-gun bullets. What ran thru their minds while it was happening? If they ever got a chance to send word back to Mexico, surely they would

70

tell their amigos that the American border was very well guarded, and in depth.

¶A way of relieving tension could be a practical joke played on someone. "Short sheeting" was a relatively harmless one. To understand it, you need to visualize the narrow bunk beds in which we slept. On top of the wire rack was a mattress, three-to-four inches thick. There was a bottom sheet, a top sheet, a blanket on top of that, and a pillow at the head of the bed.

The trick was to remove the top sheet and hide it. Then the bottom edge of the bottom sheet was folded up toward the head of the bed. The blanket was laid over this arrangement and the shifted bottom edge of the bottom sheet, which was now at the head of the bed, was folded out over the edge of the blanket, appearing to be the exposed top edge of a top sheet.

It amounted to creating a pocket with a depth of half the length of the bed. When the victim got into the bed, preferably in the dark, quite tired, possibly drunk, he could not extend his body down toward the foot of the bed. He was stuck in that pocket.

In his attempt to stretch out, he would be quite frustrated, maybe a bit noisy, and a comic sight. It was worth a few laughs and nobody really got hurt.

Potentially more harmful was a prank played on a man who had a habit of leaping onto his upper bunk bed late at night and landing with a noisy thud. The noise was loud enough to wake up and irritate the man in the lower bed and men on each side. So the offended persons conspired to play a trick on the noisemaker.

While the offender was out of the barracks, they disconnected the metal wire links which connect the wire-grid spring to the bed frame and replaced them with thin cotton strings. They covered up everything with the mattress and bedcovers and waited for the offender to return.

When the guy came back that night, the lights were out and everyone around him was very quiet, desperately trying not to giggle out loud at what was about to happen. To avoid injury, the man who had the bunk below had gone elsewhere to lie down.

With the leap, the unsuspecting victim vaulted upward, landing momentarily on top of his bunk. All the strings broke immediately and, undergirded by his mattress and the wire-grid, he crashed downward onto the bunk below. He was in shock and the guys around him were reduced to helpless laughter. But the noise of the crash woke up everybody in the barracks.

There was some danger in dropping down because he could have banged some part of his anatomy against the metal frame as he plunged thru it. Fortunately, he survived altho shaken up quite a bit. After the perpetrators returned his wire connectors, the "vaulter" repaired his rack. In the weeks that followed he was much quieter getting into bed.

Chapter 10
LIBERTY & COMPLETION
OF TRAINING

A MEMBER OF MY PLATOON, Bob Roeszler, had at least three positive things about him: he had a friendly demeanor, he was from Los Angeles, and he owned a Hudson, made in the very factory in Detroit where I had briefly worked right after high-school graduation.

The car was very fast and he would drive 95 mph coming back to Pendleton late on Sunday nights after our weekend leave in Los Angeles. Lying down in the backseat of his car and looking upward thru the windows, I would see the utility poles on U.S. Highway 101, Pacific Coast Highway, flying by and hoping that we didn't get a tire blowout or have some other kind of accident because I knew that at that speed neither one of us would survive. At least I wanted to live long enough to finish my training, go overseas and, God willing, have a life after the war.

He introduced me to two families in Los Angeles. The Balmas family had two daughters. The younger one was Barbara, about eighteen or nineteen years old. Millie was a few years older and engaged to Ray, one of the sons of the other family, the Nizibians. The Nizibians also had a daughter and another son.

I believe Mr. Balmas was of Italian extraction. The Nizibians were Armenian Americans. Back in Detroit I had grown up with people from those ethnic groups. Both families were quite hospitable to me, something very important to any serviceman who's a long way from home and bound for a war.

Mr. Nizibian had a combined grocery store and meat market that sold *lahmajun*, a type of pizza eaten by Turks, Kurds, and Armenians. I had never had it before, despite eating lots of Turkish food cooked by my father. It was great and is now one of my preferred ethnic foods. Mrs. Nizibian even cooked one of my favorite foods, *köfte* (a type of meatball); unfortunately the version she served, "kuftu yakani," didn't set well with my stomach, but I appreciated her efforts.

I never asked the Nizibians about their family name, altho interest in family names is avid among the multiethnic people of Detroit. Some fifty years later in Washington DC, I met a man named "Niziblian," just one letter longer than "Nizibian." When I mentioned my contact with the Nizibians in California, the man told me that the letter *l* belonged in their name.

He explained that his folks were from a town named Nizib in southeastern Anadolu (Anatolia). Natives of that town are called Nizibli. Armenians add "ian," meaning "son of" to form the family name, hence "Niziblian." In English we would most likely call a person a Niziber, a Nizibite, or possibly a Nizibian. So I could understand how an American immigration officer could've asked the immigrant his name and decided to write it down as "Nizibian."

I told him that his folks were lucky to bring their family name intact thru the immigration process. My dad was not so lucky going thru the immigration process in Providence Rhode Island in April 1913. The Ottoman (Osmanli) Turks and other Muslims had no family names; only the Osmanli Christians had family names.

When the American immigration officer, presumably thru an Armenian immigrant interpreter, asked my dad what his full name was, Baba probably guessed that whatever his answer, he would be stuck with it. Altho illiterate, he sensed that a simple name would be best. He must have said his real name, Hüseyin, and then added "Ali." Perhaps he liked the sound of that simple and common Turkish name.

My father got a medical exam to be sure that he had no infectious diseases and showed the immigration officer that he had the necessary funds ($20.00) to live on until he could get a job. The process ended as the official gave him a document listing him as "Sam Alli" and indicated that the immigration process was complete.

Like most of the eastern Anadoluans (Turks, Kurds, and Arme-

74

nians) who came to America before World War I, he made his way to Worcester Massachusetts, where his elder brother Mehmet lived. After they greeted each other, my dad showed the document to Mehmet and they went to the *Kızılay Cemiyeti,* the Turkish Red Crescent Society, referred to as the "society," where somebody could read English.

Actually, it was a mutual-aid society supported by dues from the mainly illiterate immigrants and revenue from the coffeehouse, where it had its business office. The society's officers helped the members with filling out all sorts of government forms and employment applications, borrowing money for emergencies, writing letters to Turkiye, finding lawyers for legal problems, prepaying burial expenses, and arranging Muslim burial ceremonies.

My uncle asked the official "What is my brother Hüseyin's name?"

The official looked at Baba's immigration papers and said, "Hüseyin's name is *Sam Alli.*"

His brother said "Hüso, you may be able to learn how to write it."

Eventually my dad learned to write merely two words in English: Sam Alli. But he went beyond that to learn to write numbers, up to one hundred.

I wonder if distorting immigrants' names was part of the immigration process. The Nizibian family of California had lost an *l* in the immigration process; my father had gained an *l*. Was it the same *l* ? I am convinced that there was no connection; my father would never consent to stealing an *l* from any Armenian immigrant.

In 1935 my father got news from his folks in Turkiye that the family had a new surname; it wasn't the one he had gotten from the U.S. immigration official in Providence Rhode Island in 1913. What was going on?

During the 1920s and 1930s the Turks were being led thru rapid—and radical— modernization under their brilliant leader, Mustafa Kemal Atatürk. [AM] In preparation for taking a national census,

75

the government ordered all Turkish citizens to adopt an officially approved surname. That was a good step toward modernization.

So, Baba's family decided to take the name *Kayma,* which rhymes with "buy Ma." Dad was officially *Hüseyin Kayma.* But there were ramifications for me and my sister, because we were officially Turkish citizens in the Turkish Government's eyes.

So the official Turkish records show that I lost the name William Edward Alli and became *Ali Kayma.* My sister, Geraldine Yvonne Alli, became *Jale Kayma,* (*Jale* being pronounced like ZHAH-leh).

But what does *Kayma* mean, if anything? My research has revealed two possibilities: (1) a landslide, or (2) the common Turkish pronunciation of the name of the first paper money issued by the Osmanli Empire in 1841, under the rule of Sultan Abdül-Mejid in 1841.

I'm not sure what to do with this information. I welcome any recommendations from readers, as long as it does not get me near any landslides nor make me stop using American dollars. Meanwhile, my father and I never quit using Alli. Who knows, it might even have caused us trouble with our own government if we had tried to make the change.

¶One day at Tent Camp One we were told about an inspection to take place the next day. I got worried because I had an unregistered pistol, a .32 caliber hammerless revolver that my dad had given to me on home leave. He told me that he had taken it away from someone trying to rob him at the coffeehouse which he briefly owned in World War II (and gambled away).

I asked Abney to get rid of it for me. I never asked him what he did with it; I just didn't want to know at the time. I was afraid of the consequences of having an illegal weapon. It was probably a mistake; pistols were prize weapons in Korea for keeping inside a sleeping bag. It is easy to shoot thru a sleeping bag with a pistol if one does not have time to unzip the sleeping bag and grab a rifle. And a hammerless revolver will not jam when fired from inside the

76

bag. But how good is a .32 caliber bullet for stopping someone who is trying to attack you?

We had received some cursory training in firing the .45 caliber Colt semiautomatic pistol, the standard sidearm for officers and gunners and assistant gunners of machine-gun units. We were not allowed to use both hands to fire it, unlike the more accurate two-handed practice nowadays. The .45 caliber pistol was notoriously inaccurate altho it fired a bullet that would stop almost anything or anyone it struck. However, the Marine Corps was not going to issue me a .45 in addition to my rifle.

One night at Pendleton we had the experience of attacking a hill; it was disastrous. Night-vision equipment had not yet been invented. Nobody knew where anybody else was, friend or "foe." Fortunately, it was only a training exercise, so we were not using loaded weapons. The likelihood of getting shot by one's own troops is very high in real nighttime attacks. I cannot imagine how such an attack could succeed. I only hoped that I would never be involved in one in Korea.

Our final training activities included: exiting a landing craft by rolling out sideways and hugging the craft's side to drop to the ground, running thru an obstacle course, crawling on the ground as machine-gun bullets were flying overhead, and "the hike." Our "hike" was a twenty-mile march, wearing a full pack, a helmet, and canteen, and toting a rifle. It was all done on a fairly level road, but at a brisk pace. I don't know how many hours it took but it was an excruciating experience. Later, the arduous terrain of mountainous Korea would make me long for the flatter and friendlier stretches of those Camp Pendleton roads, even at a brisk pace.

The cooks at Tent Camp One served us really good chow. My only complaint was that they served us some kind of potato every day; it never failed. I thought that boot camp was bad with all of its beans, but I was wrong. I never ate so many potatoes in my life as I did at Pendleton. On 10 November, the Marine Corps birthday, they served us two kinds of potato at the same meal.

I wrote to my mother telling her that, "When I go to sleep now instead of sheep jumping over a fence, I see spuds jumping. I think the general owns a vast potato plantation."

We assembled for our final inspection and got a pep talk from the legendary BGen Lewis B. "Chesty" Puller, recipient of five Navy Crosses; that medal is second only to the Congressional Medal of Honor. He had commanded the 1st Marines from Inch'ŏn to the Chosin Reservoir. "Chesty" told us that if we got shot and were "going down," we should "reach up and pull one more of those bastards down with you." It was good bravado talk, but I wasn't sure just how to carry out the details.

¶For our final weekend at Pendleton we were looking forward to shore leave. Instead, we were confined to the base. Everyone was angry. We knew we were leaving soon for Korea. They even gave us a new address: "E" Co. 6th Replcmnt. Draft c/o F.P.O. San Francisco,

So, late on Saturday evening I joined a few of my friends in an unauthorized military exercise. We put on our uniforms and conducted a reconnaissance of downtown San Diego. It required that we avoid any sentries as we left and returned to our barracks. The foray was good for our morale and improved our combat readiness. It was an act of patriotism or, at least, a morale booster.

Fig. 10-1: Col. Lewis B. Puller

If we had been caught we would, no doubt, have been punished. But since we were sailing on the following Wednesday, what were they likely to do? They could always throw us into Pendleton's brig (jail) and delay our arrival in

Korea. That didn't seem very likely and even if they did, none of us would have protested. On the other hand they could have incarcerated us in the brig of the troopship on its way to Korea. However, there were so many of us who had gone out on the town that no ship's brig could hold us all. Nobody was caught or punished.

Roeszler did not need to take that final foray into San Diego. He wasn't going to go to Korea. His next assignment was to an aviation school on the East Coast. It made sense; his high-speed driving in that Hudson proved that he was capable of piloting speedy aircraft.

Before we boarded the buses to take us to the San Diego docks, we had a little gift for SSgt Stavrue, the NCO in charge of our training. He had hectored us with all sorts of half-comical threats of punishment for whatever mistakes or shortfalls he deemed us to be guilty of.

Most often he had threatened us by saying we were "going to get the purple shaft." Nobody was sure what that meant, but it sounded painful and definitely obscene. One time he threatened us with "the purple shaft with dingleberry clusters." We weren't sure what that meant either, but we sure didn't want to have any contact with it.

Our gift to him was a broomstick, about three-feet long; it had been painted purple. We told him that we were getting revenge by giving *him* the purple shaft, but *without* any dingleberry clusters.

Chapter 11
WESTWARD HO: TO THE FAR EAST

FINALLY, WE PACKED OUR SEABAGS and went by buses to a pier in downtown San Diego. More than 2,000 of us boarded a troopship, the USNS *General G. M. Randall*, and sailed on 14 February 1951, bound for Korea via Japan. We would be at sea for about two weeks, my first ocean voyage, and it would be free of charge for me, a round-trip, I hoped.

On the pier, a small crowd of friends and relatives waved at us as the tugboat helped the *Randall* pull away. But there was no one that I knew on the pier. With our ship moving

Fig. 11-1: USNS *General G. M. Randall*

farther away, we watched the pier diminish as it was absorbed into a thin dark layer of the atmosfere, which merged with the shrinking image of San Diego's waterfront. I thought that more people should have been saying goodbye to us; after all we were more than two thousand Marines leaving for a war. I guess that most of the people on that pier lived nearby in California and most of us on the ship had come from more distant States. Our families and friends were too faraway.

I felt slightly sad but calm. I knew I would not feel better if I stayed on the deck, watching the shore receding and the ocean completing its encirclement of us. I was leaving my country for the first time. I might never see it again, nor all that it contained: my family, my friends, my memories. I began to feel some loss. I must shut it out of my mind; I had to go below deck.

¶I was the second person in my family to take a long voyage by ship. Thirty-eight years earlier, when my Turkish father left his

80

country, he too was journeying westward. Both of us would be at sea for about half a month.

Each of us was in the military. He was unofficially leaving the Osmanli army, in civilian clothes, and maybe would avoid involvement in a war; I was in the U.S. Marine Corps, still in uniform, and certainly destined for combat. We were almost the same age as we made our journeys. He could not know whether he would ever return. The same was true for me.

While aboard the *Randall*, I did not feel a special anxiety. However, that might occur the closer I got to the war. But in 1913, Baba and Veysi Kaplan, were very uneasy aboard the *Germania* in the presence of the many Osmanli Armenian passengers. The pair avoided speaking Turkish around them. They were fearful because of the growing ethnic hostility between Turks and Armenians.

The Armenian Revolt (1894-1920) had been launched by the Armenian Revolutionary Party (Hunchaks) and the Armenian Revolutionary Federation (Tashnaks) with massacres of Kurdish and Turkish villagers, assassinations of Osmanli officials, and other violent acts. Their bloody twenty-six-year drive for an independent Armenia was doomed from the start because Armenians were not the majority of the inhabitants in the territories that they wanted to rule. [LN, JM/VAN, MC]

The violence climaxed in a catastrophic civil war as the Armenians' ally, the Russian Empire, invaded Anadolu in World War One and were assisted by Russian-armed Armenian guerilla forces that attacked Osmanli military sites and non-Armenian villages thru-out the eastern regions of Anadolu. Massacres and ethnic cleansing were accompanied by famine and widespread disease among all the ethnic groups. Eastern Anadolu became a grossly depopulated wasteland for years. [GL, JM/D&E, SJS]

My father and Veysi were relieved to arrive safely in America. My hope was that I would survive Korea and be able to return safely to America as well.

¶The interior of our troopship gave us much less living space than we had back at Pendleton. It's tempting to speculate about what "quarters" really means; we're talking about 25 percent of something. I can now make the case that the writer of the biblical story of Jonah (and the whale that swallowed him) would have better understood Jonah's predicament, if he had traveled on a troopship.

Many years later I learned how ignorant I was. I was traveling in luxuriousness without knowing it. The *Randall* had an official troop capacity of 5,289 and we were only about 2,000! On her maiden voyage in World War II, she left Norfolk Virginia in May 1944 with nearly 5000 troops and arrived, via Panama and Australia, in Mumbai India seven weeks later.

Maybe that's closer to what my fellow Turkish-American, Frank Ahmed describes as the shipboard conditions on the journey from Turkiye to America shortly before World War I. He got the information firsthand from his father and other members of the Turkish immigrant community, who were all males, in New England. Most of these persons came from the Harput region, my dad's birthplace.

Frank writes:

> The journey to Marseille was a nightmare for these farmers and shepherds. All of the immigrants were herded into steerage, packed together in extremely close, often unclean, quarters. The trip across the Atlantic was somewhat more comfortable but not by modern standards. For these poor rural immigrants, who expected so little in the way of comfort, it was acceptable. The sleeping accommodations were hammocks. Food was served from large buckets into tin plates arranged close together on long wooden tables. [FA xxi]

¶My quarters on the *Randall* were Compartment C-2, three decks below the main deck. Think of Compartment C-2 as a large ships' lounge partitioned into bays, holding scores of men sleeping in racks, stacked six high, about eighteen inches apart.

A rack was a rectangular frame of one or two-inch diameter steel pipe, painted grey like so much else on the ship. The rack was about two feet wide and six-and-a-half feet long; its outside corners were curved. Like the drop leaf of an old-fashioned desk, one side of the frame was hinged to the bulkhead (wall); the outer side was suspended by a chain bolted at about forty-five degrees to the bulkhead. The sleeping surface was a sheet of dirty canvas, edged with brass grommets spaced six inches apart, laced tautly to the frame by a thin rope. All the racks could be folded up against the bulkhead to open up space for us to sweep and swab (mop) the deck.

As we first entered our quarters, the sailors advised us: "For sanitation, self-defense, or riot prevention do not occupy the upper racks, if you think you might get seasick." Perhaps they should also have told us that in case of diarrhea a lower rack would be best, for everybody around.

Thrice a day we were invited to dine in the ship's mess hall by a voice calling out over the public address system, "Chow down for Compartment C-2 and cabin-class enlisted passengers. Form port and starboard mess lines." Most of the time that was a welcome invitation, but for anyone who was seasick, it might even bring on more nausea.

The mess hall was perfectly suited for a ship that pitches fore and aft and rolls port to starboard. Thus, there were no chairs, stools, or anything else to sit on; everyone ate standing up. The metal tables were like lunch counters securely bolted to vertical metal poles that were themselves bolted thru flanges to the deck and to the overhead (ceiling). The tables had a raised rim around their edge so that food trays, etc. would not slide off. The idea was to provide a stable surface to hold food trays and an object to hang onto as the ship moved in various ways. The deck was easy to clean because the only things on it were the bottom of the poles.

Aboard ship, clean water must be parsimoniously used, hence the "navy shower." It starts by quickly wetting your body and immediately turning off the water flow. But you're using sea water; it doesn't lather up easily. Nevertheless, you rub yourself all over with the soap. Finally, you turn on the shower again to quickly rinse off. Then you turn off the water, step out of the shower, and dry yourself with a towel.

The bathroom facility (the head) is located at the stern of the ship. So if it's there, why is it referred to as "the head?" Because on sailing ships, where it got its name, it was located near the bow, meaning downwind (and downsmell) from the rest of the ship. On modern ships the wind is going from bow to stern, so the head is located appropriately.

Instead of separate commode units, there is the equivalent of a long benchlike platform running crosswise to the ship's keel and having individual toilet-seat openings. The droppings go into a gutter, running the full length of the platform. It has drainage pipes, but the speed of outflow is affected by the number of men using it and the amount of rolling that the ship is doing. The sloshing about of the sewage, the bubbling and gurgling noises, and the accompanying smell are nothing to write home about.

On vacation cruise ships, passengers have a full array of optional activities to keep them occupied; on the *Randall* participation was mandatory. We did calisthenics and even some practice with our weapons. I guess we shouldn't complain, after all we weren't paying any money for the cruise.

A select few were assigned to work in the galley (thank God I was *not* one of them) and some Marines learned to use chisels to chip off old marine paint from the ship's steel surfaces, clean the surfaces with steel bristle brushes, and brush on fresh paint. Nevertheless, most of us did have some time for reading and walking around the ship every day.

¶I do not like the sea. It is desolate and dangerous. When I look out from the railing, I see where the sky meets the ocean's surface about thirteen miles away, all around our ship; it's no wonder thirteen is an unlucky number. Nothing stable is protruding upward from the ocean. What happens to us if our ship sinks?

There is much deception in the sea's appearance. By day it reflects the sky's color, ranging from beautiful blue to glummer grey.

It is merely copying the sky's colors and can make no claim to possessing them innately. By night it ignores the countless starlites and reflects only the brightest moonlite, restricting it to a beam hemmed in by black water.

The ocean can claim mastery of surface texture. Much of the time it is smooth-rolling waves and swells. Less frequently it can be glassy-looking steppes of water; in storms it is wild turbulence.

The sea proclaims nature's power; seldom does it reveal nature's beneficence. If my mother's eighteenth century ancestors had known in advance about the dangers of the sea, would they have left England, Scotland, or Wales to cross the Atlantic in wooden sailing vessels to reach America?

Barely five months before I went aboard ship in San Diego, the first Marine Division was on ships converging on Inch'ŏn for an incredible invasion that would reverse the dire course of the Korean War. They too faced the prodigious dangers of the sea, as Tyfoon Kezia battered their ships with a glancing blow. No doubt this induced great stress among the Marines, and probably many silent prayers for safety.

But Tyfoon Kezia did not use its full fury against our ships. It spared them by changing course. There would be no repetition of the thirteenth-century tyfoons that destroyed two Chinese invasion fleets sent by Mongol Emperor Kublai Khan to conquer Japan—storms that the Japanese gratefully named *Kamikaze* (divine wind).

Altho the NKPA at Inch'ŏn got no divine wind protection, everything else seemed adequate to protect them from any American invasion. The tides varied so much, about thirty feet, that a reference table of tide levels could tell them the few dates in the year when they should be ready to repel an invasion attempt. Even then miles of mudflats (unpassable at low tide), a narrow channel (easily mined), and a fortified offshore island were barriers that would impede any attempt to land hostile armed forces.

Besides all of this, there were no beaches, only seawalls rising from very narrow rocky strips at the water's edge, plus a few easily destroyed piers. If not impossible, at least an invasion was totally impractical.

The tide data made 15 September 1950, the best date for the totally impractical invasion of Inch'ŏn; it was officially called *Operation Chromite*. It was also the nineteenth birthday of Jack Underwood, a young Marine from Alabama. Like the rest of the 1st Marines who were to storm ashore on Blue Beach, he was in the small fleet of landing craft that started out from the troopship early in the afternoon. The craft followed each other in one big circle, round and round for a couple of hours and finally straightened out to form a wave rolling toward the shore. He was not thinking that what they were doing was impossible. He did realize that it wasn't good to be landing so late in the afternoon. [JHJ]

Fig. 11-2: Inchŏn: Lt Baldomero Lopez leads his Marines over the seawall. Soon, while wounded, he sacrifices his life on an enemy grenade to protect his men.

When their landing craft noisily scraped onto the narrow rocky strip, he and the others hurried across it. Some of the 1st Marines had landed carrying ladders; they used these to clamber up and over the sea walls. Jack and his fireteam hustled up a short, steep slope and quickly went over its crest. A few Marines got wounded immediately but Jack's fireteam kept going until it reached nearby rice fields where the men set up their defense perimeter for the night.

But his birthday would not pass without some sort of perverse "gift." A mortar shell plummeted into the soggy earth right next to him, and did not explode! It sank deep into the soil so that only the trailing edges of its tail fins were visible.

For the next two weeks, the 1st Marine Division, soon joined by the first combat units of the Korean Marine Corps, plus the Army's 7th Infantry Division, fought their way thru the port city of Inch'ŏn, the next town (Yongdungpo), and the South Korean capital, Seoul. The 1stMARDIV received its second Presidential Unit Citation for the campaign.

The success of *Operation Chromite* meant that the NKPA forces besieging the Pusan Perimeter were now in danger of being trapped as the 8th Army broke out of the perimeter and attacked north-westward to link up with the surging UN forces that were driving eastward and southward thru Seoul.

On a patrol in Seoul, Bob Davis saw a shocking and sickening sight:

> Behind some peasant homes. . . we found about 30 bodies of wom-en and small children, some infants, all piked to death with North Korean bayonets. From that day on I had no hesitation in pulling a trigger without compassion.

Elsewhere in the city Jack Underwood would be wounded by a North Korean grenade and later return from the hospital to join another impossible military operation at a place in North Korea called Chosin.

87

¶Before our ship reached Japan, I saw more evidence of kooky ideas by young men. Maybe they had been at sea too long. Some Marines wanted to use nature to launder their dirty clothes. Their solution: put the dirty clothes into a seabag, tie it to one end of a long rope, throw the seabag over the stern of the ship, tie the other end of the rope to the ship's railing. Of course, the rope broke and the seabag made its way to Davey Jones's locker. My guess is that they failed because they did not put enough, if any, soap into the seabag. Everybody knows that soap makes bubbles and that bubbles float on the ocean surface. There was no need for the seabag to sink, if only they had been less stingey with the soap.

¶After fifteen days at sea I was relieved to see the coast of Japan, that nation which we had loathed so much during World War II, barely five-and-a-half years ended. But it was land, solid, firm soil. People lived there and were aware of our American superiority. Still retaining some hatred, I thought, *We beat these son of a bitches and now occupy their goddam country.* Also, they had geisha houses.

Some of the Marines had been talking about "getting some ass" (women) before we landed, on 1 March 1951. A couple of guys seem to have thought about that subject quite carefully. I remember one of them saying:

> Don't have anything to do with the women in Kobe. This is a busy international port city. A lot of ships dock here and a lot of their crews use the geisha houses here. There's a much greater chance of getting VD (venereal disease) in Kobe. That's why we're going to jump on a train and go to Osaka to visit the geisha houses there. It's much safer. The trains are cheap and fast. So why take a chance with the women in Kobe?

It had the ring of wisdom to it, but most of us were too foolish to abide by that advice.

¶Before doing anything with any women anywhere, we had to go to a U.S. military warehouse to drop off the seabags that held our regular uniforms and other gear that we would not need in Korea. After that, we were given eight hours shore leave; our first objective was to find out where the geisha house district was. Next, we wanted to know where we could do some shopping. Both of those were to be found in a section called Motomachi.

The geisha house was a traditional Japanese residence, made mainly of wood resting on posts in the ground. It had a slightly raised porch, covered by a sloping roof. We were invited into the reception room by the *mamasan* who had the geishas line up for our selection. We chose our preference and then went into a tiny bedroom to have sex.

To call them geishas is not accurate. They were really prostitutes dressed in attractive kimonos. They did not do dancing, perform the tea ceremony, or sing, as trained geishas traditionally do. At that stage of my life my hormones were far more developed than my appreciation of Japanese artistry and culture.

Afterward, I went into a department store and asked for the lavatory. I could not read the Japanese sign outside the door, and just went inside and sat on one of the commodes. There were no partitions and no one else in the room. Soon, a Japanese woman walked in, hiked up her dress, and sat down on a commode next to me. My jaw dropped, I turned my head to face the other way, and felt temporary constipation.

She wiped herself, stood up, and flushed the toilet. She left as quickly as she had come in. It was all very businesslike, altho not very ladylike, according to my cultural biases. Then I was able to quickly finish and leave that place.

Years later I learned the word "unisex." I wish the Japanese had been using some appropriate unisex logo to warn me before I entered any facility where special body functions are performed.

¶After two days in port, we left for Korea. We sailed thru the Inland Sea, where countless islands and rocky formations abound.

Small Japanese fishing boats were everywhere. I could not imagine how our ship could safely make its way thru this area. But I believed we would arrive in Korea safely.

Two days later, 5 March 1951, after having passed thru the Tsushima Strait and the main part of the Korea Straits, we saw the port of Pusan. With tugboat assistance, the *Randall* moored at the dock. We had arrived in the "Land of Morning Calm." From the ship's railing it looked more bustling than calm. It also looked shabby and smelled bad.

We went down the gangplank, got into formation, and marched to the train station. Nothing in my life before, nor anything after, compares with the next twelve-and-a-half months. Like countless ancestors before me, I was entering the kingdom of war where I might get killed, and I was too young for it all.

Chapter 12
IN THE STEPS OF THE CHOSIN FEW

AS THE 6TH REPLACEMENT DRAFT, we were a temporary organization, hardly a unit. We would be dispersed soon to fill vacancies thru-out the ranks of the 1st Marine Division. The march from the dock to the train station was to be our final display of strength.

We marched in platoon formation, a column of three men abreast, thru the drab and stinking streets of Pusan. We were in combat gear, our helmets covered with camouflage cloth, unlike the bare helmets worn by most of the U.S. Army. We had M1 rifles slung over our shoulders and our pockets filled with eight-round clips of ammunition. Our backpacks were stuffed with our belongings.

As we marched, we were more serious; no one seemed to be making any comments or whispering anything to others at their sides. I sensed some kind of collective power, without any pretensions of fierceness. Yet we were advancing toward the unknown. If any had apprehensions, they were well concealed. Maybe we were starting to develop that basic survival skill: fatalism.

How many of us realized that just eleven weeks before we arrived, 22,125 men of the 1st Marine Division, nearly all (to some degree) famished and suffering from exposure to frostbite, had disembarked at Pusan. They were survivors of the brutal winter campaign at the Chosin Reservoir in North Korea. Instead of being annihilated by the huge Chinese People's Liberation Army, they had fought an unbelievable battle against huge odds and emerged to reach the sea. Our Navy had brought them safely to the docks of Pusan. We were walking in their steps on the very streets that these Marines had been on so recently. We would be joining them at the front in not too many hours.

¶Who of us replacements could have known that the fate of our

1st Marine Division had been decided by the outcome of a small conflict within a large conflict? The large conflict was international war; the small conflict was a contest between two American generals. The large conflict had been precipitated by General MacArthur's orders that comprised a monstrous folly: UN forces were to race to China's border and intimidate the Communists by "planting the flag."

China had announced to the world that it would send its troops to defend North Korea from a foreign invasion, and had the power to smash an invasion. Soon they set in motion a campaign for trapping and annihilating United Nations forces in North Korea. In October 1950 the first phase began: stealthy infiltration of more than 300,000 Chinese troops into the mountains of North Korea.

Unaware of the looming disaster about to fall on United Nations forces in North Korea, two commanding figures, in a conflicted relationship, would make different decisions, with drastically different consequences. At stake in this "smaller" conflict was whether and how many of the Marines and soldiers of the 10th Corps (X Corps) would survive the coming violence in their sector of North Korea: the entire northeast.

The senior figure was Army MajGen Edward M. Almond, commander of the 10th Corps. The other was Marine MajGen Oliver P. Smith, commander of the 1st Marine Division, the largest division in that corps.

The differences between the two men's personalities and leadership styles were profound. Almond was energetic, ambitious, brusque, and prone to arbitrary actions. In a benign environment his impetuousness might be considered an inconvenience to his subordinate commanders. But with the menace of an aroused China nearby, his impetuousness amounted to recklessness.

Further handicapping Almond's analytical abilities was his blatant racism, well known (and documented) by both white officers and black enlisted men who served under his command of the Army's 92nd Division on the Italian front in World War II.

92

Fig. 12-1: At Inchŏn: (L to R), Gen. MacArthur, driver, Gen. Almond, Marine Gen. O.P. Smith, VAdm Struble.

He reflected his racism in Korea by discounting the abilities of the Chinese to seriously threaten American forces. Almond referred to them as "Chinese laundrymen" and "not very intelligent."

General Smith was methodical and cautious; he had been nicknamed the professor. His extensive combat experience in World War II underlay his unwavering insistence on maintaining control over the command structure of the entire 1st Marine Division and preparing in advance for serious contingencies. Smith was truly blessed with a superb staff that had proven themselves in battles against Japanese forces on the islands of the Western Pacific.

Therefore, the 1st Marine Division's northward advance into North Korea *was* slower than what Almond wanted. Smith's forces were taking time to stockpile ammunition and supplies along the way. The Division's three infantry regiments (1st, 5th and 7th) moved ahead so that they were not too strung out from each other, and their artillery (the 11th Marines) was close enough to give them support.

General Smith even had the foresight to get his Marine engineers to build an air strip for receiving supplies and evacuating the wounded. The time taken to do it was one of the best use of resources possible, as events were to prove.

Nearly 61 years later a former Marine, Rev. Hugh A. Miller, Chaplain, wrote this tribute to Gen. Oliver P Smith and his staff:

I was in one of the line companies who first occupied Hagaru, the base camp at the south end of the Reservoir. I was there standing behind my Captain in the circle who welcomed General Smith and members of the Division when their helicopters landed.

After greetings to regimental and battalion leaders, their first attention was the priority of creating an airstrip capable of handling twin engine cargo planes of the C-46 size.

'Get the engineers in here immediately,' he ordered, and an aide went to the helicopter radio to give the order.

Because of that order bulldozers were able to get up the long mountain trail before the enemy blockaded it. Because of that moment of caring for his men, more than 4000 of us were evacuated to medical care and safety.

It was an anxious moment when the plane took wing, and cleared the canal below, and began the winding climb over the mountains and down to Hŭngnam.

Because our General cared, we survived! We can all be thankful for General Smith and his staff for their caring. Because they cared, we live today! [*The Chosin Few News Digest*, July-September 2011, p.17]

A quarter century later, Army MajGen Almond expressed his dissatisfaction with Smith, saying:

I got the impression initially (and it was fortified constantly later) that General Smith always had excuses for not performing at the required time the tasks he was requested to do. [USMKW 210]

The task that Smith resisted was a northward rush of his Marines by truck on mountainous roads to the Chinese border. He also resisted orders to send a force of Marines to participate in "Operation Mixmaster," a grandiose, quixotic, and suicidal, fifty-five-mile westward detour over forbidding mountains and thru deep snows in an unnecessary display of solidarity with the already-doomed U.S. 8th Army. *Any* implementation of MacArthur's strategy was a recipe for disaster, as it would move the Marines farther from aircraft-carrier support and even the range of helicopters necessary for supply and medical evacuations.

Even before MacArthur's irrational plan was launched, General Smith wrote a letter to the Marine Commandant complaining about the Division being strung out to the Chinese border in winter and looming problems of getting supplies in and sick or wounded Marines evacuated.

By late October, all the UN's forces were strung out too much along valley roads, vulnerable to any enemy controlling the towering heights on both sides. In November, they soon encountered Chinese forces firing down on them. Then they were cut off by Chinese roadblocks behind them.

The Army's forces on the Western front should have battled to take back the heights and attack Chinese roadblocks from the upper slopes. Instead, too many Army units stuck to the roads and tried to run the gauntlet of fire from the Chinese and ram thru any road-blocks. Road traffic was totally snarled as Army vehicles were destroyed and soldiers killed. Some died immediately, some froze to death or got frostbite, many wounded died without proper medical attention; many were captured and murdered. The collapse of unit integrity and cohesion simply added to the catastrophe. The U.S. Army's divisions were shattered.

¶The 1st Marine Division was on the eastern front in late November when it reluctantly began to move west as part of MacArthur's calamitous Operation Mixmaster. MajGen Almond, derisively known as "MacArthur's boy," was the overseer that pushed MajGen Smith to initiate the operation. The first step required the 5th and 7th Marines to kick off the fifty-five-mile drive west from Yudam-ni in bitterly cold weather. And it would move the Marines farther into remote areas where escape from encirclement would become almost impossible, if they didn't freeze to death first. Years later it seemed totally preposterous and even unrational!

Before the 5th and 7th Marines could advance very far westward, the Chinese attacked them and actually prevented them from totally entering into doom, tho the Marines suffered grievously and barely escaped intact. Thru it all, individual Marine units fought to maintain unit integrity and cohesion. And thanks to General Smith's foresight, the Division's major components had coordinated their movements, staying close enough to each other to seize the heights and break thru encirclements.

With these tactics the combined Marine forces battled their way southward to the Sea of Japan (or as Koreans call it: the Eastern Sea). When a reporter asked General Smith why his division was retreating, Smith said, "Retreat hell! We're just attacking in another direction."

The 1st Marine Regiment under Col. "Chesty" Puller was ordered to conduct rear guard action and hold the passes and perimeter at Koto-ri as the 5th and 7th Regiments fought their way back from the Chosin Reservoir.

"Chesty" received his fifth Navy Cross for his outstanding performance in the campaign. He also left us with a memorable and colorful description of the military situation. He was heard to say something like:

> We've been looking for the enemy for several days now. We've finally found them. We're surrounded. That simplifies our problem of getting to these people and killing them.

¶Near Kot'o-ri, Bob Davis was looking for the presence of Chinese Communist soldiers. It was something he had done a few years earlier, when the Marines were in north China on pacification duty, following the end of Japan's World War II occupation. [GVS] But this time he was leading one of those patrols that the 2nd Battalion 1st Marines (2/1) kept sending out to maintain security for the escape route that the 5th Marines and 7th Marines would have to use in the event of encirclement by the Chinese.

The area was strange looking, a lot of hummocks all around; they were not natural. They had to be man-made, about ten to twelve feet high. It was a necropolis. Each mound must have contained the bodies of many generations of Koreans. However, Bob and the rest

96

of the patrol were not interested in signs of the dead. They were searching the area for signs of live Chinese soldiers. As in all well-laid traps, they knew that at least some of them might be killed before they knew the enemy was at hand.

Bob walked quickly around one mound and suddenly saw a Chinese officer pointing a pistol right at him. In a split second two things happened simultaneously: his mind told him that he was seeing his last image in this world and would hear only the beginning sound of a bullet firing at him; also, he jumped back. His buddies didn't understand what was happening, there was no noise. Bob was dazed; he was still in this world! He kept looking at the pistol and saw that the officer's eyes were wide open, and did not blink; the whole body was motionless. In shock, Bob saw that the officer was kneeling on one leg and was frozen to death. The sight of that corpse would stay in Bob's memory for the rest of his life.

*Fig. 12-2: Smoke from Corsairs bombing
in support of Marines at Chosin*

¶Now descending on everybody was the brutal Siberian-type winter, with nighttime temperatures bottoming out at twenty to thirty degrees below zero (Fahrenheit), packed with howling winds. Weapons froze, fuel froze, food froze, and men froze. Lacking adequate cold-weather uniforms and equipment, the Chinese suffered

Fig. 12-3: Chinese prisoners near Chosin

from the cold even more than did the UN forces. Also, they were decimated by the effective firepower of Marine infantry (when weapons were not too frozen to shoot) that was coordinated with Marine ground-support aircraft, flying dangerously low, to attack the enemy. Marine artillery units added their valuable firepower as well, in rugged terrain hostile to all use of heavy weapons.

When the Chinese cut off the Division's escape route by blowing up a bridge, all seemed lost. But the Marines brought in, by air, sections of a prefabricated bridge and then assembled it to allow the vehicles and those on foot to continue down the road.

The campaign was an ordeal of suffering and death spread out over an expanse of eighty miles at its longest extension. The battles were fitfully fought, night and day, on mountain tops and in valleys, draws, and defiles, and sometimes upon the single-lane, frozen dirt-top roadway running south from the Chosin Reservoir to the seaport of Hŭngnam, where U.S. Navy ships were waiting to evacuate any survivors.

¶Many Marines were casualties of the cold weather; others had been wounded by the enemy. They had to be transported to survive. General Almond (hastily and thoughtlessly) suggested to General Smith that he abandon most of his vehicles. This would mean abandoning the wounded. That, the Marines would not do. They were determined to defend, maintain, and operate their trucks, jeeps,

Fig. 12-4: Marines on the Funchinlin Road near the Chosin Reservoir

and ambulances while smashing all roadblocks, and bring all their men all the way to the sea.

Ammo carrier Vic Knabel knew that he had to take care of his feet because he trusted only them to take him safely to the sea. He kept his spare socks dry by carrying them under his armpits. When it was time to swap sox, he would uncover his feet and rub them hard until they were bright red. Then he would put on the next pair.

Also escaping to the sea were crowds of Korean civilians. The Marine rearguard made the civilians keep their distance, wary of armed enemy infiltrators who could use the crowd as cover for shooting or tossing grenades at nearby Marines.

During the night the civilians huddled together on the road and their mournful sounds could be heard a long way up and down the road. Most unnerving were the sounds of women giving birth or having miscarriages. Some Marines say that for years they could not totally remove those sounds from their memory.

Toward the end of the battle, the men of the 1st Marine Division were in pitiful condition. My fellow Detroiter, Manert Kennedy (a member of the old 17th Infantry Battalion), told me:

> We were wearing up to eight layers of clothing. We had not been able to change clothing or wash it for weeks. Many of us had dysentery and it had permeated our trousers. Because of the bitter cold, we were often unable to defecate or urinate properly, it would require that we remove our gloves before opening up our trousers or dropping them down and having our buttocks and penises, plus our hands exposed to the cold. The urine and watery feces that had soaked into our clothing would freeze and then gradually dry out in the low humidity of the frigid air.

> Comical in name, but unpleasant on contact, were the "dingleberries." These were the little balls of dried feces that collected on the hairs around the anus. They grew with time and could be painful each time the hairs were tugged and pulled during walking. Very disgusting. We were walking piles of stinking filth. In training we had been taught field hygiene, but that was set aside in the deplorable conditions we fought under. Our degraded condition was another aspect of the loss of human dignity in combat.

> We were hungry, we were exhausted, and we were suffering from hypothermia. Our bodies' electrolyte balance had been wrecked by the diarrhea and dehydration as well as a build-up of lactic acid. These chemical changes imposed such excruciating muscle and joint pain that toward the end of our journey to the sea we were close to joining the roster of the dead.

And we were hallucinating at times. As soon as we arrived in Hŭngnam, some soldiers carried us into warming tents and laid us down on cots. I thought that I was about to be thrown into a mass grave, like the one for our men back at Kot'o-ri.

After we had warmed up, our clothing was removed and our helpers could see the wretched condition of our skin: rashes, blisters, boils, oozing sores, all compounded by insect bites from the lice which had infested our clothing. Black frozen skin covered too many men's feet.

We were helped into warm showers. We were given new clothes.

Fig. 12-5: Marine dead at Kot'o-ri

The old clothing was put into a large pile, soaked with kerosene, and set on fire by the soldiers. Then they fed us and helped us board the ships for evacuation.

¶Upon reaching Hŭngnam, the Marines were in no mood to talk about anything to anybody, including answering questions by Maggie Higgins, a well-known U.S. newspaper correspondent. She was not in any way unsupportive of our armed forces, but her eagerness to report back to her publishers occasionally got her into difficulties. She actually got a plane ride up to Kot'o-ri and was promptly put back on the aircraft by order of "Chesty" Puller.

She waited back in Hŭngnam and approached one of the newly arriving Marines, to ask, "What was the most difficult thing you experienced?" The man's reply never appeared in the stateside newspapers but has a worthy place in the oral history of the Chosin Few:

> Lady, it was trying to figure out how to take a piss with a frozen one-inch-long cock that had to get thru three inches of stiff winter clothing.

Bob Davis had survived and boarded the ship with the rest of 2/1. Jack Underwood was there too. He had recuperated in Japan from the grenade wounds he'd gotten in Seoul and arrived after the Division was heavily engaging the Chinese at Chosin.

Among 2/1's machine-gunners embarking were Gene Punte and Vic Knabel. I would become part of their unit when I joined the Division nearly three months later.

¶The evacuation from Hŭngnam was no Dunkirk. The Marines boarded ships between 11 and 15 December. They were among the 105,000 U.S. and ROK (Republic of Korea) servicemen evacuated along with 91,000 North Korean civilians. Also evacuated were 17,500 vehicles and 350,000 tons of supplies. [USMKW 334] The last Marine casualty was a lieutenant, who died on 24 December in an accidental explosion near the harbor.

Fig. 12-6: Marines boarding evacuation ship at Hŭngnam

102

The fifty-one-day Chosin Campaign had cost the 1st Marine Division 4,418 battle casualties, killed, wounded, and missing. Their non-battle casualties were higher: 7,313; most of these were from frostbite.

Fig. 12-7: Refugees aboard ship

Marine "guesstimates" of Chinese battle casualties were 25,000 killed and 12,500 wounded. If the Chinese nonbattle casualties were in the same ratio to battle casualties as were those of the Marines, then they were about 62,000, probably up to 90 percent due to frostbite.

For the Chosin campaign the Division received its third Presidential Unit Citation of the Korean War. Later the Korean government awarded its Presidential Unit Citation to our division for its total service in Korea.

¶All the companies of the 2nd Battalion, 1st Marine Regiment arrived in Pusan on 16 December and debarked from the ship by noon. They were in woeful condition. They quickly boarded the train to Masan and by 1645 were in the Ozang-won Ta assembly area, also known as the "bean patch."

The regiment was assembled to hear a pep talk from "Chesty" Puller. According to Manert Kennedy, Colonel Puller stood up on the back of a truck bed and told his fellow Marine survivors: "This is one lousy goddam war, but it's better than no war at all." It's not clear what positive effects his words had on these men. Kennedy says, "It ended my aspirations to be a full-time active duty career officer with the Marine Corps."

¶Before they were fully recovered from the Chosin ordeal, the Marines would go into combat again. Whether they recognized it or not, what they had done at Chosin would become a towering legend in the history of the United States Marine Corps!

A person who learns about the epic battle of Chosin (a Japanese name, which Koreans resent and replaced with "Changjin") can do no better in honoring the Marines than to echo the ancient bards, who praised their warriors in verse. Despite overwhelming emotions going thru my mind, I held back most of my tears and struggled several days to write the following meager tribute:

DOWN TO THE SEA WITH O.P. SMITH

From frozen heights and reservoir,
Where Death had ruled the scenes,
Down to the welcome Eastern Sea,
Came O.P. Smith's Marines.

The U.S. Navy had its ships,
Waiting to give their praise,
To the First Marine Division,
Exiting winter's maze.

104

Not bloody corpses in the snow,
But victors – grim and free,
Shortly they'd fight the foe again,
These "Soldiers of the Sea."

Carry them onward, Oh Ocean,
To Pusan on your waves,
Don't claim these Marines, but keep them,
Safe from watery graves.

Down from Chosin (some say "Changjin"),
Eighty miles, I would say,
General Smith, and a few good men,
In history had their day.

Chapter 13
NORTHWARD TO THE DIVISION

THE TRAIN PULLED AWAY from the Pusan station platform and snaked its way thru the rail yard. Freight trains were parked on some of the sidetracks paralleling the main rail line. One of these trains had rail coaches that served as living quarters for U.S. Army transportation personnel. Along with the American soldiers, there were some attractive Korean women in these coaches; none of the women was in proper military uniform. In fact, they seemed to be doing household chores, like dumping out pails of water and hanging laundry on clotheslines. I wondered what I had to do to get the kind of military duty those soldiers had. Did they need volunteers? I was ready, willing, and able.

We quickly reached the countryside and I saw nothing much of interest. Spring had not yet arrived and the vegetation was brownish or some neighboring color on the light spectrum. There was no snow in sight, but I presumed we'd see some farther up north.

I was in for culture shock when I went to use the head in a little room at the end of the coach. It did not have the Western-style commode. It was old Asian style: a raised platform in the corner with a hole cut thru its surface. As I looked down into the hole, I saw that whatever came out of my bottom would drop straight down and land on the railroad bed. But first, I had to figure out how to sit over that hole and preserve my balance, all the while squatting in a very uncomfortable way.

Because the train rocked as it went along the tracks, the situation was quite challenging. The first challenge was to figure out which way to face while squatting on the platform. I started out facing the corner walls with my back to the center of the room. I looked for wall handles to brace myself, but there were none. I figured that I might be able to brace myself with my hands against the walls, especially if the train lurched. But I got worried that I would fall backwards off the platform and onto the floor. And my accuracy of bowel movement and urination wasn't too promising.

I then turned around 180 degrees, with my back to the corner. I figured that if I fell off the platform at least I would be facing forward and be able to use my hands, and maybe my knees, to control the direction and impact of the fall. In that "corner-to-the-rear" position I completed my dump. But now I had to figure out how to stand up from the squat.

My leg and thigh muscles were aching because I just wasn't used to squatting, which so many Asians seemed to do. I used each hand to push down against each wall to elevate myself. If that had not worked (it did this time), I was prepared to try a ninety-degree pivot on one foot that would bring the other foot over the edge of the platform where it would drop down to the floor, straightening the leg enough to help me lean far enough away from the platform to pull the other bended leg over the edge and down to the floor.

The best thing I did before attempting any of these gyrations was to use plenty of toilet paper to wipe myself as clean as a whistle and spare my clothing from getting accidentally smeared, regardless of how I managed to dismount, or fall, from the platform.

I thank God that I had only one bowel movement during the five or six-hour trip north. If I had been afflicted with diarrhea, I imagine any attempt to describe the situation in more detail would be preparing me to become a professional writer of yoga literature or maybe techniques of waste management.

Returning to the seating area of the car, I wondered what to do about the more frequent body function of urinating. I briefly toyed with the idea of opening a window and using that to relieve myself, hoping that nobody farther back in the train was sitting next to an open window to get some fresh air. But I ended up going to the head each time and developing a special leaning position that kept both my feet on the swaying floor, both hands pressed against the walls, and my body bowing low over the platform. It wasn't a pretty sight and I'm glad I had spare toilet paper to clean up the mess around the hole each time.

¶After only a few hours travel, we were close to where our division had fought "The Pohang Guerilla Hunt" (informally called *Operation Rathunt*). It was a thirty-eight-day campaign, 11January to 15 February 1951, against some 6,000 troops of the Tenth NKPA Division, a division that had inflicted more casualties on UN forces and captured more of our equipment than any other in their army.

The zone of action was a 1,600-square mile area of hilly terrain stretching from the east-coast inland about forty miles. Its southern edge was about sixty miles north of Pusan (one-third of the way to the Thirty-eighth Parallel). The "Hunt" was a textbook anti-guerilla campaign that ended the Tenth Division's effectiveness as a fighting force by mid-February, 1951, only three weeks before our train passed thru the area.

Fifty-five years later, Max Buzman (fictional name) told me about a nasty incident during the "Hunt" that had left him with disturbing memories. He knew that some Marines had done something wrong—criminally and morally wrong. [see CVL about an example soon after Inch'ŏn]

Buzman was with the 1st Marines in the northwest sector of the zone of action. On 5 February, his company advanced on a small village, not knowing what to expect. It was the site of an unmarked North Korean field hospital. As the Marines got closer, several dozen unarmed North Korean soldiers on crutches and splinted legs ran out of the houses and scampered up the nearby hills and rice paddies. The Marines had a clear field of fire at the North Korean soldiers, who kept running. It was a turkey shoot. Buzman did not like the Marines' glee as they shot down the unarmed enemy soldiers.

Buzman was a warrior; he performed his duties, including killing his share of the enemy, but killing was not something he relished. He must've been of the same mentality as Captain John Philip, who commanded the dreadnought USS *Texas* at the 1898 Battle of

108

Santiago Cuba. Philip told his crew as they passed a burning enemy vessel, "Don't cheer, men. Those fellows are dying."

After shooting the running North Koreans, the Marines made a house-to-house search. Buzman heard shooting and ran over to the house where the shooting came from. The door was open and out came Sergeant Drew Edwards (fictional name) and several members of his squad.

"What happened?" Buzman asked.

"Oh, just a few gooks inside that needed finishing off," was Sergeant Edwards's curt answer.

Buzman looked inside and saw the bodies of about twenty, previously wounded or sick North Korean soldiers lying on straw mats. Sergeant Edwards had simply gone around shooting each one in the head with his pistol.

Buzman protested, "You shouldn't have done that. They should have been taken prisoner."

"Fuck you, Buzman. They're nothing but gooks."

Buzman was getting angrier and so was Edwards; they leveled their weapons at each other. Finally, Buzman turned in disgust and walked away.

Fifty years later, at a 2/1 Marine veterans reunion in New Orleans, Buzman entered a hotel elevator and saw Edwards. "Do you remember what you did?" Buzman asked. "Fuck you, Buzman. That was war," was his response.

¶A month later, when the division was fighting near Hoengsŏng, Berthold Guenavis (fictional name) witnessed an atrocity that still haunts him, despite the passage of fifty-seven years. Appropriately, it was the very savagery implied in the name of the military campaign he was involved in: *Operation Killer*.

They had just finished defeating a North Korean unit of one or two platoons. Most of the enemy may have escaped but dozens had been killed. The Marines climbed aboard trucks and waited for the convoy to get going. One of the guys in the truck looked out at a large field and noticed, "Hey there are some wounded gooks over there."

The gunny spoke up, "Get out of the trucks. You guys come with me. You know we're not supposed to take any prisoners, wounded or not. Go finish them off." Guenavis walked around checking bodies; all of those were dead.

He heard a few shots. It was the gunny; he had found a few still alive and was shooting them, one shot to the head.

Guenavis was about ten to twelve feet away watching his squad leader, a buck sergeant, approach what looked like an older man (probably a civilian porter). The man was trying to shield his eyes from the sun. The Sergeant pointed his M1 at the man but, to Guenavis's surprise, turned his head away and emptied a clip [eight bullets] toward the man, leaving him still alive.

The gunny had seen everything. He strode over, angry at the sergeant and immediately shot the Korean man in the head. "What the fuck is wrong with you, sergeant? Can't I trust you to carry out my instructions?" Then he turned to look at Guenavis. "You're standing right next to him. Couldn't you have done the job?" The gunny walked away, clearly disgusted. "OK. Get back up on the trucks. We're moving out."

Guenavis returned to the truck. He had just witnessed something sickening. In Seoul he had seen the more numerous victims of Communist atrocities. But now he wondered what evil might be contaminating his own Marines in this war.

If I had known about the battles that had occurred so recently in this sector, and the danger of rail sabotage or attacks by surviving enemy infiltrators, I would have understood better why we were put on alert during the next three hours until we got close to our destination, Chech'ŏn. There we got off the train and boarded trucks. That ride was about two hours and brought us to Hoengsŏng, which the division had just captured. We got off the trucks and were met by someone who told us to spread our waterproof-shelter halves on the ground and get a good night's sleep so that we would be ready to

110

join our units in the morning. Some snow was still on the ground, but I had a good night's sleep.

The next morning I met my unit, the machine-gun unit, attached to Dog Company in 2/1. I was paired with Myles H. Jackman of East St. Louis Illinois and given two heavy cans of .30 caliber machine-gun ammunition to carry. My job title was: "ammo carrier." An apter term would be "beast of burden."

Chapter 14
FIRST DAYS ON THE FRONT

MY FIRST DAY ON THE LINE was peaceful. It was almost like camping days in the Boy Scouts: being outdoors, living out of a backpack, and cooking our own food over a fire. For the first time I was eating C-rations. And they tasted good. But that would gradually change as the days wore on. At least camping as a Boy Scout was short-term and we soon returned to Mom's home cooking.

As the evening approached, the ambience changed; I sensed a growing tension. I was assigned to stand guard on our "gun" (not a rifle), a .30 caliber light machine-gun. A man named "Smitty" (from Jackson Michigan, I think) was to stand guard in a "watch hole" forward of our positions. Smitty asked me to lend him my carbine because it was lighter and had more bullets in the clip. So I had his M1 rifle with me during the night.

Soon after dark I heard a lot of small-arms fire in the valley. The North Koreans were attacking a U.S. Army water-purification unit, which had a large water tub; it was getting shot up. Tracer bullets were flying thru the air. The enemies' tracer bullets had a green-colored fiery tail; ours were red.

With all the noise going on I decided I preferred to have my carbine. I called out to Smitty, "Smitty give me back my weapon." Smitty replied, "Come and get it."

I wasn't going to crawl out of my hole to fetch it and so I stayed put. Corporal Punte heard us talking and was amused. More than half a century later he delighted in recalling it when we discussed our days in Korea.

The second evening I saw "Chief" getting ready to go out on patrol. Chief was an Ojibwa (or Osage) Indian, named Augustine Oberg. He could not have been a real chief because he wasn't more than thirty-five-or-so years old. Why was he called chief? That's a nickname that all American Indians in the Marines used to get stuck with.

Fig. 14-1: Chief

Chief liked to go out on night patrols. The rumor was that he returned with the cut-off ears of enemy soldiers. He initiated these night patrols, even when they had not been ordered by his officers. Why on earth would he do such a thing?

Jack Underwood came to dread Chief's initiatives. Without realizing the consequences, Jack had revealed that one of his grandmothers was Cherokee. That was enough for Chief to see Jack as a blood brother. Naturally, Chief would prefer having a blood brother come along on the patrols and often "volunteered" Jack to go along with him.

Jack regrets having said anything about his lineage. He wonders if he might have avoided having to accompany Chief on patrol, if he had claimed that his lineage was a tribe called Leghorn or perhaps Rhode Island Red (both are types of chicken).

¶Myles H. Jackman had been in World War II as I recollect. He seemed to be about thirty-five years old. His hair was jet black and his complexion was almost light olive. His beard was sparse. I wondered whether he was part-American Indian. However, he was

113

from East St. Louis Illinois, which is many miles away from Indian country: Indiana.

The uncanny thing about Jackman was his ability to make a fire any time and any place, even with wet wood.

Fig. 14-2: Jackman

More mysterious were the reasons that drove him to build so many fires. I didn't think it was a good idea to keep making fires because I thought smoke would give away our positions to the enemy but, somehow, Jackman's fires didn't seem to give off much smoke. He enjoyed building a fire and then holding out his hands to warm them. He liked to gaze at the fire and took pride in his fire-making skills.

There must be a suitable term for people like Jackman. Pyromaniac is not appropriate, because it implies illegality, and I wouldn't want to vilify my foxhole buddy. Besides, he wasn't doing anything illegal. I've thought of "firomaniac, conflagarant, inflammator" and even "armed incendiary." However, like everybody else in our machine-gun unit, I ended up calling him "Jackman the Firebuilder."

He didn't need to build a fire for cooking because we had been issued Sterno. All we had to do to heat our cans of precooked food was to pry off the lid of the Sterno can, drop it (upright) into the stove can and drop a lighted match into it.

The stove can was made from an empty food can. Using a "church key" (the one that makes a triangular opening on the top lid of cans of liquid) we made perforations around its sides near the bottom and a few near the top rim. The can's original lid had been removed to leave an open top. We then put our can of food on it. The can of food had its top lid peeled outward to serve as a handle.

Jackman enjoyed heating wash water over a wood fire. With the liners removed, our steel helmets made a perfect round-bottom pot

114

and a natural washbasin for our faces, feet, etc. as well as for washing socks and underwear.

I had joined the unit right after it had finished capturing Hoengsŏng. A few days later we moved northward as the NKPA was retreating. We were still involved in Operation Ripper, the follow-on offensive to Operation Killer. The enemy was not making a stand against us on the east-central front. Unfortunately, the Chinese were planning a big offensive and in April we would bear the brunt of their massive fury.

The smell of some smoke in Korea was something that affected my subconscious. It was not like tobacco smoke nor any of Jackman's campfires. It was something distinct. I first noticed it passing burned-out houses. They were still smoldering as we passed by. I felt pity for the people who had been living there. Was the smell of burning flesh mixed in with that of the burned mud walls and straw roofs? For ten or so years after coming back home, whenever I smelled burning substances my mind flashed back to Korea.

As we walked along a road near Hongch'ŏn, we passed some houses where village women were lined up at the side of the road; there were no men. They were calling out *manse, manse, manse* (Hail to you!). I assumed they were welcoming us, and probably hoping we would move on.

A few of the women were wearing very short-length jackets, which did not fully cover their breasts. One of our squad smiled as he passed closer to them and reached out to gently pat upwards the underside of the few breasts he spotted. We all laughed and a few of us even blushed.

¶Right from the beginning I was having problems keeping pace on the trail with the unit. We walked close to the ridgelines, being careful to stay just below the crest; walking right on the crest would make us clearly silhouetted targets for snipers. Our elevation was hundreds of feet above sea level and I wasn't used to exerting myself at that elevation. In addition, I was burdened by the forty-pound weight of the machine-gun ammunition in those steel boxes, twenty pounds on each side of me. They were suspended from a strap that hung around my neck and simply drained my energy, hour after hour.

I soon learned to just put one foot in front of the other and never look uphill. Otherwise I might become dismayed at how much farther I had to go. Still, I was heavily laboring.

During the first week on the trail as I was falling behind the rest of the guys, one of the men ahead called back, "Hey, Alli! There's somebody here who wants to help you carry your ammo." We kept moving and I soon saw what he was referring to: the burned corpse of an enemy soldier near the trail. I was being mocked and did not like it. I disliked shirkers, and was doing my best to keep up, yet it seemed like I was dragging an invisible anchor behind me. It was bad for my morale and I felt ashamed.

It didn't seem right that the other Marines were not having the same trouble. Some were smaller than I and didn't look as strong as I. I was not a smoker, but many of the other Marines were smokers, altho they seldom smoked along the trail. My problem never went away. *What was wrong with me?*

One day we were on the trail at a higher elevation than I had encountered since joining the unit. As usual, I was having difficulty keeping up. More and more units were filing by me.

Periodically our column would stop so that the men could sit down or even lie down to rest. These breaks were usually for fifteen minutes. That would give me some time to catch up to my unit, but it also meant I did not get a full break before the march resumed.

This time when I reached my unit they were on a longer break than usual. Because the weather was a little cool and it looked like the break would be long enough, Jackman had started a fire!

I trudged toward some of our crew; they were standing on all sides of Jackman's fire, enjoying the warmth. As I reached them and

116

stood there still panting and getting kidded about my "tardiness," somebody yelled, "Hey! There's a grenade in that fire!"

Everybody scattered. I don't know where I got the strength. It must've been adrenaline kicking in, but I ran up the slope, toward the close crest of the hill, almost knocking down a few guys in my way. I leapt just over it and flung myself down on the ground and waited for the explosion. When the grenade exploded, it hurled shrapnel everywhere, but along with the shrapnel were tiny glowing cinders from the burning firewood. Fortunately, nobody was injured and nothing caught fire.

Afterward we came back to the fire site, still rattled, and tried to figure out how the grenade had dropped into it. It must have fallen off somebody's pack or slipped out of a belt loop, or whatever. Altho no one could figure out how it had happened, we all agreed that the grenade would have killed every one of us if no one had noticed it in the fire, and if we had not scattered. Years later Punte told me that Herb Hummel was the one who yelled out the warning.

The stress of the accident was reduced by a bit of humor, at my expense, by one guy who said, "When I saw Alli running fast, I knew something really bad was going to happen."

Even funnier was the "compliment" given to Jackman: "Jackman, that's the hottest fire you ever built!"

Chapter 15
A SHAMEFUL ILLNESS

EARLY IN THE TWENTIETH CENTURY, Margaret Mead, a famous cultural anthropologist, concluded from her field studies that the most critical challenge for any society is what to do about the young males. She would have had a field day studying the challenge of what to do about the young men in the United States Marine Corps.

The latest research into the human brain has yielded interesting findings that may explain risky behavior. The brain is not "fully wired" until a person is between twenty and thirty years old (males later than females, of course). Many earlier observations by harried parents, teachers, physicians, clerics, police, and others, had concluded (at least for young males) that the cause may not be the wiring of the brain as much as its chemistry, too many raging hormones flooding it and the rest of the body.

A young Marine once asked his father, a former Marine, "Dad, do you know why every young man has a nickname for his penis?" The father said, "No. What's the reason?" The son told him that, "young men want to be on friendly terms with the thing that is controlling their mind."

During World War II, the U.S. government produced movies for training the military in prevention of sexually transmitted diseases. We saw one of these at Camp Pendleton. It was a sober eye-opener to some of us but humorous to others. I honestly think that most of us were too immature to realize the seriousness of the health risks. After presenting the film, the sergeant made a few remarks, starting with, "Flies breed disease. Keep yours zipt!" Then he proceeded to answer questions, interspersed with a few more crude but entertaining remarks. One of them had to do with transmission of VD:

> If any of you guys come down with the "clap" (gonorrhea) but tell me that you got it from using a toilet seat, I'm going to tell you that you can't get it from a toilet seat. Also, that's a hell of a place to be

118

taking a girl!

A common practice of the Marine Corps was the "short-arm" inspection. For those interested in etymology, or possessing a vivid imagination, the name is intriguing.

Here's how it worked: without any advance notification, our platoon would be ordered to fall in (get into the usual formation) and the platoon sergeant, accompanied by a medical corpsman, would begin going down the line examining the penis of each man. When they came to the man, he had to unbutton the fly of his trousers, reach inside, and pull out his penis for inspection. How humiliating!

The corpsman would tell the man what to do to expose all surfaces of the organ, for example, "Lift it up," "Pull it to the left," "Pull it to the right," "Let go of it." Sometimes the corpsman would ask a question like, "What's that blemish?" and "How did you get that?" Then a person had to "milk" his penis to force out any liquid, which could be a sign of an infection. The corpsman never touched anyone's organ; the main things he was looking for were excretions and chancres. Naturally, Marines had a nickname for corpsmen: "shanker mechanics."

Each Marine was exposed for only a minute or so while the corpsman was standing in front of him. The discomfort was more psychological than physical; after all we were in the mild climate of southern California. Would they ever attempt such an inspection in the cold winter of Korea? I hoped not.

During our shore leave in Kobe Japan, we had visited geisha houses. Did any of us have any concerns based on our training at Pendleton? I don't believe so. A few weeks later, I heard about those Marines who had told us on the ship that they were going to take a train to Osaka and visit the geisha houses there, which they had claimed were "safer." It seems that a few of them contracted gonorrhea.

Ned Harpur (fictional name) got concerned about his wayward behavior with Kobe's geishas, a few hours after the ship left for

119

Korea. He checked in at the ship's sick bay and mentioned his carnal encounters ashore. A corpsman gave him a prophylactic kit and told him to follow the printed instructions. He had to use a tube of some kind of ointment and stick its tapered nozzle into the opening of his penis and then gradually squeeze the substance back into his urinary tract, not a painless process. This required Ned to squeeze his penis shaft, starting at the tip and force the ointment toward his groin (the reverse motion of milking a cow). Later he joked with a few of us that altho the medical people called it a "*pro*fylactic," it had made him "*anti*fylactic."

A month after arriving in Korea, Ned went to the corpsman because he was getting scared about a red pimple on the underside of his organ. The corpsman used a magnifying glass to study it closely and then squeezed it with his fingers, much to Ned's surprise and pain. After Ned stopped yelling, he asked the corpsman, "What is it?" "It's only an ingrown hair," the corpsman said as he took a wad of cotton, poured some alcohol onto it, and applied it to the affected area. Ned grimaced in pain. Then and there he decided that he needed to change his lifestyle. In the future he would avoid prostitutes.

¶My encounter with illness was more sudden and serious than what afflicted Ned, and mine did not involve sex. It started shortly before dawn on 22 March. I was on watch and had to leap out of my foxhole and run a few yards away, where I had an attack of diarrhea. When that was done, I went back to the foxhole, feeling nauseated. About twenty minutes later, I leaped out again, ran a short distance, and dropped to my hands and knees to vomit. I felt weak. I went back to the foxhole again, feeling worse. A couple more times I leaped out and vomited or let loose with diarrhea. I crouched low whenever moving outside the hole, aware that I could be an easy target for enemy snipers.

I felt terrible. I knew that I would not be able to walk, much less carry the heavy cans of ammo, when our unit set out on its next advance. And I couldn't hold down any food to regain my strength. Corporal Punte told me to go to the Battalion Aid Station (BAS), which was down the back slope of our hill.

Unable to stand up, I started crawling down the hill and even did some sideways rolling downhill. After maybe a hundred feet, I was in a defile and looking for the BAS. I saw somebody and they told me that the BAS was *up* the defile a short distance. I slowly crawled in that direction, feeling weaker and weaker.

I struggled a few yards then saw two men coming toward me with a stretcher. They put me on it, carried me down the draw to the road, and loaded me into a jeep ambulance that was equipped to carry up to four persons on stretchers. But I was the only person being transported. The driver started out a little too fast, I thought. As we bounced across a nearly dry creek bed, he slowed up and turned his head slightly to ask over his shoulder whether I was wounded. I replied weakly, "No. I'm not." On the rest of the ride I was only half conscious.

At the 1st Medical Battalion hospital I was put onto a cot, covered with a blanket, and examined by somebody. I must have described my diarrhea and vomiting, but I was too groggy to know what was happening. I don't know whether they gave me intravenous feeding, an injection, medicine by mouth (doubtful), or anything else. I do know I slept a long time.

One morning I heard a corpsman talking to the physician. "Doc, you remember that badly wounded captain? Well, he died last night." I was sorry to overhear that. And right away I felt ashamed that I was in the hospital not for being wounded but merely for being sick with something they called "gastroenteritis." I wanted to leave as soon as possible.

According to the records in my Marine Corps personnel file, I was in the hospital for three days. According to the 2nd Battalion unit diary for 23 April 1951, my fellow ammo carrier Burt Anderson, also a Sixth Replacement Draft member, spent time in that hospital from 3Apr51 to 10Apr51. I wonder whether just being a newcomer

121

meant more vulnerability to the stress of front-line conditions.

The jeep took me back to my unit, which had moved forward but was now in reserve and living in tents. Shower tents had been set up and I had a glorious shower. *Wouldn't it be great if we could have a shower at least once a month?*

¶Easter was 25 March and I had something to be thankful for; my health had been resurrected in three days. But I still felt ashamed that I had been unable to stay with my unit on the front line and do my duty as an ammo carrier.

The religious services were in a beautiful wooded area with the soothing sounds of a flowing creek nearby. The chaplain was a southern Baptist and he chose one of their most rousing hymns to finish the service:

> Do Lord, O do Lord, O do remember me,
> Do Lord, O do Lord, O do remember me,
> Do Lord, O do Lord, O do remember me,
> > Way beyond the blue.

> I've got a home in Glory Land, that outshines the Sun
> > Outshines the Sun; Yes, outshines the Sun.
> I've got a home in Glory Land, that outshines the Sun
> > Way beyond the blue.

> Do Lord, O do Lord, O do remember me,
> Do Lord, O do Lord, O do remember me,
> Do Lord, O do Lord, O do remember me,
> > Way beyond the blue.

> I took Jesus as my Savior, you take Him too,
> I took Jesus as my Savior, you take Him too,
> I took Jesus as my Savior, you take Him too,
> > While He's calling you!

Nevertheless, Glory Land would have to wait. A lot of things were going to happen to me here in Korea and I hoped the Lord would remember me, but *this* side of "the blue" too, not just "way beyond" it.

Chapter 16
SPRING: NEW LIFE, NEW DEATH

APRIL IS BEAUTIFUL in Kangwŏndo province; living outdoors is the way to enjoy it. In accordance with nature's cycles,
temperatures slowly warm up and the days get longer. In this
mountainous province, we saw a new layer of greenery sprouting,
new life emerging.

In accordance with man's cycles, things were warming up too.
The two warring sides were making preparations that would involve
new deaths. After all, in the military tradition springtime introduces
new opportunities for combat with the enemy and acquiring new
territory. To celebrate the coming of spring during wartime, we have
"the spring offensive." Man's red colors would fertilize Nature's
greens.

For three weeks in April we advanced north. The terrain was
getting hillier as we got nearer the Hwach'ŏn Reservoir, less than
twenty miles southwest of the mountainous "Punchbowl."

Our movements each day were a routine: setting out each morning, carefully scouting out the terrain, occasionally being harassed by
snipers, sometimes having an enemy mortar or artillery shell explode
nearby, but still no strong enemy resistance; that would come later.
In the late afternoon we would set up our lines of defense, dig
foxholes, and man the nightwatch.

We were strenuously exerting ourselves. As usual, I had trouble
keeping up with my unit while carrying the heavy ammo. But other
men had onerous burdens: the BARman was lugging the BAR
(Browning Automatic Rifle), which weighed at least twice as much
as my M1 rifle, along with a few extra loaded magazines for it. The
Assistant BARman also carried BAR magazines.

Other men were lugging even heavier weights. I couldn't believe the size of the backpack radio being carried for the company
commander. Altho the carrier was larger than the average Marine,

the expression on his face revealed sheer agony going up the slopes. In a few years transistors would be developed and future radiomen would be liberated, but the Marine Corps would no doubt have them carrying something else in addition.

Maybe the heaviest toting was by the 4.2-inch mortar men, the *Four Deuces*. That weapon had a baseplate so heavy that it had been manufactured in two pieces, allowing each half to be carried by a single person. Even its shells were heavy. They had a diameter of 106.7mm and weighed twenty pounds; an average person would be straining to carry two of these. Fortunately the Four Deuces were not moved as frequently as were the lighter mortar units.

During the first week, we learned that we had crossed the Thirty-eighth Parallel. All that meant to me was that we were passing some kind of a border. How could I possibly know, at the age of nineteen years and three months, that so much about the Korean War was tied in with invasions across the Thirty-eighth Parallel, whether south-bound or northbound?

The terrain suggested no border. In fact, I didn't see any line or markers while moving about those hills. I would have to get back into civilian life and start studying the "big picture" about the war, in order to understand the significance, or insignificance, of my participation. That would make a good project for future study. Maybe I would write a book. All it would require is that I survive this war. But my fatalistic attitude meant making no long-range plans. For now, I was guided by the common Marine wisdom of "hope for the best, expect the worst, and take whatever comes along."

¶The best thing that came along to affect the "big picture" was President Truman's firing of General MacArthur on 11 April. Getting rid of that arrogant egomaniac was long overdue. Marines were very happy.

125

General Matthew B. Ridgway was MacArthur's successor. [MBR] Fellow Marine Bob Davis's views were shared by nearly every other Marine in Korea:

Fig. 16-1: Gen Matthew B. Ridgway

> Too much has been written about that egotistical, misguided MacArthur. Ridgway, on the other hand, could not have had more of my admiration. He had only one fault: he chose the wrong service; he should have been a Marine.

Davis is being polite about MacArthur. To this day, many former Marines, and soldiers, use expletives in referring to the general and accuse him of causing the deaths of many of their comrades. Those who knew the general best saw him as an arrogant and pompous "Caesar." He ended his career causing more harm to our forces than to the enemy's.

One week after MacArthur's firing, I wrote my first letter from Korea:

> Dear Mom and Geri, It's a beautiful day here in Korea. Our whole division has been resting for a couple of weeks now. Things look pretty good on the front. The North Koreans have asked for a ceasefire order. The Chinks might be the next to ask. The boys were glad to hear that MacArthur had been relieved of his command.
>
> I'd really appreciate it if you send newspaper clippings in your letters; we don't get much news. In fact, you people back home get more news and get it quicker than we do.

Four days later something big did happen, and we got that news

126

quicker than did the people back home. It was the Chinese spring offensive, starting 22 April. Like nearly all their assaults, it was launched at night across much of the 175-mile Korean front line. The heaviest attacks were on our east-central front. I remember a lot of noise from distant artillery and watching our Corsairs with their unique, inverted gull wings swoop low to attack the Chinese. A lot of men were moving about from one hill to another, attacking or defending. The highlight for me would be the dramatic nighttime crossing of the Pukhan River.

Initially, our 2nd Battalion was in reserve position, while the regiment's 1st and 3rd Battalions were on the line, sometimes trying to repel enemy assaults, at other times attempting to seize positions. On 24 April some of us 2/1 men were sent along the ridgeline to help carry wounded 3/1 Marines back to the BAS on stretchers. I was with three other men carrying a stretcher and we looked back over our shoulders to see a Corsair making a lazy, wide turn and then coming in our

Fig. 16-2: Insignia of the First Marine Aircraft Wing

direction. It looked like the pilot was going to strafe us. We got ready to scatter for protection and I rapidly told the wounded man "We're going to set you down because that plane is coming in our direction. We'll come back for you as soon as we can."

We set him down about ten or twelve feet below the crest, ran a short distance away and hit the ground. At the last-minute, the pilot must have spotted the bright-colored ground panels used to identify our forces' location because he suddenly veered off; we were safe!

We went back to the stretcher and carried the wounded man to the aid station. Until that incident, it had not occurred to my immature mind that my demise in this war might come at the hands of our own forces, so-called friendly fire.

The near-mistake by the Corsair pilot was quite understandable.

127

The fighting was causing turmoil as the Chinese swarmed toward us, coming down the same ridge that we were on. They were attacking 3/1 all the way back; it was truly a fighting withdrawal by our Marines.

Unaware of the huge and complex drama that I was a part of, I was simply moving along without thinking what would happen next. True, there was more noise from artillery and small-arms fire, plus the usual chores, digging foxholes and serving on watch at night. But I didn't realize the full extent of the grave danger to the entire 1st Marine Division. Nor did I realize that a successful withdrawal is one of the most difficult of military operations.

¶Decades later, I read the official history of U.S. Marine operations in Korea and its calm, and skimpy description of those dramatic spring days:

> It was decided that four infantry battalions—1/1, 2/1, 3/5, and 3/7—were to take positions on the west bank of the Pukhan to protect the Mojin bridge and ferry sites while the other units crossed. The execution of the plan went smoothly, without enemy interference. After all other Marine troops were on the east side, 3/7 disengaged last of all and forwarded the chest-deep stream as a prelude to hiking to Chunchon. [USMOK IV 119]

No grand opera nor wide-screen movie can capture the drama and excitement of that river crossing, 26 April. It was nighttime and we were moving down a steep slope toward the river. We were quiet, tired, and tense. *I must not slip going downhill*, I thought. Yet all of us had to stay close enough to maintain contact with each other in the darkness and move in the right direction. Downward we continued, until we reached the riverbank.

Artillery was pounding in the distance. The engineers were setting off huge explosions of our ammo and fuel dumps to prevent their capture. The noises thundered thru the hills and the fires lit up the sky. An airplane droned overhead, dropping parachute flares to light up the river-crossing area. Close by, amfibious vehicles

128

("ducks") were carrying our wounded, along with some light equipment and their crews, across the river. Many men were gathering at the shore. I could see crossed poles near the river's edge; our column was streaming toward them. A cable had been stretched across the river, anchored on each side by those poles. Thank God for the work of the Marine engineers.

Word came down the line, "We're crossing the river, hang onto the cable, hold your equipment up out of the water, keep moving and help the other guys." Then we went down the steep bank, holding onto the cable with one hand. Somehow I was able to swing one of the ammo cans over to the other side, next to the other ammo can, and lift both of them high up against my chest, close to my throat.

Like most mountain rivers in early spring, the Pukhan had a strong current and cold water. I stepped forward and quickly sank up to my crotch. My scrotum shrank immediately; most of it was pulled up into my torso, something that evolution had produced to protect males. Extreme fear causes the same reaction, as I would learn on Hill 676 in June.

The official account refers to "the chest-deep stream." That was true for me (being five-foot ten inches tall) and most of the others; for the short guys it was disturbingly deeper. They had to bob along, especially midway, where the river was deepest. Men next to them had to grab them, lest they sink with their weighty and cumbersome loads.

We reached the other side, let go of the cable, and clambered up the bank to a road. Each of us stopped briefly to take off our boots and empty out water and then continue walking soaked, at least from the chest downward. We would gradually dry out as we moved southward thru the night, toward Ch'unch'ŏn.

We were not alone on the road. Korean refugees were also southbound, lugging their meager belongings on their backs. One of our ammo carriers, a sturdy man about 5'9" tall, deliberately bumped into a Korean man, knocking him down. "What the hell did you do that for, Lester," somebody called out. Lester Thiwman (fictional name) answered, in his distinctive Massachusetts dialect, "I'm just pist off!" Another Marine reproached him: "That's no fuckin' reason to do that, Lester!"

We kept moving along; by now we were south of the Thirty-eighth Parallel. Nobody was talking much, yet all of us must have known that we would be going back north in just a few weeks. *And how bloody would that be?*

The best characterization of our Division's accomplishments is found in a letter from our magnificent General, O. P. Smith. He wrote:

> The unit commanders and staff of the Division deserve great credit for the manner in which they planned and conducted the operations which resulted in blunting the Chinese counteroffensive in our area. In my opinion, it was the most professional job performed by the Division, while it was under my command. [USMOK IV 118]

Writing these words sixty-one years later, I can declare that *I was there! God bless you, General Smith, and all the other Marines who I served with, wherever you may be.*

Chapter 17
A TENUOUS EXISTENCE

The officers must know, the top NCOs probably know, but I do not know how to explain the movements of our forces. Obviously we want to go north because that is where the enemy is. How does the division decide which of the line regiments (1st, 5th, and 7th) to put on the front line and which to hold in reserve?

I made up a musical ditty, using a tune from the World War II Soviet patriotic song "Meadowlands" and sang it to entertain my buddies: "The Fifth relieves the Seventh; The Seventh relieves the Fifth; But nobody ree-ee-ee-ee-lieves the Fir–rr-rrrr-rst; No–body ree-ee-lieves the First." It was musical complaining and not very truthful.

I prefer to be back in a reserve area. It's quieter and usually less strenuous; we don't have to climb up and down the hills, dig new foxholes, fear stepping on antipersonnel mines, or get killed by something else. Even the weather and scenery are better. Late in May I wrote a letter home about it:

> Today has turned out to be a nice day. I went down [from] the ridge, accompanied by another guy, and took a bath in a brook. The water was ice-cold but it felt great. The weather has warmed up considerably but the nights are still cool. As for scenery we've got some of the finest. We always camp on the high commanding ground. We can see for miles. There are pine trees all over the hills.

Just being back in reserve is no guarantee of safety. Late in May we pulled back off the line and bivouacked close to the west side of the north-south MSR (main supply route), setting up our small tents along the lower slopes of a draw. One Marine thought he would be more secure putting his tent against the side of a big boulder he found midway up the draw. To this day I do not fully understand his reasoning.

During the night, a brief but heavy rain fell. Someone screamed loudly for help and the nearest men ran over to rescue the man next to the boulder; he was covered with mud that had rolled down the hillside. They started digging with their shovels and dragged him away from the muddy water coursing downhill. He was still trapped in his soaked sleeping bag, but they managed to unzip it and help him crawl out. He was badly shaken by the experience. The area he was sleeping in was a natural funnel, and the boulder had helped narrow and speed-up the flow of the runoff water and mud. He was at the top of a spout; if he had not been heard screaming, he would've suffocated.

The 8th Replacement Draft brought us a few fresh Marines, replacing men due for rotation back to the United States and vacancies caused by casualties. The new guys were all young, like most of us. One was dark-haired, wore a thin mustache, and had a Mediterranean (olive) complexion. He was handsome enough to easily attract most women.

He brought a beautiful pistol with him: a new 9 mm Walther P38. It was the world's first military semiautomatic to have a double-action trigger mechanism, a worthy successor to the German army's famous Luger. It was immaculate and gleamed as he pulled it out from its beautiful black leather holster attached to a matching pistol belt. He took pride in showing it and I believe all of us were envious.

None of us suspected how doomed he was. Just a few days later, Vic Knabel walked over to find the man curled up in a corner of their tent and tried to wake him up for morning chow. Shaking him didn't work; he was dead. The corpsman was called in and checked his condition; he died of pneumonia, without having spent a moment on the front line.

It was tragic, more tragic than if he had been killed in combat. I wondered what happened to his pistol, and the beautiful black leather holster and belt.

Tragedy was lurking for me. I was in one of the multiple tent configurations that was possible, since each one of us had half a tent (a shelter half). We could connect up to six shelter halves to give us a tent that looked like a dome. It had more headroom than the two-piece pup tent and was more comfortable for playing cards, eating or whatever.

While cleaning my rifle, I heard a gun go off and the bullet whizzed thru my tent, putting a bullet hole thru each side. The bullet had nearly hit me. I sprang out and joined other Marines trying to figure out where it had come from. The culprit was a Marine getting ready to clean his weapon. He had violated the first rule about weapons: check to see whether it is loaded!

One time a Marine was letting a Korean porter examine his pistol. Unfortunately, the pistol accidentally fired, seriously wounding the Marine. Word was passed around to *never* let a Korean handle your weapon.

Fig. 17-1: Whitten, Lohr and WEA on a battle-scarred hill

In Korea no place was safe. Fatalism was a mind-set to maintain mental health, yet war itself is a type of insanity. The tenuousness of our lives inhibited forming too close a friendship with another person. It would be easier to lose a "co-worker" than to lose a friend. My attitude must have shown in my letters. A former girlfriend told me after I got back home, "Your letters to me were

133

cold."

I could not be sure of what other changes were happening to my mind. There were so many dangers around us and the smallest detail of our behavior could have life-and-death consequences. I must watch where I walk; there may be land mines around. I must not fall asleep on nightwatch; a lurking enemy can sneak up and kill me. I must keep my weapon properly cleaned; if it jams, the enemy can shoot me (or get close enough to throw a grenade). I must stay off ridgelines not be out in the open; those make me an easy target for the enemy. Loud talking or noisy walking can attract the wrong attention.

Some veterans later told me that one of the characteristics of civilian life was how trivial and mundane so much of it was. After I returned to the States in 1952, I would find out how right they were, but I would find out that civilian life also had its own hazards.

Chapter 18
MILITARY VIGNETTES I

FROM SPRING TO MIDSUMMER the 1st Marine Division did a lot of fighting involving frequent moving around on the east-central front. Our experiences can be illustrated in many short sketches.

BEEF ON THE HOOF

War produces orphans. Sometimes they are cattle. Here's some food for thud, a hard thud.

On a cool spring day we are bivouacked in a pinewoods on a large hill. A big bull with large horns appears, without his owner. He doesn't seem to be afraid of us. Right away we see him as a way to supplement our C-rations with fresh beef. The challenge is how to do it.

Several minds immediately come up with the same suggestion, Tex is the guy to do it. *But why Tex?* The answer is obvious. The beef in our rations must come from Texas. He must know how to do it.

He is consulted and tells us "You gotta kill it first." Shooting it is out of the question; we are not supposed to fire our weapons except at the enemy.

"How do we kill it, Tex?"

"You gotta hit it between the eyes."

"With what?"

"A sledgehammer."

"Where are we going to get a sledgehammer?"

"The engineers have all sorts of tools. They must have a sledge-hammer."

So somebody is sent to Battalion HQ to bring back the sledge-hammer. About an hour later he returns with a sledgehammer and, of course, hands it to Tex. By this time most of the machine-gunners and riflemen of Dog Company have assembled to watch Tex in action. Meanwhile, the bull is still standing around, unsuspecting.

Nobody seems to have figured out in advance that the bull will have to be skinned, carved up, and cooked to have any value to us. There's no mess kitchen nearby. Is it really a good idea to do this to the bull?

The tension is rapidly increasing. The spectators are starting to move away from the bull. A few men are looking around for trees that can be rapidly climbed. Nobody knows for sure what will happen, but adding a little distance seems like the prudent thing to do.

Tex walks over to the bull. He lifts up the sledgehammer like a baseball player holding the bat. With his eyes focused on the target, he swings the sledgehammer and bangs it between the eyes of the bull. The animal snorts loudly, spins around halfway and starts running down the hill. Tex starts chasing it and everybody else is laughing. Nobody has to climb any trees. The animal disappears from sight and Tex soon gives up the chase.

It's time to take the sledgehammer back to the engineers. It wouldn't be fair to ask Tex to return it; after all, he has provided us with a unique form of entertainment. The same guy that fetched it will take it back. The audience disperses. I doubt that anyone regrets the bull's escape.

Nearly 60 years later I learned that it wasn't just Marines who were a danger to Korean cattle. A fellow Korean War veteran, Carl Collier, confessed to me about an incident that happened on the Western front where he was a soldier on guard duty one cold and foggy wintry night. Sitting behind a .50 caliber Browning machine gun, he heard a crunch on the crusty snow and feared the worst. What happened was important enough for him to put into a poem that tells,

An answer to 'Password!' was not even one word
The crunches came closer and louder: Still, no reply
With the hair-raising on his neck, he was sure he would die

136

Deeply apprehensive, he heard an even closer crunch
Causing him to fear, Chinese soldiers, quite a bunch!

A peek into the fog soup revealed, not a ghoul
But his mind playing tricks, just making him a fool
Out of the fog loomed a large cow
Use of the .50 caliber is not for now.

THE BUTT OF A BLOODY JOKE

It must've been Sergeant Punte who yelled: "Get your fuckin' ass down, Mancha, before you get it shot!" And that's how a comical tale got started.

We were moving across an open area; a few rifle shots rang out. We hit the deck, not sure where the shots were coming from. PFC Felix C. Mancha had flung himself down on the ground but had not flattened his lower torso enough. For some reason Mancha had his ass arched up. Later, we learned that he had landed on some uncomfortably hard object(s), small rocks or the stub of a plant. They were directly under his genitals. Instinctively, he moved the lower part of his body away from them, unfortunately he moved it *up*.

Eagle-eyed Punte had yelled the right thing. In fact, Punte's words were still hanging in the air as Mancha yelled that he had been shot. The bullet entered one side of Mancha's ass, crossed the narrow separation between the buttocks, entered the other cheek and came out the far side. It was *four* bullet holes from a single bullet. Mancha was taken back to an aid station and spent time in the hospital.

When he returned, he didn't want to discuss his wound (or wounds). And, he sure wasn't going to show us any scars. But we had acquired good material for humor to be used when new replacements joined our unit.

The new men were usually inquisitive and wanted to learn about conditions on the line. They wanted practical advice in order to function well (and survive). Sometimes one of us "old timers" would say something like, "Yeah, you have to be careful here. You don't want to get shot, but even if you do, it doesn't mean you'll be seriously hurt. Mancha here is an example. Mancha, show the new guys your scars."

Mancha would blow up and swear ("Fuck you" or "Go to hell"). So nobody ever got to see the evidence that justified awarding a Purple Heart to him. Moreover, one unanswered question has remained in the minds of all of us who knew about his injuries: "Had the Marine Corps made a mistake in awarding *merely one* Purple Heart to Mancha? Didn't he deserve *four?*"

COMBAT HAZARDS FOR MUSICIANS

After the Chinese spring offensive had been stopped, we started to get mail again. I received personal letters from my mother and sister and back issues of *The Detroit Times*, thru a subscription purchased by my mother. One issue described a handsome, popular, and brilliant accordion player named Dick Contino, who had been convicted of draft dodging and sentenced to six months in prison. He was quoted as saying, "Why should I risk my life in a war?"

Our reactions to Contino's statement were spirited. One man mockingly defended Contino saying, "The guy is no dummy. It's dangerous up here. A person could be seriously hurt in this war. I would rather be back in the States playing an accordion."

A few expressed fantasies about harmful things they would like to do to parts of Contino's body with an organ of their own body. Others suggested use of their military skills; these involved guns, bayonets, and even a grenade or two attached to Contino and his accordion.

Decades later I learned that Contino did go into the army after his prison term. He was even assigned to duty in Korea. On top of all that, he became a sergeant, was honorably discharged, and even received a pardon from President Truman!

138

Occasionally we got a beer ration, one or two cans of beer. It would come only when we were going to be in a fixed position for at least several days.

I was not a drinker; so I would trade my beer for chocolate bars, a can of fruit, or some other food item. That made me popular. My friends, who had nicknamed me "the Kid" would come around with offers: "Hey Kid, I'll swap you a can of sausage patties for your beer," or "Listen Kid, I'll let you have the canned pears and maybe a few crackers, for one of your cans of beer."

Soon after we occupied a high hill, the beer ration arrived. It was still early afternoon and none of us had dug our holes yet. I suspected a conspiracy as I heard, "Kid, we want to make you a bet. We'll bet you that you cannot drink five cans of beer." This was an introduction to some kind of stupid rite of passage into manhood.

At that time I had been paired with Randy Lohr from upstate New York. He had already started to dig our foxhole and called over to me, "Bill, I'm going to need your help soon." One of the guys said "Hang on, Lohr. We're making a bet with the Kid."

So what were the stakes involved? If I drank five beers, what would I win? If I couldn't drink five, what would I have to hand over? I simply can't recall now. It was all so ridiculous.

I do recall sitting on the ground and slowly drinking five cans of beer under the intense scrutiny of the conspirators. Once in a while, Randy called out, "C'mon over and start digging!" The other guys would yell "Shut up, Lohr! We've got a bet on with the Kid."

Randy grumbled each time, all the while digging out dirt for our foxhole. I kept drinking, and getting dizzier. The guys snickered and got more and more amused by my condition.

Finally I finished the fifth beer and they congratulated me, handing me whatever it was I had won. Then I stood up and staggered over to the hole in which Randy was standing with a shovel in his hand. At the edge of the hole I swayed and said "Get out of the way!"

139

Randy jumped out immediately and I collapsed into the hole. After a few hours I started to revive. I was still lying face down and gradually feeling the hot sun beating down on my back. I turned over on my back, still groggy, and tried to open my eyes. The harsh sunshine was partly blocked by the silhouette of Randy's head and shoulders looming over me. As I fully opened my eyes, he thrust the shovel at me and said "Here, start digging!"

HAIR TODAY, GONE TOMORROW

In late spring a new officer was assigned to Dog Company. He soon conceived some ideas for improving our personal appearance. After all, we didn't look well-groomed. Our clothes were not clean, we were not bathing or showering, our shoes were not neat looking and shiny, and worst of all, we were not clean shaven. What was a newly arrived second lieutenant to do in view of such derelictions?

He was faced with daunting obstacles. Our clothes were always dirty because we were living in holes in the ground on the front line. We were not bathing or showering because there were no facilities for it. Our shoes were over-the-ankle leather hiking boots, called boondockers; they were very comfortable because they were made with the finished leather's smooth surface on the inside and the rough rawhide on the outside. Only the inner smooth side could possibly be polished and even the lieutenant realized the impracticability of that since nobody, friend or foe, would see a polished shine on the inside of our boots.

But he was very resourceful; there was the matter of facial hair. All of us allowed our beards to grow until they became an inconvenience, such as catching too many food drippings while we ate or giving us an itchy face, etc. In winter we valued long beards to protect our faces.

Comfortable shaving requires warm water and sharp razor blades. To heat water we had to use the Sterno fuel that had been issued primarily for heating food. It was a slow process to heat even a pint of water in our helmets. Not many men had razor blades and

140

most of the blades were dull. Shaving with cold water was uncomfortable. In fact, any shaving on the front line was a low priority.

The lieutenant said that we had to shape up our appearance and that meant shaving every day. I wish he had threatened us with the option of "shape up or ship out." I knew which I would choose.

Nevertheless, with much grumbling, we followed his orders as best we could. I did not have enough of a beard then to warrant daily shaving so I could skip a day or two. After a week or so somebody got the lieutenant to relent; I think it was the skipper (the company commander). Happy days were here again.

I'm glad that the lieutenant didn't order us to change underwear every day. For one thing I couldn't think of whom I would want to change mine with. Moreover, I doubted that any other person's underwear, even if it did fit me, would be any cleaner or better smelling than mine.

LET THERE BE LIGHT

The most dangerous time on the line was at night. Both the Chinese Communist Forces (CCF) and the NKPA launched their attacks at night. It allowed their forces to get close to our positions without undergoing substantial losses from our artillery. They were also completely safe from our air attacks. After getting close, they would try to swarm over us, relying heavily on hand grenades to capture our positions. Nighttime was also a preferred time for them to reconnoiter our positions and to attempt infiltration. We also preferred the dark to reconnoiter, however infiltration by us was uncommon.

One night we were all surprised when the clouds above us were suddenly lit up. It was obvious that beams of light were coming from our rear areas and reflecting off the cloud cover. It was from Army searchlights, mounted on trucks. What a welcome sight. We could soon feel a lowering of the normal tension of the night.

A few nights later we were straining to see thru the darkness in front of our line. By now we were expecting the searchlights to come on, but they did not. We were disappointed until we figured out that they couldn't be used when there were no clouds above us, and we had a clear dark sky above us. That was a limitation on the use of the searchlights. Now we knew what to expect and tension was always highest at night when there were neither clouds, nor moonlight.

Fig. 18-1: U.S. Army 155 mm gun firing at nite

LOOKING FOR A GOOD NITE'S SLEEP

Early one evening we entered a wooded area just off the road and set up our bivouac. We ate and set up a 25-percent watch. I finished my time on watch before midnight and was soon in a deep sleep.

Just before dawn unbelievably loud explosions and quaking ground shocked us awake. We jumped out of our tents wondering whether we were under enemy artillery attack, air bombardment, or something else.

Across the road a U.S. Army artillery battery was firing at the enemy. They were shooting long-barreled cannons with a range of up to fifteen miles. In addition to the roaring sound, they gave off huge flashes of light. None of us infantrymen was comfortable around any artillery, even our own Marine artillery, when it was firing; we were afraid that the enemy would fire back and hit us, as well as the artillerymen. However, the Communists were not using guns with a range that could hit the Army's biggest artillery. Years later I heard that we had a minor casualty from the firing. PFC Clyde Queen reported bleeding from both ears.

Vic Knabel was neither surprised by the artillery firing nor injured by it. He was on watch when the Army artillery units arrived

142

and set up their positions. With Marine disdain, he says that, "Altho it was still dark, I knew it was an Army unit arriving, because I saw them setting up their chow tent before putting their guns into place."

A REALLY NEAT FOREST

I remember seeing something unique and unnatural, a perfectly laid out hillside forest. It covered a large area and the rows of trees were evenly spaced up and down the slope and side to side; they were as regular as the gravestones in military cemeteries.

We were moving along the trail, high up on the hillside, parallel to the upper edge of the reforested area and were able to look down and see how perfectly aligned the trees were with one another. The tops of the trees had all grown far enough outward to interweave a thick canopy which deprived the lower parts of the trunks of the sunshine needed to produce lower branches. They formed tunnels of light shining up thru the blackish-green forest from its lower edge. A bowling ball could be rolled down each of these "tunnels" and not hit a single tree before coming to rest in the valley below. It also meant that rainfall would produce torrents of water to gouge out the soil and flow unimpeded to the bottom.

Why had the trees not been planted in a staggered checkerboard pattern, to avoid the tunnel effect? My guess was that the project stemmed from the time of the Japanese Empire when the laborers had been subservient Koreans while the supervisors and forest engineers had all been Japanese.

The arrogant Japanese overlords did not countenance criticism, or even positive feedback, from the Korean subjects of the Emperor. The empire's pretentious title was *The Greater East Asia Co-prosperity Sphere,* but it was still an oppressive Japanese despotism, despite their reforestation and other public works programs.

Chapter 19
MILITARY VIGNETTES II

RICE PADDY DADDY

Who came up with the term "rice paddy daddy"? I heard it several times in Korea and imagine that it was used also in the Vietnam War, which was fought by a lot of men who had served in the Korean War.

We saw many rice paddies, or rather, land that had been used for growing rice until the owners were killed or fled from the warfare. These areas were located mainly in valleys where they flattened the valley floors. Sometimes they were on hillsides. On slopes they looked like a giant staircase. Overall they were quaint, almost picturesque. Chinese wall paintings sometimes feature such landscapes.

Absent from all portrayals is the overwhelming stench of an active paddy, which is fertilized with "night soil" (human manure). Any Marine who has been around these paddies, especially in hot weather, has a stinky story to tell. Sergeant Manert Kennedy remembers a night approach that led to our Company (Dog 2/1) digging fighting holes in a paddy. He spent the night nauseated and puked his C-rations a number of times.

With the farmers gone, the paddies were dry and hard but easy to run across. I learned that one day in May, when our machine-gun unit came down out of the hills and began crossing a small valley, in the direction of low hills on the other side. We were in our usual "formation," strung out in a zigzag line with each man at least ten feet away from the other. Most frequently, the gunner was at the front with the tripod, followed by the assistant gunner carrying the gun itself (the receiver and its attached barrel). The four to six ammo carriers were following behind.

When bullets were fired at us from the hills to our right, we started running toward the other side of the valley. I stumbled. As I fell, one of my ammo cans banged hard against the ground, broke open, and spilled out most of the ammo belt.

I kneeled down to gather it up and shove it back into the can. What a foolish, actually suicidal, thing, since we were being targeted. It could have been my Depression-era upbringing where we were taught to never waste or throw anything away.

Corporal Punte yelled at me, "Forget the fuckin' ammo! Run! We can replace it. We *can't* replace you!" I jumped up and ran, holding extra tightly to my remaining can of ammo. We reached the bottom of a tree-covered hill and started climbing it. No more shots came at us, but I was minus that can of ammo. I felt really foolish for what I had done, stopping to pick up replaceable ammo and becoming an easier target. What a way to get killed.

We had barely started up the steep hillside when a cloudburst dumped torrents of rain on us. The slope got very slippery. We had to hold onto the tree trunks and lunge upward toward the next tree, grab it and gradually pull ourselves up to the top. Our clothes were drenched. At the top we dug shallow foxholes. The rain eased up and ended a short time later.

By evening I had a shallow foxhole full of water. And I desperately needed sleep. I took my inflatable rubber air mattress out of my backpack, inflated it, and placed it on top of the water in my foxhole. It floated nicely and I lay on it, holding my carbine close to my chest and fell asleep.

When I was awakened to take my turn on watch, I got off my floating mattress and managed to stay awake till I had finished my watch and then woke up the next guy for him to take his turn. Then I lay back down on my "raft" and slept some more. At no time during the night did I get seasick.

Nearly sixty years later I learned of a far greater accomplishment with an air mattress. Altho I have been outdone, at least it was by a fellow Marine!

It was the summer of 1952, around four months after I left Korea. Our First Marine Division was now on the western end of the front line facing Chinese forces adjacent to the Yellow Sea. The Second Battalion/First Marines had been relieved from front-line duty and was taken by train from the railhead at Munsan-ni to a training area near the port of Inch'ŏn. They would engage in a practice invasion of a nearby island.

After participating in the helicopter assault part of the operation, Charles "Chuck" Lundeen and his unit were given the rest of the day to lounge around on the beach. He says:

> Everybody swam naked, to the delight of some nearby Korean girls who giggled and tried not to look as they passed by the beach.

Fig. 19-1: Charles Lundeen

> I used the waters of the Yellow Sea to wash away the caked filth that was on my body. Then I filled my air mattress and got on it and paddled away from the crowded beach. With the rays of the sun on my back and the rolling surface of the sea, I was soon in a deep sleep, oblivious to where I was.

> I was jolted out of my sleep by the sound of a boat whistle. I had floated too far from the beach and into the sea lanes.

> It was a fishing boat and on its deck some Oriental faces were staring at me. *Were they Korean? Japanese? Or Chinese?* Whatever their nationality, the crew must've been bewildered to see a naked white man on a dark grey air mattress floating in the Yellow Sea.

> I quickly turned the air mattress around and vigorously started to paddle back to the beach, praying that the crew were not Chinese communists from the mainland. I finally reached the shore and was met by howls of laughter from my fellow Marines.

> They speculated that I could have floated all the way across the sea and landed in Red China. The headlines in the Beijing newspapers

would have probably asserted 'Naked Marine Invades Motherland; People's Army on Alert.'

The next day we left for the port of Inch'ŏn and headed back to the front. Our vacation was over.

SERVICE FOR FOUR AT THE COMMODE

Sanitation is a critical part of maintaining military readiness. Disease can incapacitate or even kill an infantryman just as surely as an enemy bullet; it had put me into a hospital for three days in March. In the field, sanitation regarding toilet functions is unburdened by personal modesty. Proof of this is to be found at the "four-holer."

The four-holer is a small, outdoor platform of mainly plywood, having a six-foot by six-foot flat top with four oval-shaped holes serving as commodes. The platform is supported by low (some eighteen inches high) walls on all four sides. It's like a big box with no bottom, and it's placed over a hole in the ground.

Four-holers are usually placed downslope (hopefully downwind and level), away from any tents, foxholes, roads, brooks, creeks, or other watercourses. However, it is totally out in the open; there is no partition to provide privacy from the rest of the world. It has nothing overhead to give shelter from rain. But it does have its advantages.

An approacher can look ahead to see if there is a vacancy. Since one of our frequent problems was the "Korean krud" (diarrhea), we might get desperate and have to race to the four-holer. A person often had to guess whether he could reach it in time, assuming there was a vacancy there. And anybody on a commode could see anybody else desperately running toward the four-holer and decide whether he should (or could) remain any longer. At all costs, one must avoid getting in the way of the oncoming rusher. If there was no vacancy, the afflicted person could also decide how far and in which direction to run for another place to squat and let loose.

Fig. 19-2: Bob Davis

The four-holer has been given at least three other names: "the can," "the throne," and the "shitter." I have some problems with "shitter." What then do you call the person who is using the four-holer? An "appendage?" An "operator?" In our current age of unfettered capitalism I wouldn't be surprised if somebody suggested "stakeholder" or (God forbid) "consumer." My solution was to call the user the "shitter" and the four-holer itself the "shittery."

My most vivid experience while sitting on it was one day in May. We were in reserve north of Ch'unch'ŏn. I was sitting on the four-holer, overlooking the valley. Our camp was on its western slopes. I could see the MSR running the north-south length of the valley. The road ran along the valley's eastern side. My vantage point was 300 to 400 feet higher than the MSR. I looked down upon supply trucks moving along the road. I was quite relaxed and enjoying a normal bodily function (meaning free of the "Korean krud"). Suddenly, an explosion on the road blew up a truck, almost flipping it over. There was much smoke but no fire. My body reacted with eyes stretched wide open, jaw wide open, faster breathing, and a tightened stomach. Nearby trucks stopped and men jumped out to help. At least two men had been killed.

The road had been secured for several weeks and a lot of traffic had used it since. Why had there been an explosion now? Had the enemy sneaked in at night to plant the mine? Was it really a mine explosion? Had the engineers failed to fully clear the road before opening it to traffic?

Later, everything was explained to us. Our engineers used metal-mine detection equipment, but the Chinese used wooden "box mines" that were not detectable. The enemy had covered these mines loosely with dirt, not daring to compact the soil. Passing trucks gradually compacted the soil and built up pressure on the mines, finally causing detonation.

Bob Davis was going down the road near Hongch'ŏn during Operation Ripper and saw a friend, a jeep driver, at the side of the road jacking up a wheel to change a tire. Bob says:

> He stopped the jacking a moment as we joked about his position as driver being an easy one. I left him to rejoin my unit and was about twenty-five yards or so away when I heard the explosion and turned to see his body flying thru the air and the jeep blown apart. Another close call for me. His jack was on a pressure landmine and one-hundred pounds of boxed black powder. If he hadn't stopped the jack to talk to me, I would've been gone too.
>
> You can do nothing to protect yourself from that kind of hazard; all of us were vulnerable. That's war.

WAR TROPHIES

Back north of Ch'unch'ŏn again in May, we were in fixed positions for a week or so. Things were quiet, no shooting or other angry noises. I noticed several Marines looking out toward the enemy lines. A couple of them were using binoculars. What were they looking at?

I walked toward them, staying well below the ridge line, and saw a North Korean soldier sitting on the ground, about twenty or thirty feet down the slope on our side. Apparently he had just walked over and surrendered. I saw no weapons on him but as I got closer, I saw a Soviet burp gun on the ground next to him.

Quickly I sprinted toward the gun, reached down, and grabbed it. Why had nobody around him taken the weapon out of the prisoner's proximity? I realized that he had brought it over with him, no doubt slung over his shoulder, and if he had tried to use it, he would've been blown away by all the firepower of our men. Still it bothered me that his burp gun was so close to him and nobody was assigned to guard him.

I slung his weapon over my shoulder and looked him over. This

149

was the closest I had ever been to a live enemy soldier.

He wore a leather belt that had a brass buckle, probably made from an empty artillery shell casing, and I wanted it. I reached down, unbuckled it and pulled it out of his belt loops. He seemed distressed, maybe wondering whether I was going to harm him.

I removed my own web belt, the standard USMC issue, and tossed it at him. Then I used my hands to indicate that he should put my belt thru his belt loops, meaning he was to wear it. Tho I had forced him to do it, I considered it an even swap. I

Fig. 19-3: My trophy NKPA leather belt

didn't see anything else on him that I wanted so I went back to my hole.

I was fascinated by the burp gun; it looked like the 1920s-era Thompson submachine-guns ("Tommy guns") used by gangsters and FBI teams. However, the burp gun shot a smaller-size bullet, .30 caliber (7.62mm) compared to the .45 caliber of the Tommy guns. How eager I was to fire it as soon as possible. Of course it would be a fatal mistake to dare use it in a firefight with the enemy because of its distinctive bur-r-r-r-rup sound. Every Marine knew that sound and would instinctively shoot in my direction.

With permission from our officers, a few of us went many yards behind our line, and each fired a few rounds. The burp gun jammed repeatedly. That might explain the enemy soldier's decision to surrender to us. A prudent soldier would be better off surrendering than trying to use a defective weapon against so many of us and our non-jamming weapons. Unfortunately, most burp guns did not jam when they were being fired at us.

Fig. 19-4: "Burp Gun" Bill (WEA)

Later that day I was told that I had to hand over the burp gun "because of regulations." My adventure was over, except I asked a friend to take a photograph of me holding it. It's one of my favorite fotos. But nobody asked me to give up the leather belt. I still have that trophy. It's a cheap unattractive brown leather belt whose sole value is as a memento of an interesting time in Korea.

I am curious about what happened to the prisoner when he was taken back to a POW camp. Any American seeing him wearing a standard U.S. issue belt might suspect that it was seized from an American and get angry, maybe hitting the guy, or worse. And if I were ever captured, the Communists might look at my leather belt and think that I had taken it from one of their men. They could get very angry and do some unpleasant things to me.

Something more sinister was at work. At the UN's sprawling POW camp on Koje-do Island, a revolt was brewing. The Communists were using their surrendering soldiers as messengers to transmit orders to their POW conspirators. When the revolt erupted, the POWs were well organized and U.S. combat troops had to be brought in to subdue them. The Communist countries launched an international propaganda campaign, accusing UN forces of cruelty to POWs.

151

"Practice random acts of kindness and thoughtless acts of beauty," goes an inspirational message that appeared on automobile bumper stickers in the late twentieth century. In war there is no beauty and acts of kindness do not seem random, if at all.

Before April ended, the Chinese offensive was at the end of its punch. We had stopped one day on our slow withdrawal and were near Ch'unch'ŏn. The land was less rugged. The rice paddies had dried out. The only people to be seen were our own troops.

I was walking around looking at the ground, hoping that it was free of antipersonnel mines. I kept glancing around and was startled to hear a voice using words I did not understand. I spun around with my rifle aimed, ready to fire, and saw a ragged-looking Korean man and a ragged woman holding a dirty-faced child. I kept my weapon aimed at the man, my finger still on the trigger. Were they a threat? Where had they come from? How had they gotten so close to me?

Fear was in their eyes. They were trembling, not knowing what to expect from me. The man was obviously begging. It had to be for food. I kept my rifle aimed at them, pressing its side close to my body to support it with my right hand while lifting my left hand toward them in a gesture meaning "halt!" Then I began stepping backwards about five paces and set down my backpack. With my eyes still fixed on them, I knelt down, having to slide my right hand to keep the rifle balanced yet ready to fire it. I reached into my pack with my left hand and pulled out a can of food.

I approached them about three paces and bent down to place the can on the ground. I stood up and pointed down at the can, thrusting a finger at it quickly. I stepped backwards toward my backpack keeping my rifle aimed at them. They shuffled slowly and warily toward the can, their heads slowly nodding up and down and saying something I interpreted as "thank you." They were careful not to make any sudden movements picking it up. Then they turned around and walked away, but where to? What were they living in? How was any civilian surviving in this devastated area?

Later I wondered how they were going to open up that can. I had not given them a can opener.

What had happened? I could easily have killed them; their fate was in my hands. In this war, life is very cheap; it is taken or spared, by whim, if not at random. All I had done was give them some food. I did it deliberately and very warily. It was neither a "random act of kindness" nor a "thoughtless act of beauty!"

Chapter 20
A BUNKERED HILL

AMONG THE ARCHIVES of the United States Marine Corps is a paper record of what the 1st Marine Regiment commander told his men they had done in early June 1951:

> The missions you have been called upon to accomplish during that period have been very difficult. Added to the rugged terrain has been a dogged and fanatic resistance from a competent, resourceful and heavily-armed enemy estimated to have been, at the very least, three regiments in strength. You have attacked him in his prepared positions in very rugged terrain and you have never been stopped. Even considerable losses have not turned you from your objectives, nor shaken your morale. And the losses you have inflicted on the enemy have been tremendous. You have counted many hundreds of dead in the various positions taken in spite of the enemy propensity for burying his own dead, so that is most probably only a small part of his casualties. His wounded will probably die, ours won't.

> In accomplishing this you have demonstrated professional skill of the highest order. You have used ground and cover with consummate skill, as I have personally observed; you have used your organic supporting arms very intelligently; you have used your attached supporting arms, including air, tanks and artillery, to their maximum potential; you have used patience, common sense, and good judgment in regulating the speed of your advances; and, when time was of the essence, you have used sheer guts and determination to close with the enemy and destroy or rout him with grenades, bayonets, clubbed rifles and even with bare hands on at least one occasion. [WSB]

No paper record can convey the intensity of men at war as they fight and die in bloody struggles for summits and hilltops named for their height in meters, such as Hill 676. Shouldn't there be more details about the contrast between the carnage and the beautiful setting of green hills where it all takes place? Shouldn't we know more about the report writer, whose effusive praise and adulation for

154

his troops might be masking some feelings of anguish over the death of so many young men? Because his son is also a Marine in this war, what is it about the colonel that will allow him to continue doing his duty without being emotionally overwhelmed by so much loss of life, which may one day include his own son?

Should we presume that the writer is mindless of the tragedy that both sides are enduring in this conflict or can such a consideration be tolerated in the mind of a warrior whose success and survival depend upon dehumanizing the enemy to ease the task of killing them or at least ordering other men to do so. Is he merely boasting about his units, and showing arrogance?

¶By midmorning of the lovely spring day of 10 June, we were advancing across a small sloping field at the base of Hill 676. The unit was spread out in the usual fashion: at the leading edge was the tripod being carried by the gunner, the machine-gun being carried by the assistant gunner, and the ammo being lugged by the ammo carriers strung out behind.

Suddenly the first shell exploded and we all hit the deck. It was "incoming mail" from enemy mortars behind the hill. We could actually hear as each mortar fired its shell. The launching sound is a metallic *thawmp.* And soon there is a quick fluttery noise, like one or two flaps of a big bird's wings, as the shell arrives and then explodes against the ground.

The terror is unbelievable. Panic is starting to control me, my whole mind and body say "run!" But I cannot run; I'll get hit by the shrapnel if I'm on my feet. I cannot raise any part of my body to start digging a hole and it's too late to start. I pray, "Oh God, don't let me get blown up!"

Then I hear more mortars launching their shells and dread their quick arrival. My whole body is so tightened up that I am trembling; I feel like one big muscle under maximum load. My innards are all squeezing together; I'm afraid I'm going to shit in my pants. My balls have shrunk up into my torso.

155

I'm clamping my jaws against each other and I think my teeth will start cracking. I'm squeezing my eyes shut with enough force to crush my eyeballs. If a shell lands on me I will never know it; I'll be blown to pieces.

Mercifully, the shelling stops. I strain to hear sounds nearby. Nobody is moaning in pain. Nobody has been hit. We've all survived. We get up and start climbing up the slope, into a wooded area. A firefight is underway higher up on the hill; we hear gunshots and grenade explosions. It doesn't seem to be directly in front of us. We continue climbing and then hear shots directly ahead. The assistant gunner gets shot in the chest, dropping the gun and falling down. Randy is ordered to "get up there and bring the gun back."

Randy races up the slope and gets wounded by grenade fragments grazing his jaw and neck. He tries to stagger down the slope and I rush up to him. Blood is flowing down the side of his face and neck. *How can blood be so bright a red?* I rip open a bandage and press it against the wound with one hand and put my arm around his body and tell him to hold the bandage, if he can, while I support him in moving down the slope.

He keeps hanging onto me and we finally get to the aid station.

Fig. 20-1: Medical Aid Station with helicopter landing pad

The medical corpsman starts treating him and I can do nothing but just watch. Then an officer arrives, looks over the situation, and says, "What are you doing?" I said "I'm here with my buddy. I just brought him down."

"Well, you're not needed here. Get back up there!"

I had no idea whether Randy would survive. But there was nothing I could do now. I climbed back up the slope. I assumed I would soon be killed.

After Randy recovered he rejoined us several weeks later. He told me that the doctor at the aid station had removed grenade fragments and he was soon taken by helicopter to the hospital ship offshore. His jacket was blood soaked; one pocket was filled with blood and it ruined the watch he was carrying in it.

I got back up the hill in time to experience a group insanity. The order came to "fix bayonets!" I attached my bayonet and dreaded what might come next. Then we were told to get ready to charge up the hill. Next I heard "Charge!" We jumped up and began running while yelling, hooting, howling, screaming, each man making his own weird noises. Then we got to the top; the bunkers were empty; the North Korean soldiers had fled.

That charge was one of the stupidest things I had ever been in. If just one enemy soldier had been there with an automatic weapon, he could've cut us all down. In an age of rapid-firing weapons, nobody in his right mind would charge with bayonets. And certainly no move against an enemy should be accompanied by yelling and screaming.

To this day I wonder how the folly got started. Was it a quirk? If so, then we had survived by a quirk, an ominous thought for my future.

Chapter 21
PRELUDE TO SUMMER

AT THE END OF JUNE we were on the Kansas line, strung out east to west on some high hills. In front of us were irregular draws, meadows, and rolling land. Behind it, three to four miles from us, was the enemy's defense line along a range of higher hills.

One hill was prominent and gave them a vantage point for looking down upon us and seeing our positions quite clearly during the day. Also, they could see movements a long way behind us, including the MSR. That made our forces vulnerable to their well-directed artillery fire. Our supply storage areas had to be constructed at night and kept well-camouflaged during the day. Our trucks could bring supplies only at night.

Late one afternoon we got word something bad was going to happen to the enemy on that hill. B-29s were coming from Japan to blast it. We would be told when to hunker down in our holes.

Evening came. We were expecting a spectacle, but what kind? The darker it got the more ill at ease we got. How could the pilots hit their target at night? What if they missed and hit us by mistake? I realized that I shouldn't worry. I didn't expect to survive this war anyway.

The order came and we got down into our holes. I crouched as low as I could as tho I would get extra safety by pushing hard against its bottom. And we waited, and we waited, straining to hear the sound of B-29 engines.

I heard a distant and muffled droning, hardly louder than the sound of a mosquito, but lower pitched. Was I really hearing something man-made? I strained to hear, wondering when the planes would be directly overhead.

Then I heard the sound of a wind rapidly becoming a gale. I got up onto my knees to peer over the edge of my hole. A huge explosion erupted, shaking the ground. I saw flashes of fire interspersed with billows of smoke, covering the entire top half of the hill. The noise went beyond a thunderbolt's; it was loud and rumbling fast, without the echoing and diminishing reverberations we hear in heavy thunderstorms. It ended abruptly.

I was dumbstruck and probably holding my breath during that fast bombardment. I thought, *Thank God they didn't accidentally drop bombs on us.* But I pity those poor bastards on that hill.

¶Early in July we were told that we would be leaving our positions and to be packed and ready to go in the morning, 6 July; we were going to be relieved by the 1st Battalion 1st Marines and go into battalion reserve. Would it be another case of "hurry up and wait?" It was, but not too many hours.

In the afternoon we got the familiar order: "Saddle up and standby to move out." I stood up, put on my cartridge belt with its canteen, first-aid kit, and bayonet. Next I put on my backpack; my entrenching tool (small shovel) was hooked to it. Then I reached down for the strap on one ammo can, put my head and right arm thru the loop and hung it close to my right side. Then I took the other ammo can, put my head and left arm thru it so that it hung at my left side. Next, I put on my helmet, picked up my rifle, and waited for the command, "Move out!"

We went down the rear slope of our hill and got on the MSR. We were moving south in full daylight, staying on the road in two columns, each column hugging its side of the road. I was uneasy, knowing that we were visible to enemy observers back on that high hill, if any of them had survived.

We were moving faster than usual. I kept anticipating "incoming mail." Sure enough, some artillery shells exploded a few hundred feet on our left flank. We picked up the speed of marching, but there was no more enemy fire. All the while, I saw the skipper, our captain, looking calm and almost nonchalant. His job was to set an example of confidence for us to follow, but I still felt anxious until we were a few miles farther away from the front line. A few more miles and we boarded trucks to take us to our bivouac area where the mess kitchens had been set up and, close by, those very welcome shower tents.

On the march back, I wasn't concerned about road mines. I thought that the Chinese box mines were a menace only to vehicles. Later I learned that whatever weight bore down on them, increased the pressure so that eventually even a light weight, such as a man's footstep, could detonate them, like the proverbial "straw that broke the camel's back."

Chapter 22
CLUB HONGCH'ŎN

"EVERYBODY WANTS TO GO TO HEAVEN, but nobody wants to die," or so I have heard. In the Korean War there was no heaven, but we probably had the best it could offer to the 1st Marine Division: nearly two summer months of a "working vacation."

It started on 6 July when we were pulled off the Kansas line for an 11-day stint in regimental reserve. On 17 July trucks brought our bat-talion south to the Hongch'ŏn area, about forty miles below the MLR (main line of resistance, the front line). This is where our division would be in X Corps reserve. Our front-line sector was being taken over by the Army's illustrious 2nd Infantry Division, the famous "Indian-head Division."

Fig. 22-1: Randy & WEA carrying hot food

We were leaving a life of living in foxholes, eating canned food rations, staying awake at night on watch duty, constantly on guard against a nearby enemy, unable to wash our clothing or shower, constrained from exercising outside our foxholes, subject to being shot by enemy snipers or bombarded by their mortars or artillery.

We were going to a camp in a peaceful valley. It had field kitchens to serve us hot chow, mess tents with floors and good drainage, shower units to get us clean, and nighttime showings of the latest Hollywood movies. We had aboveground sleeping areas in tents, a shallow, slow-flowing river where we could safely swim, and a narrow, clean sandy shore for sunbathing.

And the scenery was fine, rolling hills on the east side, palisades on the west side (the river's far bank), and a few square miles of farmland with many dried out rice paddies, hence no problem with mosquitoes.

The native population, tho sparse, was friendly and unobtrusive, quite understandable since their new visitors were thousands of foreigners, most of them young adults and all caring lethal weapons. Our main contact with the Koreans was paying the women to wash our clothes. There were some Korean laborers attached to our battalion, but language differences impeded any attempt at communicating.

Fig. 22-2: Bourassa, WEA, and Mancha

And then there was "Sam." He was a boy, about 10 years old, living with one of the washerwomen. He seemed to like being around us, maybe because his family expected him to get things from us. We did give him some cast-off clothing and occasionally some candy or other goodies. We also played around with him and even took fotos of our times together.

It seemed that we had gone from "Club Dead" to "Club Med," Marine Corps style, or maybe it is enough to call it "Club Hongch'ŏn."

Fig. 22-3: WEA and "Sam"

¶Down the middle of our camp ran a 15-foot-wide dirt road with a border of white-painted rocks. Tents were on each side, some two-man "pup tents" of paired shelter-halves in camouflage color and some olive-drab canvas pyramidal tents, holding six men.

New replacements arrived and had the luxury of time for a peaceful transition before having to go to the front line in September. They would be quite busy in Club Hongch'ŏn. As on most cruise ships or at vacation resorts, a variety of activities were available. Nearly all of the activities were mandatory, and few were for recreation or entertainment.

Wake-up call (reveille) came at 0600. We quickly got dressed and assembled in formation for calisthenics. Then we had to collect any ground litter. By then we were able to have breakfast between 0700 and 0800 and start our classes or training exercises. We had lunch around noon and some more training during the early afternoon. The free time after that was when we went swimming.

The new routines and the arrival of warm summer days, and maybe something mental, decreased my appetite. I started losing weight and my waist dropped from thirty-three inches to twenty-nine inches. I was at my skinniest, when some photos of us were taken. The fotografic film was mailed to Japan for development and printing. I sent a foto to my mother, hoping it would cheer her up. When she saw how thin I had become, she cried, according to my sister.

Fig. 22-4: WEA getting ready to go on a training exercize

¶Our machine-gun section leader, Corporal Punte, was determined to make us proficient at operating and maintaining the machine-gun. He was impelled by his first experiences in Korea, during the Chosin Campaign, where he had been assigned to a machine-gun unit without enough training. And he was right about me and the rest of the ammo carriers; we really needed the training.

Our World War I vintage machine-gun was a recoil-operated, belt-fed, air-cooled weapon, weighing thirty-one pounds. Its tripod mount weighed nearly twenty pounds. It was long obsolete. The Germans had a far superior light machine-gun as early as 1935, and yet we were still using our old weapon in 1951.

Punte was a good guy, conscientious, patient, and fair. But before I could know much about him, I had to adjust my ear to his East Baltimore dialect; he was uttering sounds which I had never heard before. Fortunately, by the time I heard Punte, I had become much more tolerant in language matters. Besides, it is unrealistic to expect everybody in America to learn to speak the high-quality American English one finds only in my hometown of Detroit.

Punte showed us how to change the barrel. It took too long because of its design, and was hazardous to attempt during active combat when sustained firepower was crucial. He showed us how to adjust "head space." That's the gap needed for the internal mechanism, the bolt, to properly strike the firing pin of the cartridges and

Fig. 22-5: Our MG Section: L to R: Standing - Eugene Punte (1), WEA, hatless (2), F.C. Mancha, hatless (9), Burt Anderson (11), Don Newell (12); Squatting - William Hicks (1), Larry Moore? (3), Henry Thompson (6). Fotografer – Vic Knabel

continue a steady rate of firing.

But the funniest sight was when he conducted a "trigger-pull" class. He stood in front of us and, with his right arm outstretched, said, "Stick out your arm like this." We did it. "Now act like you've got hold of the pistol grip on the gun, but you have not yet touched the trigger with your index finger." He placed his hand on the

165

machine-gun's pistol grip with his index finger pointing stiffly forward.

"Now, slowly curl your trigger finger toward the palm of your hand. Do *not* jerk it back." While we imitated the motion, we knew that in the heat of battle we would never be slowly curling our trigger fingers, or anything else; we would be furiously pulling the trigger to shoot at the enemy.

Watching our practice from nearby was the machine-gun platoon leader, 2ndLt Ernie Brydon. He was an energetic and savvy officer who favored frequent and realistic training. Brydon was a "mustang," Marine slang for an officer who had been promoted from the enlisted ranks. Being short (and nicknamed Mouse) he was used as a sniper on Bougainville in World War II. He was standing nearby while we were practicing trigger pull and had to control himself to avoid laughing out loud. He knew that Punte was right about the need for training, but it sure looked funny to see all of us pretending to be shooting.

It looked like what we did as young boys playing games with pretend guns, shooting at each other. I'm glad that during the instruction, Punte did not ask any of us to yell "bang, bang" or "rat-a-tat-tat," or, even funnier, practice falling down as tho we had been shot.

¶In and of itself, training has value that goes beyond keeping healthy young adult males from getting bored and into mischief, or worse. We needed to maintain our combat skills and to integrate the new replacements that came in each month. Before returning to the front, we would have a manpower turnover of about one-sixth.

To improve morale and help us sharpen our skills, the Second Battalion held a machine-gun shooting contest. Dog Company's machine-gunners won and when asked what they wanted as rewards, they said, "women." So it was arranged to take them by truck to a house in Wŏnju, where they spent an evening with seven prostitutes. No ammo carriers were involved in the "award ceremony" in Wŏnju.

I'm glad because nine days later a few of the gunners showed signs of having contracted gonorrhea.

Fig. 22-6: Cleaning my rifle

¶In July the United Nations had begun negotiating with the Chinese and North Koreans at Kæsong. The purpose was to achieve a cease-fire. President Truman and the United Nations wanted to minimize the fighting during the negotiations. This policy did not take into account the Communists' philosophy that negotiations were part of waging war, not merely a means to ending it.

Because the Communists were using stalling tactics at the cease-fire negotiations in Kæsong, our top military planners were preparing an amfibious invasion of North Korea on the east coast. If successful, it would cause their front line to collapse and give us more territory, possibly as far as their capital, P'yongyang. But, no matter how many U.S. divisions might be involved, I had no doubt that the first wave ashore would be our 1st Marine Division. Fortunately, for me and my buddies, the invasion was canceled.

Several weeks before the Communists suspended negotiations, an announcement was made that volunteers were needed to become truck drivers. Wow! That sounded like my ticket to a safer and softer life, no more travail as an ammo carrier in dangerous conflict with the enemy. But I needed to ask some of the older and more experienced guys for their advice.

None of them had much of an opinion about it, and I said, "Well, I guess I'll volunteer." That's when one of them asked me, "Why would you want to do a thing like that?" I said, "Because it's safer and easier. Look what happened to us on Hill 676."

"Have you thought this thru?"

"What's there to think about?"

He was in his early twenties, maybe three years older than I, and therefore I felt he was smarter. "Listen kid, don't you know about the peace talks going on now? You know what that means? There's going to be a cease-fire soon and then there won't be any more need for combat troops. All of us will be rotated out, maybe to Japan. But the support guys, like truck drivers, are going to have to stay much longer. Do you really want to stay here longer? Think it thru."

His logic seemed impeccable. So I did not volunteer. In September's violent fighting on Hill 749, I repeatedly regretted my decision: "*Why the hell did I listen to him?*" A Turkish proverb leaps to my mind: "In the land of the blind, the one-eyed man is king!"

¶Summer rains came and some of the pyramidal tents leaked. So men had to move over from under the dripping. But the real deluge couldn't be avoided; heavy rain came rolling down those nearby hills and flooded our area

Our tents, the company street, and our equipment all got drenched and we had a lot of drying out to do. But we were still enjoying our days.

¶Our time in reserve seemed to benefit some Marines who have an acute business sense; I call them "bizners" (seventy-one percent of the letters in "bizners" are also found in the word "Marines"). One of them designed a shoulder patch and sent it to Japan for manufacture. When it came back it was an

Fig. 22-7: Official Division patch

168

instant success but the bizner was ordered by his superiors to stop peddling any of the patches to his fellow Marines.

Fig. 22-8: Unauthorized patch

The problem was that the new patch was an unauthorized variation of the official 1st Marine Division patch. The official patch is a four-sided diamond shape, with a thin red border and a field of dark blue. On the field of blue running straight down the center and most of the length of the patch is a big red number 1 (one). Straight down the center of the large number 1 is the word, in white thread, "Guadalcanal." Around the number 1 are depicted the stars of the Southern Cross constellation.

The bizner's patch was identical in shape, color, and representation of the Southern Cross. However, it lacked "Guadalcanal." It replaced the numeral 1 with a red human fist making a rude gesture with the middle finger. Straight down the center of the fist, starting at the top of the extended middle finger, and going across the palm, was the word Korea in white thread. The patch is now a collector's item. I believe that the bizner deserved to receive an award, official, of course, for initiative, artistry, and courage, and maybe punished for vulgar taste in art.

¶Marines have an aesthetic appreciation for "wine, women, and song." In our lingo you could translate it into "booze, sex, and music." Manert Kennedy showed some entrepreneurial skills in the alcohol business.

It started with his hiking trips among the hills. He found a few small Buddhist temples and, more important, a shallow well with cool water. He came back to it with two cans of beer and a pair of long johns (winter underwear) that had been knotted at the end of each leg. After putting a can of the warm beer into each underwear leg, he used a rope he'd brought, and lowered everything into the well.

After the beer was very cold, he pulled it up, put it into his knap-sack, and quickly took it back to camp, where he traded one can of cold beer for two cans of the warm beer that was our standard ration. Soon he had enough cold beer for himself and his valued customers.

The women were a very secret operation that began rather late in our Club Hongch'ŏn stay. I did not know about them until fifty-five years after leaving Korea. One or two bizners in Dog Company were able to keep three or four Korean women in one of the tents and offer sex with them to the other guys, for a price.

In early September it was time to move north. The bizners load-ed the women into a truck, hidden in the middle of some baggage. Unfortunately the women weren't used to bathing and did not have access to (or the practice of using) sanitary napkins or tampons. Most of them were menstruating and there was an overwhelming smell that permeated the vehicle during the trip.

They were released when we reached the forward staging area. Unable to support themselves there, they were forced to do road work with the Korean laborers. It was a dangerous area and about half of them were wounded by enemy shrapnel.

¶For music in Hongch'ŏn, there were few options. Somebody had a Zenith Trans-Oceanic shortwave radio. But broadcast recep-tion was poor. The age of transistors and communications satellites was years away and music by shortwave broadcast was too wavering in volume and interlaced with static to be truly enjoyable. In fact, most of what we listened to were news broadcasts. Radio Moscow came in strong and we learned the latest Communist propaganda, f. ex., that we were engaged in "germ warfare" against the peaceful Korean people. None of us believed it and we all made negative comments during most of their broadcasts.

Steve Lacki arrived with the 10th Replacement Draft that summer and teamed up with a few amateur musicians. They were able to bor-row some musical instruments from an Army unit. Steve played the bass fiddle as part of a group called the Rice Paddy Ramblers.

More professional entertainment was provided by the USO. They always featured very attractive women. Fellow ammo carrier Burt Anderson, the first member of Dog Company to publish a book about our experiences in Korea, describes one of the stimulating shows and reflects the reactions of many of us horny young men to a well-known Hollywood actress and dancer:

Fig. 22-9: Detroiters Charlie Ford and Manert Kennedy

> On a beautiful, vibrant afternoon, I managed to work my way up close to the stage of a Betty Hutton show. I no longer remember the other performers because Betty Hutton grabbed my fancy and I became oblivious to all the rest. The object of my tunnel vision was more specific than the whole of Betty. It centered on her thighs. She simply had the largest thighs that I had ever seen. Not fat by any means, she was a dancer with muscular legs. To say her torso was gorgeous was an absolute understatement. I remained open-mouthed, sexually aroused, transfixed throughout her performance. [BFA 296-97]

But nothing in Hongch'ŏn compared with an unexpected, and dangerous, adventure I would soon experience that summer. And it all started with the arrival of an odd gift from a distant relative whom I had never met.

Chapter 23
PREPARING FOR MISUNDERSTANDING

AT MAIL CALL ON AN AUGUST DAY, I got a package from Elâzığ Turkiye, the "modern" town adjacent to my father's ancestral hometown, Harput. Inside was a book and a letter from my dad's eldest nephew, Sıtkı Samancıoğlu, a primary schoolteacher. The letter was in barely adequate English, no doubt written by somebody else since cousin Sıtkı did not know English. He must have gotten my mail address from one of my father's letters to his family in Turkiye.

Sıtkı wrote about how proud he was that I was performing military service against the Communists and was glad that Turks and Americans were allies, serving side by side in the Korean War. He urged me to visit the Turkish Brigade (Türk Tugayı) and, because I did not understand much Turkish, he was enclosing a book for me to learn it.

I was moved by his words and appreciated the gift of the book. It would be great to visit the Turks and get to know them. They would be glad to see me, after all, my father was Turkish. Thanks to the book from cousin Sıtkı, I would have speedily acquired a basic knowledge of the language, more than the few Turkish words I had learned from my father and his friends while I was growing up. Besides, we were in a reserve area and I believed that I could get permission to make the visit.

I would have no trouble finding them. From recent copies of the Army newspaper *Stars and Stripes* and the *Detroit Times* that my mother was sending me, I knew the Turkish Brigade was attached to the U.S. Army over on the western front (they were part of the 25th Infantry Division, "Tropic Lightning," thru-out the war). The Korean Peninsula was only about 175 miles wide and I would be able to hitchhike over to them.

If ignorance and naivete protect nineteen-year-olds, then I must have been the safest person in the world. Perhaps some measure of stupidity and bravado was residing in my brain, at least at a subconscious level. Another ingredient in this mental concoction may have been my immaturity.

Every experienced language teacher will tell you: "Never try to learn two foreign languages at the same time!" To that I would add, "Even if you have the wrong book for one of the languages and no book at all for the other. A consequence could be that you will get into a lot of trouble. You could even lose your life."

Consider the matter of the book itself. Yes, it was a language-instruction book. No, it was not written for Americans to learn Turkish; it was written for Turks to learn English. That meant that the explanations of grammar rules, etc., were all about the English language but written in Turkish. While I could see translations side by side, I had no English explanations of Turkish grammar rules. Unfortunately, it was probably the only "relevant" book Sıtkı could find in Elâzığ's bookstores.

Consider my surroundings. I was getting acquainted with Korean villagers as well as with some Korean Service Corps (KSC) laborers assigned to our regiment to carry supplies, do construction, etc. From them I was trying to learn some Korean words. I found it fascinating that some of the Korean sounds were identical to Turkish sounds. Years later I learned that Korean and Turkish (as well as Japanese, Mongolian, Tatar, and many others, including some North American Indian tongues) are all relatives, stemming from a common ancestral language that developed somewhere around the Altai Mountains in western Mongolia.

¶I told Corporal Punte that I wanted to visit the Turkish Brigade and I showed him Sıtkı's letter and the book. Punte took me to the platoon leader and I made the request to him. In doing so, I mentioned that it was good for our United Nations forces to have friendship visits by personnel who had some ties with allied countries.

174

The lieutenant asked me, "Where are the Turks?"

I said, "West of here."

"Alli, we're on the eastern front; *Everyone else* is west of here. How are you going to find them?"

"I'm going to hitchhike and just ask along the way."

"How much time do you want?"

"I think I'll need three days."

"Well, we're in reserve and not going to go anywhere for a while. So I'll have the clerk type up the orders approving it."

"Thank you, sir."

I decided that I didn't want to lug my heavy M1 rifle with me and I went to Tex to see if he would temporarily swap his .45 caliber pistol for it.

"Why?" Tex asked.

"I'm going to be hitchhiking over to visit the Turkish Brigade and a pistol would be much more convenient for me to carry around."

"Why are you going to visit them?"

I explained about the letter from my cousin, my dad's ancestry, my curiosity, etc.

"OK," he said and handed me his pistol and its holster.

I saw that the holster was different from the standard Marine Corps issue (the 1916 model) that our officers wore. It did not have the grommeted hole at the bottom for a lace to be passed thru and tied to the leg. Instead the holster was connected at its top by a brass swivel to a belt hanger, a short, wide leather strap with the hooks for attaching to the cartridge belt that we wore around our waist.

I asked him, "Tex, what kind of holster is this?"

"It's a cavalry holster. This brass-hanger swivel allows it to always hang straight down, whether you're standing up or sitting on a horse."

Not until 56-years later would I learn that the holster was the 1912 model USMC cavalry holster. And it was shown in a November 2007 *Leatherneck* magazine advertisement (p. 93) as:

"You won't believe these authentic replicas! Fabricated to original Rock Island drawings. Absolutely authentic down to the latest detail."

¶Still thinking in stereotypes about people from Texas, I wasn't too surprised that he had some kind of connection with horses and cowboys who carry guns (but *not* M1 rifles). So I wasn't all that mystified that he would have this kind of item.

"I never saw a holster like this before."

"Yeah, it's probably the only one in Korea."

Tex also lent me a canvas-web magazine pouch to hold two extra magazines of pistol ammo. I put on the holster belt. I liked it, but I could not imagine that the brass hanger swivel was really needed. The era of horse-riding was long-gone and it wasn't needed in a vehicle, no matter what its horsepower was.

Fig. 23-1: Tex in an amfibious truck

¶Soon after morning chow the next day, I walked over to the nearby road to hitchhike, westward, to where I thought the Turks were. On my belt I had the pistol in its holster; in the top left pocket of my dungaree jacket was my typewritten official orders for three-days' leave. In my backpack I carried some C-rations. Also, inside my backpack was the letter from Sıtkı and that book for Turks to learn English. Who knows, I might want to leave it with the Turkish Brigade to help somebody who wanted to learn my language.

I stuck out my thumb as a jeep with two Marines approached. They asked me where I was going and said they could drop me off at some crossroads, where I should be able to hitch a ride west. They dropped me off and I started walking away. One of them called out, "Hey! Your pistol fell out of the holster." I walked back and looked at the floor by the backseat and saw the .45 on the floor. It must've made a noise as I was getting out of the jeep and I had not noticed it but one of them had heard it.

I thanked him and put it back into the holster wondering what would have happened if they had driven away with the weapon. I would be unarmed and catch hell from Tex when I got back to my unit. From then on I was more careful when moving about, often keeping my hand pressed against the flap of the holster.

Soon, a U.S. Army transport truck approached and I stuck out my thumb. The driver stopped. He was alone in the cab; I had no idea what was in the back of the truck.

He was an African-American, wearing the standard U.S. Army fatigues. They were quite different from our Marine Corps dungarees in fabric weave, color and type of pockets. I could not tell which army unit he was with, because I was sitting on his right side and army unit insignias are customarily worn near the top of the left sleeve.

I tried to start a conversation with him, but he seemed too attentive to the road to respond to me. That made sense to me; we were on a narrow gravel-covered road. At least we seemed to be driving west. I chattered on but he didn't acknowledge anything I said; he acted like he didn't understand a word of it. So I decided to ask him a question, no response.

Finally, he stuck out his right arm and pointed with his index finger at the lower-right corner of the windshield, right in front of me. There was a decal of a flag with three horizontal stripes. He said, "eet-yohp-yah, eet-yohp yah, eet-yohp-yah." Then I understood; he was *not* an American. He was an Ethiopian soldier. They wore U.S. Army uniforms. I smiled, nodded my head up and down, and stopped talking.

The terrain was hilly; the road was steep and winding. As we were going over a range of high hills, I looked down upon a narrow river with a bridge. We were going to cross it. The far end of the bridge dead-ended at a road running alongside the river.

I spied a convoy of jeeps that had come from the right and were waiting to allow our truck to complete its crossing of the bridge. As we got near the far end of the bridge, I saw that the front fenders of the jeeps bore little red flags on short posts; they were Turkish.

The truck driver began to turn left. I yelled out, "Stop! Stop! That's them."

He couldn't have understood my words but he stopped the truck and I got out. I smiled and thanked him, hoping I had shown my gratitude for the ride.

I wish I could've expressed my thanks to him by giving him a language book: one written for Ethiopians to learn English or maybe for English speakers to learn Amharic.

I walked the short distance to the front jeep, smiled, and said, hello in Turkish: *merhaba*. The occupants seemed startled. In retrospect, I think of a Shakespeare quote: "And thereby hangs a tale," adding only: "of danger."

Chapter 24
ENEMY AGENT

EXPERIENCED EDITORS HAVE GOOD ADVICE for all writers: "Put yourself into the place of the reader." This is intended to sensitize the writer to the discrepancy between what the writer *thinks* he is expressing and what the reader actually perceives.

Similar advice applies when an armed stranger approaches a group of armed soldiers. For example, I wanted to be viewed as their friend, but I was wearing the Marine Corps combat uniform. The Turks were not familiar with it. Being part of the U.S. Army's Twenty-fifth Infantry Division, they were wearing U.S. Army-type uniforms, which I was familiar with.

Fig. 24-1: 25TH Inf. Div. "Tropic Lightning" shoulder patch

In pronouncing Turkish words, I do not have an American accent. I speak like my father. Also, the Turkish dialect of his region, eastern Anadolu, has sounds in common with Azeri Turkish, which is spoken in what was then part of the Soviet Union: Azerbaijan.

I do not look like most Turks. Most of them are like my father, short to medium height, brown-eyed and dark-haired, having the typical Mediterranean "olive" complexion. I am average height, blue-eyed, light brown-haired, and have a pale-olive, complexion. My *merhaba* didn't comport with my appearance.

Adding to my jeopardy was a rumor circulating among UN forces (it may have appeared in U.S. newspapers) that the Communists were planning to infiltrate UN lines using English-speaking "white" Eastern European soldiers wearing captured American uniforms. I knew nothing of this rumor as I approached the people in the jeeps.

Fig. 24-2: USMC 1912
cavalry holster

I tried to speak some Turkish to them and say I was there for a visit. I was vaguely aware that I was mixing up some Korean and English with my poor Turkish. None of them smiled and they didn't seem too friendly. Nevertheless, they invited me into one of the jeeps and we drove back to their camp. During the drive they were talking to each other in a rather suspicious way.

At their camp one of the Jeep-riding Turkish officers got out and started talking to another officer who looked just like an American Army officer. That officer asked me, in perfect American English, "Who are you?" He *was* an American, the U.S. 8th Army's official interpreter for the Turkish Brigade.

"I'm PFC William Alli, Dog Company, 2nd Battalion, 1st Marines."

"What are you doing here?"

"I've come to visit the Turks."

He looked puzzled and began talking Turkish with the other Turkish officers who had been in the Jeep convoy. They all kept glancing at me and I started feeling apprehensive.

In a slightly sterner voice, but with a forced half-smile, the interpreter said, "Come into this tent with me," pointing to a large tent nearby. He was right behind me as I entered the tent and ordered, "Hands up!" He had drawn his pistol and was aiming it at me. So I raised both hands over my head.

He lifted up the flap of my pistol holster and took my pistol away. "What kind of a pistol holster is this?"

"It's an old cavalry holster that I borrowed from Tex. It's probably the only one like it in Korea"

"It doesn't look right. It's not standard issue for American forc-

180

es."

"I know. It's a cavalry holster. This brass-hanger swivel pin allows it to always hang straight down, whether you're standing up or sitting on a horse."

Fig. 24-3: NATO Supreme Commander Gen. Eisenhower visiting Istanbul.

He did not react to my statements. He made me hand it over to him.

"Who are you and what are you doing here?" he demanded.

I repeated my answers. My arms were still raised high and I added, "I've got the letter from Sıtkı, my Turkish cousin, and the book he sent. It's in my backpack." I was bending my right wrist to point my index finger down toward my jacket's left breast pocket, "I have official orders from my outfit to be on three-day's leave to come here."

He unbuttoned my pocket and took out the orders. He also searched the rest of my pockets and backpack. Then he sternly said, "Go face the corner of the tent and squat down." I did so. Before he went out, he raised his voice and angrily said, "I don't know who you are, but we're going to nail your ass." I got scared; I knew what had happened to Jesus.

In the painful position of squatting, I waited. I sensed that some Turkish soldiers were outside the tent guarding me.

Frightful thoughts went thru my head: Are they going to shoot me, because of some misunderstanding? Is this the way my life is going to end? I won't be twenty years old until January 3. Is my mother going to get a telegram from the Defense Department saying that I was accidentally killed, arrested for desertion, etc.? Maybe the best thing for me would be if they packed me into a jeep and took me back to my outfit immediately.

My knees were really starting to hurt. In fact, most of my legs felt the muscle strain. I was afraid I would keel over. What a mistake I had made! And to think, I had started out with the best of intentions: to be an international goodwill ambassador. But then I recalled one of my high school literature courses and a famous verse by Bobbie Burns: "The best laid plans of mice and men, aft gang agley." Now I realized what "aft gang agley" could mean: can get oneself killed.

After at least an hour, I heard some sounds outside the tent. It sounded like several people walking. I hoped it wasn't a firing squad.

¶In came the interpreter and some Turkish officers; all were smiling. "You're clean. We checked on you. Here's your stuff," and he handed back my backpack, my official orders, and the pistol belt with the pistol in it. "This *is* an interesting holster," he added. I thought, W*hen I get back, I'm going to tell Tex that his goddamn cavalry holster almost got me killed.*

We walked out of the tent, my wobbly legs still aching from the squatting, and they had me climb a few steps onto a wooden platform at one end of an

Fig. 24-4: Turks sailing to Korea from Izmir, 1952

182

open area surrounded by tents. Turkish soldiers, in formation, were facing the platform. Most of them seemed to be about my age, nineteen years old. Later I learned that nineteen-year-old Turkish males, with very few exceptions, must enter their army for two-year's service. Looking at them, I got an idea of what my father must have looked like when he first came to America in 1913.

"Say something to them," a Turkish officer said in English. Obviously I was a special guest. I smiled, looked out at the troops and said, "*Merhaba*." They all roared back in unison, *Sağ ol,* startling me into jumping back a step or two and putting all the Turkish soldiers into a fit of laughter. *Sağ ol* means "be strong." It's a standard response of a military unit to a greeting or some orders from their commander. We had a similar custom in the Marines; ours was "Aye, aye, sir."

Then I said a few words about my Marine division, where we were, and why I was visiting the Turkish Brigade. Without mentioning my father's army desertion, I explained when he had come to America and expressed my hope to visit their country someday. As the American officer interpreted my words, the soldiers were smiling and nodding their heads.

For the next two days I was hosted as a long-lost brother. It was a hospitality that would warm the coldest heart. Food was a glorious part of it because the Turkish Brigade had wonderful cooks. I had great meals, good solid Anadoluan food, the kind my father used to cook: plenty of casseroles with chunks of meat and vegetables, with plenty of garlic and no lack of oil or salt. And there was lots of bread, the yummy Turkish style, with thick crispy crust and tender textures inside. It was the kind that you ate chunk by chunk, holding it in your left hand to push the food onto the fork or spoon in your right hand. And of course the chunks of bread were used like little sponges to sop up the last bit of broth or microchunks of solid matter at the bottom of the bowl or around its sides, after spoons and forks had finished their functions.

What an improvement over the canned C-rations. It tasted better

183

than the best food I ever got from the Marine Corps' mess kitchens. When will the rest of America learn that a meal without garlic is like a day without sunshine?

The 8th Army Quartermaster Corps had to deal with differences among United Nations forces. For the Turks this meant no pork products. Plus, the Turks ate a lot of bread, which required large amounts of wheat flour. On average, Turks were a little bit shorter and stockier than Americans and needed appropriate clothing sizes. And most of them needed wider boots. The Greek contingent had the same supply needs, except that the Greeks did eat pork and had fewer troops (10,000 versus 14,000 Turks) during the course of the war.

¶Years later I learned what the Turkish government's first response was to the United Nations' plea for its members to help South Korea, right after the Communists invaded on 25 June 1950. They told U.S. military advisors in Ankara that Turkiye would send a division "as a starter."

Some Turkish government officials were hoping that their actions would persuade the North Atlantic Treaty Organization to accept them as a member. That acceptance required approval by British Prime Minister Clement Atlee. In World War I Atlee had served in the British Army against the Turks at Gelibolu (Gallipoli) and later in Mesopotamia (Iraq) where he was seriously wounded.

Atlee agreed that Turkiye should be accepted as a NATO member and was reported to have said he would "rather have Johnnie Turk with us than against us." In 1952 Turkiye did gain its membership.

U.S. officials strenuously objected to the initial Turkish offer saying that the North Korean invasion was meant by the Soviet Union as a ploy to draw our forces to the Far East and thereby weaken NATO's strength in Europe. The American advisors asserted that Turkiye had to maintain the strongest defenses along the southern borders of the Iron Curtain: Bulgaria, Armenia, and

184

Georgia, as well as the entire southern coast of the Black Sea.

"Send just a token force, to show allied solidarity against the Communist aggression," the U.S. advised. The Turks decided that a brigade would suffice and called for volunteers. There were ten volunteers for each opening.

¶The brigade left Turkiye by ship under the command of Tahsin Yazıcı, a veteran of the 1915 Gelibolu (Gallipoli) campaign, who took a reduction in his general's rank, in order to qualify for command. Landing at Pusan on 19 October were three infantry battalions and an artillery regiment. They soon went into bivouac near Tægu where they received training and US equipment. On 26 November, they were sent, without receiving adequate briefing by US officers:

Fig. 24-5: Gen. Walker awarding medals to Turks

". . . to guard the East flank of the U.S. 2nd Division against an expected Chinese attack. . . They marched east toward Wawon, near Kunu-ri in North Korea, with no idea of what was going on around them. . . The main body of the Chinese offensive slammed into the Turkish Brigade. Many Turks fought to the death or launched bayonet counterattacks against the Chinese. When the brigade finally fell back. . . it had been all but destroyed. About 1,000 of the Turks were dead or missing and only a few of its companies were still combat effective. [MJV 146-47]

Of the miscellaneous UN forces (excluding U.S. and ROK), the largest were those of the British Commonwealth; the Turks were the fifth largest, but they had the second

Fig. 24-6: Mortar training of Turks   highest number of casualties for this UN group during the war.

General MacArthur praised the Turks as the "bravest of the brave." President Truman awarded the Brigade a Presidential Unit Citation.

¶I soon learned how modest Turkish soldiers are in performing their toilet functions. They require a full partition between individuals using urinals and commodes. I don't know what they would do if they had to use one of our "four-holers" to defecate (what they call doing "kah-kah" instead of our "puu-puu"). Any Turkish soldier seeing one of our four-holers would probably restrain himself as long as he could, before suffering the indignity of using it. He might even attempt to wait until dark.

Because these troops were in reserve, they were housed in squad tents that hold about ten men. They did not have individual air mattresses, and they slept in parallel on a raised wooden platform. I slept quite comfortably on it.

On my second day with the brigade I was treated to a musical performance by their folk music ensemble. They had the common Turkish musical instruments: saz, darbuka, etc. and they were really great players.

There's nothing quite like the folk music of Anadolu, where most of Turkiye's people live. I especially like the catchy dance tunes. Of course they have their laments, but the authentic village

186

music of Anadolu is pleasant to my prejudiced ear. Most of it is mercifully free of the nasal wailing that characterizes much of the music in other Near Eastern countries.

Fig. 24-7: Turkish
Army national patch

The soldier-musicians were entertaining us, as did bards thru the ages. They sang about clashes with the enemy, emphasizing their first, and bloodiest, encounter in Korea: Kunu-ri. They played on native instruments, yielding musical sounds that their ancestors had developed centuries ago. The sounds captivated me too; the resonant plucking and strumming of strings and the beat of the drums lured me into smiling, rocking my head side to side, snapping my fingers and rhythmically tapping out the rhythm with my foot.

Soon after breakfast on my final day I got ready to leave and a few of my new friends gave me fotografs as souvenirs. They gave me their addresses and asked me to come to Turkiye and be their guest.

I accepted their invitation but had no idea when I would ever visit them. But two years later during my summer vacation from Wayne State University in Detroit, I spent a week in Ankara as the guest of one of these soldiers: Erdoğan Başaran.

In 1974, I was made an Honorary Member of the Turkish Veterans of the Korean War Association (Kore'de Savaşanlar Derneği—KorSavaş). If they had demanded to see my identification first, it would be no problem because then I was an employee of the U.S. Agency for International Development. I was traveling with an Official U.S. passport on an inspection visit of our agency's programs in their country. Also, I was carrying no pistol or holster. The veterans' hospitality was most gracious.

The Brigade gave me a special gift, their circular shoulder patch, a white star and crescent on a field of red, indicating the nationality

187

of their army. Later I learned that the Brigade also had a unit patch that reflected their name: the North Star Brigade. It displays Polaris with its neighbors. I had not seen them wearing that unit patch in Korea. I wish they had given me that patch too.

Years later when I did get their Brigade patch, I mulled over its resemblance to my 1st Marine Division patch; both featured constellations. We were the "Guadalcanal Division." Our patch displayed the Southern Cross, which our Marines were able to view only after nearing and then crossing the equator in World War II, bound for the 7 August 1942 invasion of Guadalcanal.

¶Two soldiers had a special gift for me, slender, sharp daggers: one with a ruby-red plastic handle, hiltless, and a blade having a tip like the end of a carpenter's nail. The other dagger had a yellow, all-metal handle, inlaid with polished, colored stones; it had a slightly curved blade tip and a small hilt. Both were easily concealable.

Fig. 24-8: Turkish North Star Brigade shoulder patch

As the one soldier reached forward to offer his dagger to me, I instinctively reached out for it and he stopped me by pulling it away from my reach, disapprovingly clicking his tongue once and tipping his head back once. He was telling me the equivalent of, "Just a minute. Never reach out to accept a dagger as a gift from someone who is still holding it!" Then he went thru the motion of holding the dagger by its handle and showing me how a malicious person could thrust it into me as I reached for it.

Finally, he picked up the knife to show me the proper motions. He placed it down on a blanket between us (we were in a tent) with the axis of the knife at right angles to each of us. *Böyle* (like this), he told me, smiling with the satisfaction of having taught a younger brother some special etiquette. I recognized it as a safety lesson and was grateful. I picked it up by its handle, and thanked him, *Teşekkür ederim*, trying to imagine what ancient experiences had precipitated this etiquette with knives.

The final gifts were presented to me with obvious reverence. Both embodied Koranic prayers for God's protection (they were in Arabic, not Turkish). One was handwritten on a small piece of paper which could be carried in my shirt pocket. The other was a necklace that seemed to be made of brass. The chain was thin; its pendant was a thin, rectangular tablet on which a prayer had been engraved.

I was quite touched by their gifts. They had not inquired about my religion and were merely wishing safety for my future. I said, *Çok teşekkür ederim* (thank you *very* much), and they smiled. All I had to offer was my language book. It might help one of them learn English in the future.

The interpreter told me that a jeep would take me back to the main road where I could hitch a ride back to Hongch'ŏn. I thanked him and the other Turks for their hospitality. I said, "I hope to visit all of you in Turkiye someday." I was presuming that I (and they) would survive the war and that I would be able to afford the expense of the long sea journey from America to Turkiye. I could not have foreseen low-cost commercial flights starting in the late 1950s.

It was time for goodbye, Turkish style. I climbed into the jeep and said: *Allaha ısmarladık* (We entrust you to God); they replied: *Güle güle* (Go smilingly). Then the jeep pulled away, they waved goodbye and I waved back, being sure to use the Turkish gesture, a side-to-side wig-wag (semafore) motion, instead of the wrist-hinged up-and-down hand flutter that we Americans use.

It had been a remarkable visit and I promised myself to visit their country and learn a lot more about the Turks and their Korean War experiences. [MKÖ, AKD] I vowed to study Turkish and contribute to better understanding between Americans and Turks. How well would I be able to learn Turkish? I couldn't be sure. The American interpreter was the first non-Turk I could remember who spoke

189

Turkish. He had an enormous vocabulary. But his heavy American accent pained my ear as he mangled nearly every one of the thousands of Turkish words he seemed to know, and the few I had learned from my father. If there is such a thing as a language crime, then that American was a mass murderer.

Nevertheless, the Turks seemed to understand him, proving that native speakers can tune their ear to a foreigner's accent and get the correct meaning of his speech, regardless of how unusual it might be.

Yet I can't help but wonder what went thru the minds of the Turks when they first heard him speaking their language. Did they think he was drunk or that it was some kind of a practical joke by the U.S. military? I doubt that they suspected him of being an enemy agent.

Chapter 25
NEARING A DEADLY RENDEZVOUS

FOR A RENDEZVOUS WITH HELL, a Marine in Korea should have a shot of whiskey and get a regulation haircut (short and neat). At least that's what we did. But where should the rendezvous be? Kangwŏndo is alpine, so it should be on some ridges and hilltops. The more scenic, the better.

How about near a valley, so steep-sided and circular that Mother Nature could call it her punchbowl, and satellite fotos in a future era could confirm it? But this punchbowl was dry in September 1951; it seemed that Mother Nature was not interested in filling it. However, puny humans with too many ambitions that exceeded their grasp, were on hand. As warriors, they could shed a lot of blood around the Punchbowl's rim. But Mother Nature's scale is infinite and man's bloodshed is too scant to even moisten her punchbowl, tho Man would certainly strive his utmost.

At the end of August, General James A. Van Fleet, the 8th Army commander, ordered UN forces into offensive action. The purpose was to bring the Communists back to negotiating and to strengthen our bargaining position. Of course, Chinese and North Korean resistance would now be much stronger. Our division would move north to add a new and violent chapter to its history: the battle for Hill 749. And I would regret not having volunteered to be a truck driver, when I had the opportunity, back in reserve near Hongch'ŏn.

In early September, our 1st Marine Regiment packed up and got on trucks. The summer vacation was over. To us "grunts," it was just one more move to a new locale, new scenery, moving around on some hills, nothing extraordinary. To the generals, it was "assembling forces at a forward staging area preparatory to seizing favorable tactical positions on the east-central front."

We rode on trucks till we were north of the Thirty-eighth Paral-

191

lel, a little bit southeast of the Punchbowl. We spent a few days in this staging area, a small valley secure enough for us to sleep on the ground, in our two-man tents set up in parallel rows. We were at a higher elevation than in Hongch'ŏn. Fall was approaching and giving us cooler nights.

At night we were reminded that the war was close by. An artillery unit on the other side of the valley started bombarding enemy lines. Randy Lohr remembers it as an exciting spectacle, featuring thundering noise, bright flashes of light, and trembling ground. Such a sight was not worry-free for us; the enemy might fire back with his own vengeful noise, flashing lights, and flying shrapnel. That is when the spectators stop thinking that the sights have entertainment value.

By now we had dug some shallow foxholes. Our apprehension was still at a low level, tho we felt that we would be moving out soon.

Early in the morning of our last full day at that site, before he had put on his boots, Randy saw an unwelcome guest. I was still asleep. The guest was a small snake, close to the edge of our hole. While looking at it, wondering whether it was poisonous, Randy fumbled for one of his boots, got hold of it, and hit the snake's head. Then he announced to me that he had killed a snake. My groggy reply was, "Don't show me any snakes!"

At mail call, Randy received a package with a most-welcome gift from home. It was evidence of support from the "home front." It was proof of the ingenuity of the American people, 86 proof, to be exact. It was Kentucky bourbon whiskey, and it had been properly sealed inside two quart cans of commercially labeled orange juice. How could that be? Was the American consumer being subjected to deceptive packaging?

When he first looked at the cans, Randy thought he had received orange juice. With his can opener, the "church key," he opened one, took a quick drink and spat it out in a split second. Quickly realizing that it was whiskey, he took a more deliberate swig and passed the can down the line of tents, telling us: "Each guy take a swig but save enough for all the others."

There was enough for all the machine-gun unit members. And it felt great, flowing over my tongue and down my throat, spreading a comforting warmth. I couldn't believe how much I enjoyed it. After all, my only intake of whiskey was eleven years earlier, when it was mixed with honey and lemon and given to me to treat a bout of the flu. Even my anti-alcohol dad had permitted it. I puked it up right away, that may have been the purpose. I moaned, "I'll never drink alcohol again." That pleased Dad.

Somebody brought us a barbering kit and asked, "Who knows how to cut hair?" Without thinking, I said, "I know how." I really didn't know how, but I thought it would be fun to try. I soon realized that I ran real risks in cutting somebody else's hair, especially if they carried firearms. First, they might get very angry and quarrel with me, or worse. And if I butchered too many men's hair, or did God knows what to them, what would happen to my hair when it came time for one of them to give me a haircut? At least I had enough sense to know that I couldn't give myself a haircut.

Surgeons are more fortunate than barbers. If a surgeon makes really serious mistakes, the incriminating proof may be buried with the patient. But the barber's mistakes are on display for all the world to see. The good thing about our situation is that we wore helmets most of the time and there wasn't much concern about how our hair looked. Besides, some of my victims might not survive the upcoming battle.

Fig. 25.1: WEA practicing haircutting

¶Early on 11 September, we got ready to board trucks for the last few miles to the front, several miles northeast of the rim of the Punchbowl. It was noisy up there. The 5th and 7th Marines had gone ahead of us and the 7th was desperately trying to capture Hill 749. We heard artillery sounds, ours, and, in at least one case during the battle, came under artillery fire, also ours. We learned the definition of friendly fire: "Isn't!"

Randy still had the other can of whiskey (alias "orange juice") to dispose of. He asked the Sergeant what to do with it. "What's your problem?" asked the Sergeant. "It's whiskey," said Randy. "What?" "Yeah, it was sent to me in this can." "Give it to me."

None of us knows what happened to it. We guess that it was shared with those of higher ranks, noncoms and the serving officers, altho Randy observed no change in their behavior toward him. Years later Randy told me, "Good USMC officers and noncoms cannot be bribed, and we had good ones."

In Elizabethan England, the poet John Donne claimed "No man is an island, entire of itself. Any man's death diminishes me." But I believe that each person *is* an island separate from the others. Yet while we live, we have links with other persons, friends and enemies, thru sounds and sights, and smells and touching.

In the coming battle these links would be most intense. New linkages would be made and others permanently severed. The survivors would carry potent memories for the rest of their lives. And John Donne would be proven right; they would be diminished.

194

Chapter 26
POUNDING AT DEATH'S DOOR

I CLAIM TO BE A WORLD-CLASS EXPERT in a subfield of Korean War history. Specifically, it is the entire body of knowledge relating to: (1) what was happening within six-feet of my foxhole, while I was awake; (2) my position in a column of moving men, while there was enough light to see, and, maybe, (3) a few other microsituations. That means that during the battle for Hill 749, I was *un*aware of, at least, 99.9 percent of what was happening elsewhere in the battlefield area.

Now, so many years later, I know that the attack plan was quite simple. We in the 1st Regiment were to pass thru the 7th Regiment's positions on 12 September, and one of our battalions (3/1) would take Hill 854 on the east side of the Soyang River and Kanmubong Ridge. My battalion (2/1) was to pass thru the 7th Marines' positions on Hill 673 and Hill 749 in order to attack and take Hill 812 to the west on the Kanmubong Ridge. In effect, Hill 749 was to be our line of departure for the attack on Hill 812.

Our battalion commander, LtCol Brooke Nihart, writes,

As we approached the crest of 749 to pass thru supposedly friendly lines, our lead elements were hit with a storm of fire. Moreover, Hill 749 was not a North Korean outpost line, as we had been informed by intelligence, but their main line of resistance, heavily bunkered with permanent log-covered machine-gun emplacements, deep trenches, and well-organized defensive fires. [FBN]

What followed was the biggest battle I was in; we were pounding at death's door. My memory and my friends' memories are more able than any archival records to tell people about the fury and the agony and the sorrow embedded in the battle for Hill 749.

But let's start with my unadorned and bloodless summary, before getting into the rawness of the violence:

195

12 September was the day that the 1st Marines were in position to start attacking the enemy. By midnight, 14 September, they had taken Hill 749. On the fifteenth, they consolidated their hold on the hill and built up their strength to resist an imminent all-out counterattack by North Korean forces, which began late at night and continued thru the early hours of 16 September. The days that followed were much less eventful.

¶A moral conscience commands us now to flesh out the story.

We start moving up toward the jump-off point. In some places, there are paths leading to ridgelines and ridgelines leading to higher hilltops. These routes are difficult to move along. They are steep and blocked in places with broken bushes or fallen trees. We stumble into small craters from uprooted trees or larger holes from artillery explosions. We slip on wet slopes.

Everyone in the machine-gun section is heavily loaded. As usual, the gunner is carrying the machine-gun tripod plus one twenty-pound can of bullets that are belt-fed to the gun. The assistant gunner is carrying the heavy gun. Each of the ammo carriers is carrying two cans of ammo.

Everybody has a personal weapon, an M1 rifle or M1 carbine (or the new M2), except for the gunner and assistant gunner who each pack a .45 pistol. We're wearing steel helmets and carrying clips or magazines of bullets for the personal weapon. On our cartridge belts is a bayonet, a canteen of water and a first-aid kit. In our backpacks, we have cans of C-rations, maybe a can of Sterno fuel, a few socks and skivvies (underwear), various personal items, and maybe one or two grenades.

Put yourself into ammo carrier Vic Knabel's place as he approaches the ridgeline:

As we were going up the trail toward Hill 749, we saw a dead gook lying on the trail, with an attractive sword in his hand—an obvious booby trap. The sergeant called out, 'Don't touch it. It's booby-trapped.' We bypassed it and were uphill from it when somebody

196

managed to tie a long rope around the gook and pull the body, resulting in a big explosion.

Bypassing an obstacle on the trail is sometimes hazardous; mines had been planted by the North Koreans well before we arrived to attack them. One man stepped off the trail to take a shit and tripped a mine; it blew him to pieces.

Section Chief Punte recalls,

> On Hill 749, I saw a dead gook officer propped up in a sitting position in a shallow clearing on the ridge. The body looked like it had been dead for at least a few days. The officer was wearing a leather holster belt, and it looked like the Russian Tokarev pistol (a highly prized war trophy) was still in it. As much as I wanted to take that pistol, I knew for sure that the body was booby-trapped, so I moved on.

Later in the battle, Lieutenant Brydon captured a Tokarev. He gave it to LtCol Nihart, who was a collector as well as a skilled pistol marksman.

Some things are totally unexpected. As our unit was moving forward on the wooded ridge that led to Hill 749, in front of us I saw some Marines racing back toward us.

They were terrified and snapping quick glances backward; something horrible must be pursuing them. A few passed me and kept running. A few others jumped into a shallow depression a few feet in front of me and aimed their weapons at whatever was approaching. We too hit the deck and pointed our weapons up the ridge. *What the hell is chasing these men?* I asked myself. The fear on their faces made me think the worst.

We waited. I thought, *Well, when the enemy attacks us, I'll use my bullets, then the few grenades I have and then maybe I'll have to use my bayonet, if I survive that long.* So we waited. Nearby on the ridge was a lot of rifle and machine-gun fire, along with frequent explosions. And we waited. No enemy was coming in our direction. Finally, we got the order: "Let's go!"

197

Besides the main ridge we were on, two lateral ridges were connected to Hill 749. Seen from the air, it was like a huge letter *T*, and we were coming up from the bottom of the main stem, frighteningly vulnerable to enemy fire all across our front, coming from left to right, the horizontal line at the top of that *T*.

It was 13 September, and 2/1 had entered a cauldron of fury. Before we could actually assault the summit, we had to get closer to the slopes, where the decimated 3rd Battalion of the 7th Marines (3/7) was dug in, waiting for us to reach them. Only then could we launch our assault and then fight for the top. Thru-out the day 2/1 fought its way toward 3/7.

Burt Anderson, formerly an ammo carrier with my machine-gun section, found himself more exposed to enemy fire because he was serving as a runner, carrying messages between 2/1's Dog Company Headquarters and other units. He writes:

> Since the hills were alive with gooks, it is not surprising that spotters, gook observers, were behind our positions. This would have to be an explanation for a salvo right on target, particularly on the reverse slope . . . I heard the "swoosh" an instant before it hit and I fell to the bottom of the hole. But it wasn't fast enough. After the explosion, I felt stinging in my back. With one hand, I reached around and could feel pieces of metal. When I looked, my hand was bloody.
>
> Then I realized that the Corpsman was lying there outside my hole, face down. The front part of his body had been gutted; he was killed instantly. I looked downhill at the mortar section. Most of them had been blown out of their holes. The barrage was a direct hit. In an instant most of the mortar section was killed or wounded. [BFA 352-53]

The battle for Hill 749 was taking its toll. We had sustained more casualties than anticipated and were facing serious depletion of ammunition, food, water, and emergency medical supplies. If we were to make a successful assault the next day, we would have to be supplied right away. But it would take about 400 KSC porters, working all day, to bring up an adequate supply.

Our deliverance came in only three hours, thru a remarkable new technology; the supplies were brought in that afternoon, by transport helicopters for the first time in a military campaign. Operation Windmill brought us nine tons of supplies, with twenty-seven flights. They evacuated 74 casualties. It was another "first" in United States Marine Corps history.

By 2030 (8:30 p.m.), 2/1 reached 3/7 and dug into place. That night we were on a full watch, not expecting a big attack, but rather, enemy attempts to scout out our lines and maybe infiltrate them.

Vic says,

> It was the night before I was hit. I killed a gook that was crawling near my foxhole. The only reason I was able to kill him so easily was that one of our flares went off in the air nearby, and I got off about twenty rounds of my carbine. It shredded him to pieces. It's my only confirmed kill in Korea.

The machine-gun platoon leader, 2ndLt Brydon, had an eventful night:

> I looked out of my hole to see a gook moving directly toward my position. I must have shot seven or eight bullets into the man before he dropped. He was wearing a padded jacket. He was getting some protection from that thick jacket and because the carbine bullet had such a low mass and muzzle velocity, the man was hard to stop. The next morning I got rid of the carbine and got myself an M1 Garand rifle, a much more powerful weapon.

"We were dug in and feeling jittery," Randy Lohr said, adding:

> There was a hole in the back slope behind us, like a cave or mine shaft. I asked, "Has anybody checked it out?" Somebody replied, "Nobody would be in there now. They would have no way of sustaining themselves." In the morning, mortars landed around us soon after an exchange of troops on watch. Later, somebody did check the hole with a flashlight, going into it and then firing a bullet. He came out and said, "There *was* a gook in there." He was carrying the gook's rifle— the biggest one I ever saw. The gook must've been wounded or out of

199

ammunition, otherwise he would have shot the Marine as he came in with a flashlight.

¶On 14 September at 0800, 2/1 continued the attack on Hill 749, against a heavy volume of well-aimed North Korean mortar, artillery, and automatic weapons fire. According to Second Lieutenant John Gearhart, commanding Dog Company's 3rd Platoon:

> A mortar shell landed behind me, and I got shrapnel in my shoulder and arm. When I looked behind me at the hole caused by the mortar shell, I was shocked to see another mortar shell stuck in it, unexploded. About forty-five years later, I was still wondering whether I remembered a detail about the incident accurately, and I asked my buddy, Mike LaMas, whether he recalled anything unusual about the hole where the mortar shell had landed. He said, 'Hell yeah. It scared the hell out of me because another shell unexploded was stuck in it.'

Fig. 26-1: 2dLt Ernest Brydon

Dog Company's skipper, 1stLt George H. Benskin Jr., was behind a rock and wanted to survey the situation. Hunkered down near him, Brydon saw that a North Korean machine-gun position dominated their area. Brydon yelled at Benskin, "Don't leave your spot. You'll get shot!" But Benskin did move his left leg out in preparation for moving over and getting a better view; right away he got two bullets thru his leg. Brydon said, "You dumb shit! I told you not to do that!"

200

Later, stretcher bearers were able to evacuate Benskin. Soon after that, LtCol Nihart designated Brydon to be Dog Company's commander, even tho Brydon was only a second lieutenant.

Dog Company really got hammered. Just after we had secured Hill 749, Nihart told Brydon to go over and comfort Lieutenant Woodruff who had been crying for nearly two hours at the decimation of his platoon. Brydon went over and started talking to him, trying to distract him from his anguish.

Vic Knabel was hit by mortar shell fragments, "my helmet taking most of the impact." He adds:

> I was knocked unconscious and then when I came to, I was blind and could feel my eyes bleeding. Also, I heard a lot of noise; I was riding thru the air, strapped to one of the two stretchers that a helicopter was taking back to an army hospital, which was treating Marine casualties.
>
> When I was able to see in the hospital, I looked over at the wounded guy next to me. It was my friend from Tacoma, Bagby, who had joined the Marine Corps when I had, altho he was not in the same unit with me in Korea.
>
> I still have tiny fragments of shrapnel in various parts of my body. My dentist asked me around 2006 about a black spot in my upper gum. I told him it was probably a piece of shrapnel, and he was amazed to find it there, so many years after the war.

Randy looked over at a ridgeline about 300 yards away and saw some NKPA soldiers, so I looked also and saw one of the soldiers running down the ridgeline. I got him in my gun sight, following him as he ran, and fired all eight rounds of my M1 clip at him. He kept running; I had missed. The distance was beyond the M1's effective range. I had just wasted eight bullets. Instead of hitting him, I think I speeded him up.

Soon somebody yelled: "Don't shoot! Don't shoot! They're our men over there!" I was almost in shock. I had nearly killed one of our own men.

Ten or twenty minutes later somebody shouted: "They're *not* our men! Shoot! Shoot!" I looked out at the ridge, but nobody was in sight.

I decided to move over about ten yards to my right; I don't know why. I just thought I might find a better position for firing at that ridge.

Randy was near my previous firing position. While standing and watching the action, he felt a burning in his left shoulder. He had been hit by something. He went to the aid station, and they evacuated him to a hospital. It was his second wound in Korea.

Randy said, "Not everyone at the aid station was physically wounded. Some men had become 'unglued.' It was battle fatigue."

Corporal Gene Punte, our gunner, was on the ridgeline with Henry Thompson as his assistant gunner when,

Enemy mortars began landing about 100 yards or so away from us. Then they began "walking" the barrage toward us, clicking the angle of the mortar so that each succeeding barrage was farther away from them and closer to us. You could see the measured distance between the impact zones and estimate where the next explosions would take place. When it looked like the next one would land on top of us, the enemy stopped firing and redirected their fire toward where one of our medical evacuation helicopters had just landed. For this new target they switched from fragmentation shells to "Willie Peter" (white phosphorus), which would be more likely to ignite fuel, or other supplies.

¶By midnight we had taken the summit. However, the enemy was still on a slightly lower crest about 300 yards away. And it was another night of jitteriness. Some men fixed bayonets.

The night brought welcome moonlight along with some windiness. Tension was high all along our line. Strange things can happen to one's eyes, especially with exhaustion from the noisy mayhem of the day. I kept looking down the slope in front of me to see whether any gooks might be creeping up. Occasionally, a Marine somewhere down the line would fire a round, thinking he had seen an enemy. That added to the tension.

I kept looking ahead, blinking my eyes, rubbing them, squinting, and saw a strange shape. *What's that?* I thought. *It's ten yards away. Is it a man standing or is it a tree? What is that lighter-colored, curved object sticking up at one side of him. It can't be, or can it? It looks like he's raised a curved sword. I can't be sure of what it really is. Should I shoot it?*

I whispered to Punte, "I think there's a gook out there."

"Are you sure?"

"No, but there's not enough light for me to tell. Should I throw a Willy Peter grenade?"

"If you want to."

I pulled out the ring and threw it as far as I could in front of me. Dumb move.

It exploded, throwing burning phosphorous bits all around. It really gave off no additional light, but now the wind carried its acrid smoke back toward our lines. Everybody was pissed off at me.

"Why the hell did you do that? You should've shot it," said somebody nearby. I said, "OK." And I fired one round from my rifle.

Nobody slept very well that night, and the next morning's daylight confirmed the accuracy of my shot. I had killed a young tree. It had already been wounded by some artillery fire that had stripped part of one branch leaving the appearance of a light-colored, curved sword. It was my only confirmed tree-kill of the war.

¶The next day, 15 September, would be a costly one as we moved forward to seize the nearby crest. According to Ernie Brydon, in the morning some P-51 Mustangs flew over our position from an unexpected direction and fired machine guns toward us. Fortunately, none of our men was killed. The pilots were South Africans and, after they learned of their mistake, sent us their apologies, along with some booze.

At 1710, following heavy artillery bombardment by our 11th Marines, 2/1 tried to advance but was stopped within an hour by a terrific pounding from enemy mortars and artillery, plus crossfire from gook machine-guns in hidden bunkers.

Punte says that about that time,

> Thompson was carrying the gun, and I was carrying the tripod. We're going down the slope and three mortar explosions landed: one in front of us, one to the back left, and one to the back right—a triangle, with us in the middle. Thompson's forehead was grazed. I got a fragment in the right shoulder and one in the left leg. Later, while Thompson was squatting to crap, a fragment from a nearby explosion hit him in the ass. For Thompson, it was his third wound in only five months on the front line.
>
> Both of us were evacuated, and we ended up on a hospital ship, the *Consolation*. Henderson was hit the same day and taken to the *USS Consolation*. I spent about a week on the ship and returned to the United States in October 1951. Thompson had temporary duty back at division headquarters, then back to the United States, after a short stint in Japan.

¶Bob Davis remembers this:

> . . . grappling up the hill; it was awful. The enemy was entrenched on the forward slope with their officers behind them at the top, and we heard they were shooting any of their own troops trying to retreat. Not only were we crawling, but we were grabbing anything we could get a hold of. All hell broke loose because coming down from the hill were grenades, rocks, and even logs. I remember the explosions and both Marine bodies and enemy bodies rolling past us. I don't recall just how it all ended. However, there is one thing I noticed at daybreak: it was the number of new ponchos covering a lot of dead Marines. Some of them were newly arrived replacements and had been in combat only a few hours.

With dusk fast approaching, we pulled back a little bit to more defensible positions and began preparations to meet an all-out nighttime counterattack by the North Koreans. A tense lull set in; it

204

would last five or six hours. Thru ferocious mayhem, we Marines had won the bloody day. Soon there would be more fury and more death to decide who would win the bloody night.

Chapter 27

MORE FURY, MORE DEATH

IT WAS OBVIOUS that the NKPA were going to attack down the ridgeline—straight toward us. All our machine guns were positioned there and word was passed: "All ammo carriers bring your ammo up to the guns."

Over on our right flank we had an unusual weapon: a Quad-50, a tracked vehicle with a set of four .50 caliber machine guns. It was developed in World War II as a defense weapon against low-flying enemy aircraft. The vehicle had become disabled and then abandoned by the U.S. Army a few weeks earlier.

Fig. 27-1: LtCol Nihart's forward command post just behind the summit of Hill 749 soon after its seizure. Handwriting at top: "My base"

Enterprising Marine Corps mechanics had gotten it combat-ready, with appropriate U.S. Marine Corps insignia. It was devastating when used against infantry.

We were dug in, well supplied, waiting for their assault. Nobody would be sleeping that night either; it was a 100-percent watch.

The North Korean presence was not quiet. LtCol Nihart summed up the clash:

> . . . first, a heavy bombardment by artillery and mortars, then flares and bugles. By first light they gave up the attack, leaving several hundred dead scattered in front of our positions. My Marines hadn't given

up a yard of their defense. Our position held thru heroic efforts of all. As casualties were suffered, they were quickly replaced by Marines moving up the ridge from the rear and manning their positions. [FBN]

The noise was overwhelming—machine guns blazing away, big explosions, little explosions, occasional brief lulls. And it continued for four hours. I knew our men were catching hell up on the ridgeline. I was convinced that if they needed more ammo and I had to carry it up to them, I would be a goner.

¶We have the Marine Corps' official history of the action:

The NKPA hurricane barrage that preceded the attempt, according to the Division report, 'reached an intensity that was estimated to surpass that of any barrage yet encountered by the 1st Marine Division in Korea.'

The thinned companies of 2/1 took a frightful pounding from 76 mm, 105 mm, and 122 mm artillery supplemented by 82 mm and 120 mm mortars. Bugles and whistles were the signal for the onslaught. It was stopped by weary Marines who demonstrated at NKPA expense that they too could put up a resolute defensive fight.

Wave after wave of attackers dashed itself at the thinned Marine platoons, only to shatter against a resistance that could be bent but not broken. The fight was noteworthy for examples of individual valor. When one of the forward Marine platoons was compelled to give ground slowly, Corporal Joseph

Fig. 27-2: At right, LtCol Nihart in his HQ.

207

Vittori of Fox Company rushed thru the withdrawing troops to lead a successful local counterattack. As the all-night fight continued, 'he leaped from one foxhole to another, covering each foxhole in turn as casualties continued to mount, manning a machine-gun when the gunner was struck down and making repeated trips thru the heaviest shell fire to replenish ammunition.'

Vittori was mortally wounded during the last few minutes of the fight, thus becoming the second Marine of 2/1 within a forty-eight-hour period to win the Medal of Honor. His predecessor was PFC Edward Gomez of Easy Company. When an enemy grenade landed in the midst of his squad on 14 September, he 'unhesitatingly chose to sacrifice himself and, diving into the ditch with the deadly missile, absorbed the shattering violence of the explosion in his own body.'

Not until 0400 on the sixteenth did the enemy waves of attack subside on Hill 749. NKPA strength was estimated at a regiment. A combined assault by an estimated 150 enemy on 3/1 positions to the west in the vicinity of Hill 751 was repulsed shortly after midnight, as were three lesser efforts during the early morning hours of the sixteenth. [USMOK IV 192-93]

Much of the fighting on Hill 749 was so chaotic that LtCol Nihart had to make his way to different positions and personally coordinate supporting arms and aircraft. He was exposed to North Korean fire, and it is a miracle that he survived. By being in the action he was able to ascertain the difficulties facing the units in their attacks and issue appropriate orders to deal with them. For his leadership he received the Navy Cross.

Lieutenant Brydon says that the next morning,

We had to move out in an area where there were a lot of antipersonnel mines around. They were Russian "shoebox" mines, and I told my exhausted men to step into the footsteps of the man ahead of them, in order to pass thru the area.

Unfortunately, one of my men tripped and his rifle hit the ground, causing a bullet in the chamber to go off and hit the man in front of him—right in the back of the head, killing him instantly. We had to keep moving so we put the man's body at the side of the trail.

I asked LtCol Nihart how I should report the incident. He said, 'We can't be too flowery and write up that some kind of heroic action took place. Everyone was exhausted, and his buddies will be writing letters back to the dead man's family also.'

¶Our machine-gun unit moved to new defensive positions, a little bit to our north. The sergeant came along and spaced off the distances where he wanted us to dig our holes. My designated position was among at least a dozen enemy corpses, targets of one of our artillery shells during their counterattack. Their uniforms were saturated with blood. The top of several skulls had been blown off, leaving a jagged edge all around its rim, and their brains exposed. Maggots had already started their work inside what was left of their skulls.

Seeing all the unburied enemy corpses, Sergeant Rowan Kalpsher (fictional name) got a bright idea—bright as gold. It was in the tradition of gold prospecting, but much easier, and maybe more rewarding.

He went around examining the mouths of the dead NKPA soldiers, looking for gold teeth. He had a clever way of knocking them out from what remained of their skulls. With his left hand, he placed the end of a stick against a gold tooth and, while gripping that stick at its opposite end, used another stick with his right hand and banged it down on the first stick to knock the tooth out. Sometimes it took a few whacks to knock it out. He had to be careful not to hit too hard, otherwise the tooth might drop down into the corpse's mouth, and he would have to fish around with his fingers to retrieve it.

Kalpsher soon got rotated out of Korea, and I didn't see him again for fifty-six years. It was at Fort Meade Maryland, where I was a guest at a luncheon meeting of The Chosin Few. In fact both of us were sitting at the same big circular table, accompanied by our wives. He had never been acquainted with me.

While dining we talked about some of our times in Korea. I decided that it would not be in good taste to ask him about his "gold prospecting" on Hill 749. I'm sure none of the others at the table would've welcomed it, nor be able to continue eating their food.

It was time to get the hole dug, even tho I was extremely tired from lack of sleep. So I used my entrenching tool to pull some corpses back away from where I had been ordered to dig. Nobody was going to use any energy to bury enemy dead.

After my hole was ready, I felt famished. I opened up some cans of food and had a late breakfast. It was delicious, even tho it was the same old C-rations. During the remainder of the day all of us took turns trying to catch up on our sleep.

After dark, Ernie Brydon was in his foxhole listening for any movement nearby. He heard an odd scratching sound, like something an animal might be doing. But there were no animals around Hill 749—and no intact trees either. He had his .45 pistol cocked. At very close range, it was one of the best weapons to have. Finally, with the help of the moonlight, he sees a human figure crawling on all fours and scratching the ground in front of them. Ernie asked, "Who are you?"

"I'm the lineman," says the man. "The telephone line is broken, and I'm going to find it and repair it."

"Dammit. I almost shot you. Get into this hole and wait for some daylight to find it."

The lineman had been only a split second from being shot. "During those few minutes the stress was almost unbearable," said Ernie.

We had one instance of the 2nd Battalion's 81mm mortars mistakenly firing on our own men. The mortar officer was an activated reserve officer who had been a news reporter in Philadelphia and had never had training with mortars or experience with them. He was immediately sent back to the regimental supply unit, and all of us felt relief at his transfer.

A few days after we had taken Hill 749, the Marine Recon Battalion made a helicopter-borne attack on a hill behind us. Of course there were no enemy soldiers on that hill, so the battalion had to be taken back by helicopter to their base, quite upset at the unnecessary operation.

The next few days were much quieter. Both sides had been worn out. It was time for them to assess the new situation.

Soon after the heavy fighting, a young lieutenant, James Brady, joined the 7th Marines on Hill 749. In 2003, Brady revisited the area and later produced a book, *The Scariest Place in the World* (2006). Fifteen years earlier he had written a highly acclaimed personal memoir about Korea, *The Coldest War*.

According to Colonel Nihart's widow, the Colonel was especially disappointed with James Brady's 2006 book. He said that Brady had failed to acknowledge the central role of the 2nd Battalion 1st Marines in the capture of Hill 749. All the 2/1 veterans agree with their Colonel.

Chapter 28

TAKING STOCK

DESPITE MY LOW RANK and limited perspective, I could assess the situation right after we had captured Hill 749. We had lost a lot of men, taken very little territory, and the mountains ahead were far more than we would ever be able to conquer.

Our forces and the enemy's forces were facing each

Fig. 28-1: Before Hill 749

other astride the same ridgeline. The distance between us was too damn close. Hill 1052 was still in the NKPA's hands, and it would be tougher to take it than it had been to take Hill 749. Even that small rocky area nearby—Luke the Gook's Castle—was still occupied by them.

Marine Corps records show that during the four-day battle for Hill 749, the Division's losses were: 90 KIA, 714 WIA, and 1 MIA. During the 24-hour period of 13 September 1951, the First Marine's Second Battalion, Easy Company had 92 casualties, the highest sustained by any Marine Company during any 24-hour period in the Korean War.

Fig. 28-2. After Hill 749

Among our 2/1 dead were two Medal of Honor winners: PFC Edward Gomez of Omaha Nebraska, and Corporal Joseph Vittori of Beverly Massachusetts. In the 5th Marines, Jack A. Davenport of Kansas City Missouri was awarded the Medal of Honor posthumously. The NKPA lost 771 KIA, according to our count of bodies. However, the total is estimated at around 1,600.

Four members of our machine-gun section had been wounded: Gene Punte, Henry Thompson, Vic Knabel, and Randy Lohr. Punte and Thompson would not return to front-line duty. After recuperating in the hospital, Randy would be assigned back to the Division's headquarters area. Only Vic would return to our unit.

Fig. 28-2, taken before Hill 749, shows 42 members of Dog Company's 2nd Platoon (the Company our machine-gun unit was attached to) during the final days in reserve at Hongch'ŏn. Platoon Sergeant Manert Kennedy is in the front row, far left.

Right after Hill 749, a foto reveals only twenty able-bodied men, at least two of whom had been wounded, tho slightly. The platoon leader, Lieutenant Pierce Powers, was one of the wounded who had been evacuated.

More than fifty-five years after his combat experience on Hill 749, Manert Kennedy told me, "It was vicious. It was the most vicious fighting Dog Company had ever done, even compared to the Chosin campaign. Chosin just lasted longer and was an awful lot colder."

213

The bloodiest days for our division near the Punchbowl had ended. However, for another month, there were smaller conflicts, mainly raids and attacks on outposts.

Fig. 28-3: In reserve soon after 749, left to right: LtCol Nihart, Maj Jack Lanigan (Exec. Officer), Maj Carl Walker (Supply Officer)

Half a century later, Colonel Allan R. Millett wrote:

If one stands along the Demilitarized Zone today—as the author did in 1994 and 1998—in the sectors in which the Marines fought around the Punchbowl, the mountain ranges stretch off without visible end into North Korea. It is difficult not to feel that there must be a better way to conduct war than to mount one attack after another against those forbidding (and still fortified) mountains. Surely the same thoughts came to the Marines of 1951 as they felt the first chill winds of winter on the Hays-Kansas Line. [USMKW 463]

Fig. 28-4: Dog Co., 3rd Platoon men after 749, left to rt.: Sgt Bill Rogers, PFC Jack Underwood, 2dLt John Gearhart.

The writer is right, and the lesson had been learned in World War I, thirty-seven years earlier, where human-wave

214

attacks were mowed down by machine guns and other modern weaponry. World War II saw the "blitzkrieg" (lightening warfare: infantry assaults supported by armored vehicles coordinated with air power), yet there were stalemates, especially in mountainous areas, such as Italy and Burma. Korea also showed the power of terrain to offset the power of war technology. Never again in Korea did U.S. forces repeat a frontal attack like we did on Hill 749.

¶Miraculously, Vic returned in early October; he seemed completely recovered! After just a few days, he was asked to carry the machine gun back down to battalion headquarters to get the armorer to repair the barrel; it had gotten bent when the gun was accidentally dropped. He went down the trail with the KSC porters after they had delivered their supplies.

Fig. 28-5: WEA and Vic Knabel in H&S Company

The armorer, Staff Sergeant Smith, needed an assistant armorer and asked Vic whether he would be willing to take the job. Vic said yes—immediately.

During the remaining two weeks before he was due to be rotated back to the United States, Vic got some recreation. He shot a deer and, with Smith's help, lugged it to the mess hall for the cooks to dress and cook it. He says, "It made a fine meal for a bunch of us in the H & S (Headquarters and Services) Company." I don't remember eating any of it.

One time an officer asked Vic and Smith to wreck some overrun North Korean fortifications nearby; they were facing south and would be useful to the North Koreans, if they ever broke thru our lines. Smith had received a new explosive that Vic remembers as

215

having the name *tetracol*. He decided to use it on the bunkers, without realizing how much more powerful it was than the familiar TNT. The explosion was huge and scared everybody. After recovering from their shock, they laughed. Smith would be more careful in the future. Vic left Korea soon after, carrying in his body some tiny fragments of shrapnel from Hill 749 and, in his mind, a lot of bad memories.

¶Later that month, it was time for 2/1 to be replaced on the front line by South Korean troops. We stood up in our holes as a single column of ROK soldiers moved by us until they had every replacement waiting next to each foxhole on the line. We suddenly became aware of how much garlic was in the South Korean soldiers' rations. We were smelling not a mild Mediterranean-type garlic but something much more powerful and stinky. It was horticulture's equivalent to *tetracol*. We weren't used to it, and we didn't want to prolong the exposure. Thank God the word soon came for us to climb out of our holes and wait near the back edge while the Koreans got into them.

Soon we started down the back slopes of the hill. The slope was slippery because of recent rain, but nobody got hurt slipping, and we were glad to be able to move without being fired at.

At the foot of the hills, we halted in a wooded area and waited for about twenty minutes. Then, a strange order was passed down the line: "Get down on the deck, shut your eyes, and cover your ears!" It sounded ominous.

There wasn't much time for too many crazy thoughts to go thru my head. I was baffled and apprehensive as I hugged the soil. Were we near some large artillery, like the big cannons that the Army set up at night near our bivouac last spring and began firing while we were still asleep? That was a dreadful noise and shocking vibration. But what was going to happen now?

Then a loud reverberating *whoosh, whoosh, whoosh* started, and bright flashes of light lit up the area. Thru my closed eyelids I could

216

see some of the light. We were right next to 4.5-inch rocket launchers, firing a barrage at North Korean positions.

At the time, I didn't realize the potential harm to us, but both of our officers (Lieutenants Brydon and Gearhart) were aware of it. Just before the rockets were launched, both of them complained to the rocket-unit officer. Gearhart said, "Don't fire now! You'll get counterfire, and our whole battalion here will get hit." The man replied that he had his "orders from Division" and was going to launch the rockets anyway. They launched the rockets, hitched up the launchers to the jeeps, and raced away."

We marched out as fast as we could; there was no enemy counterfire. A few miles down the road, we boarded trucks for the ride back to a bivouac area. There we ate steak dinners prepared for us by the mess-kitchen cooks. Delicious.

Back in the States a few years later, Gearhart was hitching a ride on an Air Force plane and met a Marine with some service ribbons on his uniform; one was for service in Korea. They started chatting, and Gearhart found out that the man was one of the rocket-launcher guys he had confronted during that incident after we left Hill 749. Small world!

Chapter 29
BECOMING ARI SAN

A SAFER LIFE AND A DIFFERENT CULTURE

Fantastic good fortune was to come my way nearly a month after Hill 749. Of course, it was enough that I had survived that battle. My closest buddies had all been wounded, but I didn't get a scratch. Yet I was convinced that my future could not stand many more or even *any* more combat experiences. And I still had at least four months to go before rotation back to the United States. My prospects didn't look good.

My salvation arrived in late fall (the actual date of the confirm-

ing documents is 5 December 1951). I was told that I was being transferred from the Machine-Gun Platoon to H & S Company. I was to become the new "gook herder" for our battalion; the official term was Civilian Labor Leader. I felt it meant a new lease on life. I would be back at the

Fig. 29-1: WEA with Lt Dong

battalion's headquarters just behind the front line and not on it, when our time in reserve ended. At least the new assignment meant a new occupation. And I wouldn't even have to take training for it. I was going to be "back in the rear with the gear."

Like many Americans, I carried my share of racism, which requires large doses of ignorance and arrogance. Racists have derogatory terms for members of other groups—ethnic, racial, religious, etc. We called Asians "slant eyes," "slope heads," and most often, "gooks."

218

But in Korea, the laugh was on us, linguistically speaking, because the proper Korean phrase for an American (literally an "America man") is *miguk*. A Korean is a "Korea man," *hanguk*; a Chinese is a "China man," *chunguk*. Thus, *all* of us were a type of "gook."

Fig. 29-2: WEA with KSC officers

Altho my official position was "Civilian Labor Leader," I never knew of that title until fifty-five years after leaving Korea. If I had been told the title at the outset, I might have conjured up thoughts about organizing a union. I believed in labor unions and had been a member of the United Auto Workers in Detroit, working at the Hudson Motor Car Company during the two months between high school graduation and the call-up of our Marine Reserve unit.

My new "unit," with me as leader, was about 120 men of the KSC. Most of these men were too old to be conscripted into the South Korean army. They wore light-blue cotton uniforms and were organized in military fashion, by platoons. The Korean commander was a former military officer, Major O In Tæ. He had several lieutenants, including a young English-speaking man named Dong, who was assigned to be my assistant and interpreter.

The KSC was an important part of the supply system. They were sometimes called cargadors or bearers, occasionally, "porters." They did the backbreaking work of carrying boxes of food and ammo, cans of water, and sundry supplies up to the front line areas, all of which were on the highest elevations of the hilly terrain. Sometimes they carried supplies on a *chige* or "A-frame," an A-shaped traditional backpack made from barkless tree limbs attached to shoulder straps fashioned from woven ropes. Hence, the men bearing these items were sometimes called "chiggie bears."

During the fighting for Hill 749, the KSC was indispensable, and our regimental commander, LtCol Nihart, included them when he mentioned how the supply officer (Lieutenant George Stavridis) "kept the ammunition, C-rations, and water coming up the mountain on the backs of 400 Korean Service Corps bearers."

I haven't an inkling why I was selected for the job. My ego tells me that my interest in the Korean language was apparent to others in the battalion and, somehow, I was recommended to fill the position when the previous gook herder was rotated back to the States. On the other hand, it was also apparent to those around me that I had great difficulty lugging my load as an ammo carrier. From that I could infer that transferring me to the new job was little or no loss to the machine-gun unit and would give them a chance to get a more robust person to replace me.

¶My gook-herder predecessor was favorably described by LtCol Nihart as:

Sergeant Richardson, in charge of one company's Korean bearers, who insisted on wearing a field hat—instead of a helmet—and carried a heavier load than any Korean, thus motivating them (as they would lose oriental face if they could not keep up). [FBN]

With me, the battalion was getting somebody quite different from Sergeant Richardson. He was a reddish-brown-haired man, taller and stockier than I, and wore a handlebar mustache. Sometimes he would appear with a pirate's head scarf and an earring. A few times I saw him wearing the field hat—the wide-brimmed, World War I vintage hat worn by boot camp drill instructors.

I did not have a field hat, and even if I did, I would never wear it in place of a helmet in a combat area. Also, I would never wear a

220

pirate's head scarf or earring. In addition, I could not conceive of being able to carry a load heavier than that of *any* KSC porter. However, I would be able to accompany the supply trains up the hills, carrying my own weapon. And I resolved to do a conscientious job of managing the supply operations and the KSC personnel. Doing a good job might ensure that I could keep my position and not have to go back on the front line. I might be able to survive and return to the United States when my tour of duty expired in March 1952, two months after my twentieth birthday.

When it was time for me to be introduced to the KSC personnel, Major O In Tæ had them all assembled in military formation. I looked out at this multitude and thought, *How on earth am I going to be able to learn their names or even recognize one from the other? They all look alike.*

The major made introductory remarks, which Lieutenant Dong interpreted for me. He had told them that my name was Ari San (Mr. Alli). It didn't occur to me that I should ask why they were using the Japanese term *san*, instead of the Korean *sŏnsængnim*. It was no doubt a carryover from Japan's colonization of Korea, which included forcing the Japanese language on the population and requiring the Koreans to show deference to their Japanese occupiers.

But entirely new to me was having my name pronounced with an *r* in place of the *l*. Why were they doing that?

EXPLORING AN ORIENTAL MYSTERY

I asked a few Marines, "Why can't they pronounce my name correctly?" Several said, "The gooks can't pronounce *l*'s." Others said, "I thought they couldn't pronounce *r*'s."

The mystery deepened. Sometimes when the Koreans were talking in their language, I heard *l*'s and sometimes *r*'s. I didn't understand why. And my interpreter, Lieutenant Dong, when speaking English seemed to be incorrectly using one of the letters in place of the other. I needed to do some "ringuistic lesealch."

221

Altho I had no instruction book for Americans to learn Korean (or even for Koreans to learn English), I did have Lieutenant Dong teach me the Korean alfabet, *hangŭl*. Thereby I might gain enlightenment. Maybe I could help improve communications between Americans and Koreans.

Hangŭl is a brilliant invention—a fonetic alfabet that foreigners can learn in a few days. God bless Sejon Dæwon (Great King Sejon, 1397–1450) for overseeing its creation and launching the process of freeing the Korean language from slavishly imitating and laboring under the onerous Chinese writing system—and for making my Korean language study more manageable. Centuries later the great Kemal Atatürk would make the same kind of reform to liberate Turkish from Arabic.

One *hangŭl* letter is shaped like the digit "2" on LCDs (liquid crystal displays). Its name sounds like "ree-ool."

So I asked Lieutenant Dong to write my name as I pronounced it—with the *l* sound. He wrote the equivalent of "ah, ree-ool, ee." I asked him to pronounce it, and he said "ah-ree sahn." He didn't have to add the "mister" part, but he was being appropriately Korean, hence appropriately polite.

Then I asked him to write "ah-ree sahn," and he wrote it down the same way. I asked him to pronounce it, and he said "ah-ree-sahn." So I had gotten the same spelling for my two different pronunciations.

Lesson learned: if the English word has a vowel on each side of the *l* or *r*, then it is pronounced by Koreans as an *r*. What if the *l* or *r* is preceded by a consonant, for example, "play" and "pray," "fly" and "fry"? I heard Dong use only the *r* after the *p*; thus "play" and "pray" were *both* "pray." But he used the *l* after the *f*; thus "fly" and "fry" were *both* "fly."

Enough. The lesson I had learned was this: "ree-ool" is elastic. The *p* turns it into *r*, and the *f* turns it into *l*. To be adept with *hangŭl*, I had to learn which way to push "ree-ool."

That was all I wanted to learn about "ree-ool." I would remember it and try to make allowances for the Korean accent when they spoke to me in English. And if a Korean actor was planning to appear at a Friday performance of a stage play, then I should have no trouble understanding him if he said he was going to "be in a pray on Flyday."

Chapter 30
ARI SAN IN ACTION

ON THE TRAIL

Our supply trains were called "gook trains." We delivered supplies a couple of times a week. The KSC men strapped the loads onto their backs, and we followed narrow trails leading up toward the front line. These columns would be on the move for several hours, taking fifteen-minute rest breaks about every forty-five minutes, depending on the difficulty of the trail.

Much of the trail was thru wooded areas and always below any ridgelines where the enemy might see us. Each side of the trail was deemed unsafe. We suspected that booby traps or trip mines might be present, so we warned all personnel not to stray far from the trail in order to urinate or defecate. Whenever we saw evidence of a mine—like a trip wire—we passed the word down the line, from man to man along the trail. Sometimes I would stand near it and point at the danger while the men passed by and then catch up with them. One time a porter did go off the trail and hit a trip wire, setting off a mine and getting badly injured.

We were in beautiful mountain country on our trips. We saw squirrels, chipmunks, and a variety of birds. One time we even saw deer, and after fifty-seven years, I still remember a porter pointing to it and telling me its name: *noru*. But we were in a war zone, and our enjoyment of the natural setting was always inhibited and fleeting.

One time one of the carriers deliberately dumped his heavy load, and it fell down the slope. I came up to him raging and pointed my carbine at him. I yelled that I would shoot him if he did that again. I knew I had to calm down, or else I would kill him then and there. Just then I saw a chipmunk off to my left and expressed my rage by firing a short burst of bullets at it, shredding it to pieces. Only then was I able to begin getting control of myself. I never again encountered dumping of supplies while on the trail.

I mentioned another problem in a letter to my mother:

Yesterday [morning] we went up to help the 1st Battalion with their supplies. Two of the Koreans faked illness in order to escape work. Their lousy lieutenants knew they were bluffing, yet they defended them.

Yesterday evening I had a talk with the Company Commander about his boys. He must have done something about it because today they seem to be more on the ball. The lieutenants are using the stick on men late in falling-out. It's a policy I endorse as far as the gooks are concerned. We are firm and just in all we do.

Late one morning we reached the end of our trek to bring supplies to the line—actually, to the cleared areas on the rear slopes, about seventy-five feet below the ridgelines. After unloading the cartons of C-rations, boxes of ammunition, and cans of water, we would rest about half an hour and then start back down the trail to our base.

But first I wanted to look out at the scenery north of us. Lieutenant Dong and I crouched down and peered over the ridgeline. The air was clear and we could see a long way. On the horizon were high mountain peaks, a few quite jagged, others round topped. Dong exclaimed, "*Kŭmgangsan!*" He seemed in awe. Then he translated, "It's Diamond Mountain."

"What's so special about *Kŭmgangsan?*" I asked.

He told me that every Korean knows about the beauty of *Kŭmgangsan*. "It is important in our history." But he didn't seem to know much about that history. "They have temples there," he added.

I assumed they were Buddhist. I could imagine the religious ceremonies, maybe the involvement of kings and other notables.

I had no idea what a rugged, beautiful area it is. Nothing in Korea, North or South, contains such a combination of forest cover, waterfalls, deep ponds, and picturesque stone formations. The mountain is mainly granite and diorite and towers more than 1,600 meters above sea level. It offers breathtaking views all around the

225

mountainous area and the adjacent Eastern Sea. It would be a sacrilege to wage war in that area; it would also be impossible.

Kŭmgangsan is part of Kangwŏndo province, about thirty or forty miles north of the present-day demilitarized zone. The powerful pull of *Kŭmgangsan*'s history, both real and mythical, brings thousands of South Korean tourists there each year. They are required to pay in U.S. dollars—the one currency acceptable to the impoverished North Korean government.

We started back down the trail, and Dong taught me a few lyrics of a catchy Korean folk song about *toraji*—a beautiful white flower that grows around Diamond Mountain:

> Toraji, toraji, pæk toraji,
> Kangwŏndo kŭmgangsane,
> Pæk toraji.

> Toraji, toraji, lovely toraji,
> In Kangwŏndo's Diamond Mountain,
> Lovely toraji.

For sixty-one years I have gladly hosted the words and music in my memory.

BASE-CAMP LIFE

Starting in November, our battalion was in reserve and at Camp Tripoli, in a valley on one side of a creek running most of its length. A road ran parallel to the creek, about fifty yards from it.

The KSC were located in tents between the creek and the road. We Marines were on the other side of the road where the valley's side began sloping upward.

A Marine officer complained to me about the health hazards he saw early each morning when the KSC men woke up, crossed over the creek, and relieved themselves on the slopes overlooking the valley. From a distance, the many men in light blue clothing looked

226

like a large flock of big blue squatting birds. But it was not their appearance that was upsetting our medical personnel; it was the piling up of uncovered feces. I was ordered to make the KSC men use shovels and cover up all human excrement with soil. They did so, and sanitation was better.

When we were not taking supplies to the front line, Commander O In Tæ made the men do close-order drill. He taught me the commands, and I had a hand at it. It was quite a sight to my fellow Marines. They made comments about "Alli and his Asian hordes." They asked me, "What kind of empire are you creating?" I guess it all looked weird for a nineteen-year-old Marine to be in charge of so many Korean men in uniform.

Lieutenant Dong, Major O In Tæ, and I shared the same tent. One night my right arm got stuck in a folded position as I was sleeping, and the blood circulation was restricted so much that I cried out "help!" Dong jumped up and rushed over to ask, "What I do?"

Not fully awake and almost panicking, I said, "Unzip my sleeping bag," and he did so. "Pull out my arm. Now rub it."

Soon my arm was back to normal, and I said "Thank you." I slipped it back into my sleeping bag, zipped the bag shut, and quickly went back to sleep, aware that he was still standing there, confused about what had happened.

¶Americans and Koreans were treated to a comedy, the funniest incident I remember about Korea. It all started after one of our Marines got sick and was taken to the hospital. His tent mates noticed that he had left a small pack on the floor near his cot. One of them opened the pack and saw several war trophies: Chinese hand grenades, all live and dangerous!

As word spread, everyone nearby got jumpy and wanted the explosives immediately removed from the area. We did not know how stable the grenades might be. One of the Marines carefully picked up the bag and brought it out of the tent and asked the others how it should be disposed of.

I said I would take care of it, and he handed me the bag. I called over to Lieutenant Dong and said to him, "Lieutenant Dong, I want you to get rid of these," and I opened up the bag to show him what was inside. He looked inside, his eyes widened, and his jaw dropped.

"What I do with this, Ari San?"

"Go throw it into the middle of the creek, away from any tents. And I want you to do it *yourself.* Do not give it to anybody else."

During the rainy season of spring there might be torrents racing along, even overrunning the banks, turning the creek into a small river. But now it was late autumn, the creek did not have much water flow. It was filled with rocks and boulders and could be easily crossed by hopping from one rock to another.

More and more Marines gathered around to watch the grenade disposal process that I had so thoughtlessly set into motion. More and more KSC spectators appeared. No one knew what to expect. There might even be a spectacular explosion. Lieutenant Dong might disappear in that explosion.

As Lieutenant Dong continued walking toward the creek (and farther away from our tents) he continued holding the bag away from his body with an outstretched arm, and the mood of the Marines changed from nervousness to anticipation. Live theater was in process.

Getting closer to the creek, he spied one of the low-ranking porters and called him over. He said something to the man and handed him the bag, quickly distancing himself from the man, and the lethal bag.

Like Dong, the man held the sack in one hand stretched stiffly and horizontally forward of his body. Obviously, he realized that there was danger in the bag and didn't want to have it too close to his body. But he would need an arm about one hundred yards long for safety (except to that arm) in the event of an explosion.

Now he had reached the very rocky edge of the creek. All eyes were on him. None of the onlookers was talking. An event was unfolding. It might be exciting. It might be bloody. And it might be very noisy.

The suspense was building up. He began hopping from one rock to another, working his way toward the center of the stream. Somehow he was trying to aim his outstretched hand in the direction in which he was turning his head in order to select each new rock to hop to. Occasionally he would teeter on a rock, slip into the very shallow water on one or both feet, then leap back out like a dolfin.

Finally, he was close to the center and swung his arm back, trying to keep it straight, yet parallel to the general terrain. As he did so, he slipped on the rock and went into the water, up to his knees. Quickly he popped back up, swaying to keep his balance, and launched the pack into a low trajectory, no more than eight feet high.

We spectators had our jaws open, our eyes intently following the trajectory of the pack while still able to watch as the man pirouetted on the rock and begun racing back, jumping rock to rock—fitfully slipping into the water and regaining traction on the rocks—all in a desperate splashy dash to safety.

By now all of us were roaring with laughter at his comical dance with death. It was the nervous laughter of a movie audience witnessing a combination of slapstick, ballet, and impending disaster. Of course it was funny—to us. And there had been no explosion. Many of us must have speculated that by the time the poor fellow had gotten back to the shore, his trousers were not only wet but, because of his fear, quite full of shit. To this day I wonder whether that bag ever exploded.

INFLATED CURRENCY

The KSC was paid monthly, in Korean paper money, the Wŏn. It was brought to us by armed guards. My job was to keep track of the payroll. That required me to keep a roster and an account of the amount of money paid and the date. Also, each recipient had to sign his initials on the payroll list.

229

I used the list, which had been developed by my predecessors. The hardest part of my job was to recognize the spelling of the men's names and learn to pronounce them. Whoever first listed the men's names must have been an American who did not know the Korean language. If a native Korean speaker had assisted in preparing the list then he must've been unaware of the principles of Romanized spelling.

I did my best to pronounce their names as my interpreter instructed me. I must admit however that several names did sound hilarious. I saw names like "Joe Wun Kock," "Ree Suck Bok," and "In Sick Jung." When I told my Marine buddies about the names, they roared with laughter.

Each KSC man received the Wŏn equivalent of only a few dollars per month, but because the Wŏn was so inflated in value, each man was receiving a small stack of bills. I looked at all the bills that had been delivered to me and thought that the muscles of my hands and wrists were not up to the job of counting out the entire payroll.

Soon I found out that Koreans had learned to cope with handling highly inflated paper money. They showed me how to hold a stack of bills in my left hand curling them back on themselves in such a way that with my right hand I could slightly lift the edge of each bill while counting it. I learned quickly and was astounded at my ability to go thru hundreds of bills without too much stress on my hands and wrists.

South Koreans preferred to use U.S. military scrip, a U.S. currency printed on paper that was half the size of standard U.S. paper money. There was a thriving black market in the country, despite laws against giving or selling scrip to Koreans.

A PROCUREMENT TRIP

The KSC's food rations were large quantities of rice and lentils with vegetables. They got it from their supply depot in Wŏnju, about sixty miles south of our base.

230

A Marine truck and driver were assigned to us to make the monthly trip to Wŏnju. We planned to stay overnight and come back the next day. Wŏnju was a city that had partly recovered from the war's destruction and, for U.S. troops, had all sorts of attractions—mainly prostitutes.

Major O In Tæ told me that he had a present for me when I arrived on my first trip to Wŏnju. He assured me that I would have a very enjoyable time. I wasn't sure what he meant, but he left the rest to my imagination. Naturally, I conjured up fantasies of luscious possibilities.

As we drove south on the MSR, we passed thru the areas where the Division had fought during the drives north, beginning in February 1951. Farm families were moving back onto the land. The roads, altho still gravel-topped, were in good condition. In fact, Army engineers had built a long sloping highway to bypass the narrow, riverside winding road that we had fought over on our way past Hongch'ŏn and on to Ch'unch'ŏn near the Thirty-eighth Parallel.

We arrived in Wŏnju after a few hours and the major made arrangements with the suppliers to load the truck the next morning. He and I and Lieutenant Dong walked around to look over the town. The buildings were ramshackle; the streets were filthy and stinky, but there was the bustle of people at markets, and a lot of Americans in uniform accompanied by young Korean women who wore U.S. military clothing.

In the evening, we went to a house where the major said I would be spending the night. There was no bed, but there was an area for me to roll out my sleeping bag. He brought in a young woman and said, "Here is Myung Ha" (or a similar name). He translated it as "Pretty Flower" or "White Flower" or maybe "Bright Flower." Then he left us alone.

She was a short woman who seemed to be in her early twenties. She was a bit stocky and dressed completely like a U.S. soldier. She had the OD (olive-drab) field uniform, meaning, visored field hat,

231

field jacket, fatigue trousers (the kind with cargo pockets), a wool-blend military shirt, army combat boots and wool socks. Around her waist, she had the standard military web belt with a dull-finished buckle. She was carrying a rolled-up sleeping bag.

She did not speak English and I did not speak Korean. We smiled at each other awkwardly but said nothing while we looked at each other. I guess, each of us was wondering what the other was thinking, or maybe *knew* what the other was thinking.

I did not feel any stirring of ardor, desire, or even plain lust. What the hell had I been expecting?

Doesn't every U.S. Marine (or other armed service member) in Korea have sexual fantasies? Maybe meeting a woman with a name like Pretty Flower could be one of them, but never if she was dressed up like a U.S. male soldier.

Perhaps my time with her would best be spent learning more about the Korean alfabet. Maybe she could give me her favorite kimchi recipe, in Korean of course, which I would eventually have translated into English and mailed to my mother. I did not drink alcohol, but in this case, I might ask for enough of the native brew to pass out right away. Maybe she felt the same way.

I began thinking about how we saw training films at Camp Pendleton, warning us about the dangers of venereal disease. And Wŏnju was the very town in which our 2/1 machine gunners had contracted gonorrhea in August.

It was getting late and I wanted to sleep. I started taking off my clothes and she started taking off hers. As she got down to her U.S. military long underwear, she started looking more like a woman, and I realized that I wanted to learn more about her. Language barriers could be overcome; besides, I had brought a condom with me. I invited her into my sleeping bag and blew out the candle.

The next morning Pretty Flower got up early and left. I woke up later when Major O knocked at my door. I thanked him for "introducing" me to Pretty Flower, and we had our breakfast together (C-rations) before getting into the truck to drive over to the supply depot. We got the truck loaded with sacks of rice and lentils and cans of cooking oil. Then we drove back up the MSR to our base.

My fertile mind came up with a name for this type of logistical operation. Before taking future trips, I told my envious Marine friends that I was going to Wŏnju to procure sacks and sex. Upon return, I had all of the food sacks to prove what I had done. As to the sex, they would have to take my word for it. Unlike our machine gunners who had gone to Wŏnju in August, I had avoided any physical ailment that could have verified what I had been doing.

BRIDGE CONSTRUCTION

Our work was routine. The biggest job was transporting supplies up to the line. Sometimes the KSC workers unloaded trucks, dug ditches, and cleared away debris.

Once we used them to build a footbridge over the narrow creek. They used logs and boards, constructing it on the bank before shoving it into place. I was surprised to see that the workers used a chant to coordinate the final placement of the bridge. They chanted, "Eysha, usha. Eysha, usha. Eysha, usha."

I really did not see the need to chant, but I was wrong. It was the perfect way to coordinate their efforts. The custom must have come from long years of experience. Americans used to do it on sailing vessels. The sailors sang sea chanties to coordinate the crew's raising and lowering of sails and other tasks. I remember a recording by

Fig. 30-1: WEA with Sgt Farquhar and a KSC worker

233

American folk singers in the 1960s: "Way, haul away. We'll haul for better weather. Way, haul away. We'll haul away, Joe."

THE CAMERAMAN

I had requested a camera from home and was eager to take fotos of important scenes. I thought I had a good opportunity when our platoon was sent up to a helicopter-landing pad near a ridgeline. The chairman of the chiefs of staff for the U.S. armed forces, Army General Omar Bradley, was supposed to land there, and we were the security detachment. Unfortunately, the plan fell thru and the General did not show up.

I did take some pictures at a band concert for our battalion early in October. It was performed by musicians of the 1stMarDiv Band (now there's a fine job for Marines; I would love to have it). Everything was going well until the enemy threw some artillery rounds way over on the other side of our broad valley. Obviously they didn't like our band. Therefore the band ended the concert by playing *The Marines Hymn* faster than normal, finished it, packed up, and moved out swiftly.

¶My cultural horizons were being broadened. I could not predict what kind of a person I would be when I got back to the United States, if I made it back. I resolved that I would be more tolerant of other ethnic and racial groups.

Chapter 31
SHORT TIMER

SO NOW IT'S THE LAST MONTH of 1951. How long before I get rotated back to the States? They say we're supposed to stay in Korea just twelve months. That means I leave Korea in March 1952. How do I survive until then?

What could happen to prevent it? If the gooks attack and break thru our lines, I will definitely end up back in the machine-gun unit, or somewhere else, most likely a rifleman.

What is the significance of my promotion to Corporal? I hadn't expected it and I had not sought it. It took effect 18 December 1951. Was I going to be put into a job that would delay my rotation out of Korea?

If I get sick, I could wind up back in the hospital. But I've already done that, and it's no problem. However, I remember that new guy who joined us back in the spring; he got pneumonia and died less than two weeks in Korea. I doubt that I'm really going to get sick.

The gooks don't have any long-distance artillery that could hit us this far behind the front line, and they don't have any way of knowing where we are and, besides, it would make more sense for them to use heavy weapons just to break thru the front line.

But I'm not entirely safe because I'm the gook herder; I lead the gook trains when we carry supplies up to the front. We know there are North Korean mines planted in unmarked places. Lieutenant Brydon said that my predecessor, Sergeant Richardson, had sent a porter off the trail to take a shit and the man was blown apart. Even if I was on the trail, an explosion nearby could get both of us killed or wounded.

Also, there's always the possibility that a gook infiltrator would be able to shoot at us. Seeing me on the trail, an American leading a

235

column of Korean porters, it's for damn sure I would be the first one he would aim at.

Is there something I can volunteer for, something to take me farther south of here? Do they still need truck drivers? Maybe something back in Division headquarters? Do they need guys back in Japan? What a dreamer.

I wonder whether God answers prayer. If so, I would pray for my personal safety. I know that just before a game starts between two opposing high-school football teams (usually in Texas), each prays for victory. And I believe that God answers both of them. But what is his answer? Maybe He says yes to one and no to the other. Or maybe He says no to both or yes to both. If both pray fervently, then He must say yes to both. And if you ask me how that can be, I will tell you: it's a mystery, like the Trinity. It's also possible that maybe one team was praying to win and the other was praying to lose. Why would they do such a thing? That too is a mystery.

I was still "hoping for the best, expecting the worst, and taking whatever came along." It did give me some comfort. I also remembered the Marine Corps adage, "never volunteer." I was trying to take just one day at a time.

Of course, a person's conduct and actions are obvious to his buddies. Mine knew that I had become a "short timer," but I don't remember anyone criticizing me. I do admit some short timers didn't care much about anything but leaving.

¶One morning in December, Corporal Frank Daunie (not his real name) boasted to me about one of his "exploits" the previous night. It was a sordid story and I wasn't sure how to deal with it. I was a corporal by then and must have had responsibility for reporting it, but the victim had not made an official complaint.

The victim was Sergeant Neninsky (fictional name), a soft-voiced sergeant, noticeable by his effeminate mannerisms. That's something that Marines don't like. To the best of my knowledge, he had never done anything offensive to anybody. I honestly do not

236

know whether he was a homosexual, but that seemed to be the conjecture among the Marines.

Daunie was very aggressive. Occasionally, you would see it in his body language: a false smile with squinted eyes, hands that seemed too often balled up into a fist, lips too often clamped shut, and head thrusted forward a little bit, almost ready to crouch into a boxer's defensive stance.

He told me, "Yeah, I got Neninsky to come with me behind one of the big tents and roughed him up a little. He didn't fight back. I pushed him down on his knees and shoved my cock in his mouth."

With a smug grin he added, "I know what kind of a queer he is."

Daunie looked surprised when I angrily asked, "Why the hell did you do that?" But I didn't wait for his answer. I shook my head and walked away. I was disgusted. The corporal seemed more perverted than the sergeant.

¶Winter came with its special combination of beauty and hardship. The beauty was a layer of snow that covered the slumbering mountains and valleys of Kangwŏndo. Sunshine made the cold more bearable and allowed the snow and ice to sparkle. Even so, anything attractive in winter is merely masking winter's basic hostility to all life.

We still had to take supplies up to the front line. Our energy drained rapidly as we trudged thru the snow on the trails. The trips took twice as long and slipperiness was a constant hazard both ways. The heavy loads were more cumbersome going up slopes and on the return. Each man ran the risk of becoming a runaway human bobsled going down the slopes. Men fell off the trail, and we had to pull them back on. We were lucky no one set off any antipersonnel mines.

Fortunately, there was almost no fighting on the line. That meant that ammunition was not being rapidly depleted. We still carried ammunition supplies but at a reduced rate.

The troops on the front line suffered the most discomfort. They were living in bunkers at high altitudes and had to maintain body warmth while unable to walk. It was dangerous to get out of the bunker in daylight and dangerous to attempt moving about at night.

They were eating C-rations and had to heat each can using Sterno. That was inconvenient, and it took more time in the cold weather.

We wondered what front-line life must be like for the North Koreans. We concluded that they must be getting lousy chow. Proof of it was what happened whenever a Marine discarded the "deadly three."

The "deadly three" was corned-beef hash, meat and beans, meat and noodles. Because the individual boxes of C-rations had been packed with a random selection of three, out of the ten or twelve available "entrees, a person stood about a 10-percent chance of getting at least one of those three in his box. The chance of getting all three was much less and most unwelcome. Whenever a box was opened and it contained the "deadly three," the recipient usually exclaimed something like, "Oh no, the deadly three!" Another reaction was to turn to one of the more fortunate around him and ask, "Who will trade me one can of anything for all of the deadly three?" If there were no takers, the victim could either eat the food (with difficulty) or throw it away.

On the front line, Marines have reported tossing the "deadly three" down the front slopes. The next morning they would look down to see enemy footprints in the snow, and the cans gone. That proved that our opponents were endangering their lives in front of our positions, merely to recover food.

For us back at the base area, life in the tents was much easier, but it was still a drab existence. The food was definitely better than eating C-rations. One thing new in our diet was loaves of baked bread. We warmed it up on our kerosene stoves and ate it plain. Several times we had it with canned Danish bacon that came packed in a lot of solid pork fat.

We emptied the cans into the bottom half of our mess kit, which became a frying pan, and cooked it on the stove. As the solid fat melted, the bacon strips started cooking. We were deep-frying bacon.

When it was ready, we speared the strips out of the fat with forks and placed them on thick slices of the bread and when the strips were all eaten, we took chunks of the bread and sopped up all of the fat that was left. It was scrumptious! Heavenly! Salty? Certainly. High cholesterol? Yes. High calories? Yep. But it was winter, and the weather was cold, and we—and our arteries—were young.

We were spending most of our time inside the tents. We socialized a lot, talking about past events, and speculating about the future. One of my buddies then was former Detroiter Robert M. Westfall; he had been a corporal in our old 17th Infantry Battalion. Because cease-fire talks were underway between the UN and the Communists, the prospect of peace seemed a real possibility. But when? The war had gone on for a year-and-a-half and World War II had lasted just over three-and-a-half years.

We had time to read books and newspapers, but lighting was so poor in the tents that we had to use candles or kerosene lanterns. What I needed to read were materials that I had gotten after registering for two self-study courses thru the Marine Corps correspondence school: use of the slide rule and advanced algebra. I did very little study in Korea, and by the time I got back to the United States, I just wanted to avoid studying until after enrolling in college.

With fresh snow came snowball fights. It released pent-up energy and was a total distraction from our situation. One time a few guys tried to make a toboggan sled out of packing crates. They took several spills on the contraption, and it broke up after only a few runs down the slope.

A new type of winter "thermal" boot was issued to us. They were made of synthetic rubber, containing many tiny air sacs and resembled oversize galoshes. Unlike the previous winter boots, they had no interchangeable wool flannel inner soles ("shoepacs"), which

239

could be removed and dried out. In fact, they were made for the foot to slosh about and stay wet in its own perspiration. The larger size allowed for such movement. Because of their large size, we called them Mickey Mouse boots.

I wrote to my mother: "If you can get it I'd like a fifth of *mild* brandy to keep me warm. It gets cold here on watch. Peppermint Schnapps is a good mild drink too. I think it's milder than brandy." She dutifully bought it, carefully wrapped it to avoid any breakage, and immediately mailed it to me, even tho it was illegal to send alcohol thru the mail. I was grateful to her and wrote her: "It went over big with all of the guys in my tent as well as those who were at that Xmas party."

Back in Detroit, my mother had remarried. She and her new husband, "Augie" (August Shuman), had bought a house on French Road, a street I had never heard of, on the east side. In a letter, I asked for fotos of the house—inside and out. My long-time boyhood friend, Henry Tazzia, took the pictures. When they arrived, they made me happy; they showed me just one more good thing that awaited me at home.

I was elated at her good fortune. It would be the first time in Detroit, out of a dozen places where we had lived during my first eighteen years, that our family would own our own home. Baba would never remarry and always lived in tiny rooms of rooming houses close to downtown.

¶I do not understand the workings of the Marine Corps' personnel system. In late January or early February 1952, the platoon sergeant told me, "Congratulations, Alli. You're now a buck sergeant."

I asked, "Am I getting a different job?'

"No, you're still the "gook herder.'"

"How about my MOS?"

240

"No change."

I wondered whether my salary would increase. "Is there any-thing else?" "No."

Actually there was something else. And I didn't find out for fif-ty-five years! My "civilian labor leader" job was just a work-assignment title, lasting from 1 November 1951 until my last day in Korea. It was not my MOS. Not only that, but I was not officially appointed sergeant until 11 March 1952, five days before departing Korea. I am glad that in my future career I would never have to work in personnel administration, military or civilian.

As March arrived, the weather was getting mild. That helped to boost my morale, but the prospect of being rotated out of Korea soon was my main focus.

The war was at a stalemate, and no cease-fire was in the offing. I couldn't imagine what would follow after I got back to the States. Would I be kept on active duty by the Marines? For all I knew, another assignment in Korea was in my future.

A Marine from North Carolina (named Griffin, I think) was as-signed to be my new assistant. He would take over my job when I ro-tated out. During that short period, he had a lot of questions about work-ing with the Koreans and I enjoyed being able to answer them. I gave him my U.S. address, in case

Fig. 31-1: Leaving Korea with two buddies

he wanted to write to me. He did write to me, but I didn't write back; I wanted nothing more to do with Korea.

Finally, on 16 March 1952, I got on a truck in the convoy that would take me and the rest of the able-bodied survivors of the 6th Replacement Draft from our base at Camp Tripoli to nearby Sok-ch'o-ri, the small port city on the Eastern Sea. The trucks wound

241

their way along the mountainous roadway and then began descending down to the coast, where an LST would ferry us from the small dock to the big troopship anchored in deeper water nearby.

Fig. 31-2: George Coyle

Big plans had been made for my First Marine Division, but I was totally unaware of them as my assignment was winding down. After dropping us off at Sokch'o-ri, those Marine truck drivers would soon be helping to deliver 6,000 truckloads of troops, supplies, and equipment westward—all the way across the Korean peninsula. There our division would take up positions on the Jamestown Line, spanning more than thirty miles. That was twice the length of our sector against the NKPA in Kangwŏndo.

They would be engaged in frequent bloody combat with the heavier armed and more numerous Chinese forces; the violence and its constancy would reach a level unparalleled in the Korean War. It did not decrease until virtually the last day before the official ceasefire was to take effect: 27 July 1953. Since no one wants to be the last casualty in a war, just imagine the stress on all the combatants during those final days. [JS, GVS] Not until April 1955 would the 1stMarDiv be reassigned to the United States.

George Coyle of New Jersey experienced the danger and stress most acutely, starting on the night of 24 July. He transports us back to those final days:

242

We were under constant bombardment. It seemed I was bouncing off the deck every minute and eating a lot of dirt. During this night, I helped carry out three wounded Marines of my squad. One was a Marine from Philadelphia, Angelo Afilani. He would have bled to death—he was wounded so severely. Part of the trench line we had to pass thru was no deeper than ankle height, and we were exposed to small-arms fire. The trench lines at other points were so narrow that my hands were badly scraped for several months after.

When I returned to my fighting hole, I discovered it had taken a direct hit. While I was not too happy about digging out my fighting hole, I realized that I had been saved because I was carrying out a wounded Marine.

I guess the CCF were out to get me because I was wounded the last night of action, actually the early hours of 27 July 1953. I was treated and returned to my fighting position because of expected enemy activity. The truce went into effect at 10 p.m. on 27 July 1953.

I was recommended for a Bronze Star for my actions and carrying out the wounded under such intense artillery, mortar and small arms fire but never received it.

For me a new chapter in my life was unfolding. I was boarding a troopship, the USNS *General W. H. Gordon*. I regretted most that I had not killed any Communist soldiers. I was puzzled and ashamed that my strength and endurance, compared to that of the other Marines, were so inadequate, whatever the cause(s).

Soon we were underway, crossing the Korea Straits and threading our way thru the Inland Sea bound for Kobe. I had survived Korea.

Chapter 32
SAILING EAST FROM THE FAR EAST

WHAT THOUGHTS WERE GOING THRU the minds of the Marines aboard the *Gordon* as it pulled away from the Korean coast? Like most survivors of a war, they were probably thinking as I was, "I never want to see this place again. I never want to remember this stinking war. Just take me home." Also, where can I take a shower right away.

But in my old age, I began harboring a mysterious notion about Korea. Perhaps it first entered my subconscious in 1951, when I visited the Turkish Brigade and looked at the young Turkish soldiers of my age.

Or maybe it was while visiting the United Nations Memorial Cemetery in Korea (UNMCK) in Pusan in 2000. The UNMCK is a permanent resting place a for 2,300 military personnel representing eleven United

Fig. 32-1: *United Nations flag*

Nations members of the coalition that fought to save South Korea from communist military conquest, 1950-53.

I saw that 443 Turkish fallen were buried in five plots. As I walked the paths alongside the rows of their tombstones I realized that most of them were very young men when they died. During the war they were my age. I was surprised at how many tombstones bore the words *meçhul asker* (unknown soldier).

I spent some time looking at the two Turkish memorials nearby. One of them featured a bronze plaque bearing a Turkish poem. Its title was *Pusan'da Yatıyorum*. I wrote down the words and brought them back with me to America, determined to have someone

Fig. 32-2: Ceremony for fallen Americans and Turks at future UNMCK

translate them, because my Turkish language knowledge was too meager to deal with poetry. I had the feeling that the words might have profound significance for me.

At that time I was aware of something rooted in certain events taking place in September 1932, when I was only nine-months old. America was in the grips of the Great Depression and Detroit was one of the hardest hit places. My unemployed father saw only a bleak future for us in America.

But then a glimpse of hope appeared when the Turkish government sent a ship, the SS *Gülcemal*, to bring Turkish immigrants back to Turkiye, free of charge and with no questions asked. After their return the Turkish government would help them find jobs.

Baba told my mother he wanted the family to go. My mother refused. That is why I grew up as an American and went to the Korean War in an American uniform. If I had been brought up in Turkiye, I might have gone to the Korean War in a Turkish Army uniform. Thus it looks like going to Korea, one way or the other, was in my future. But dying in Korea was not to be my fate.

One of the Turkish immigrants who did return that year was Mustafa Şişli, my father's nefew. I met him on my first trip to Turkiye in the summer of 1953. He lived in Elâzığ, near Harput and was employed by a mining company. He told me that life had been very hard on him since he had returned to Turkiye. He wanted me to help him emigrate to the United States, with or without his family.

For the Turkish immigrants who did return to Turkiye in the depression, life was still difficult, tho not as difficult as it had been for them in the US. When World War II began, America was out of the worst years of the Depression but still in a recession. During the war we had full employment and growing prosperity, tempered by rationing of food, etc., and limited production of civilian goods.

Life was harder for the people of Turkiye during World War II, even though they were not active belligerents. They had a huge burden in keeping large military forces on all their borders, not knowing which side would invade them. After Germany withdrew its forces from the Turkish border with Bulgaria and Greece, shortly before the end of the war in Europe, the Turkish government declared war on Germany. But the Soviet Union's aggressive demands for Turkish territory and military bases soon after the war's end meant that Turkiye would not be able to reduce its defense costs. A few years later the United States began the "Truman Plan" of providing economic and military assistance to the Republic of Turkiye (and the neighboring Kingdom of Greece).

¶In Kobe, they gave us sixteen hours of shore leave, twice as much as we had gotten on our way to Korea in 1951. We would waste no time. I believe most Marines had a three-item checklist of what to do: go shopping, visit a geisha house (a form of shopping), and—except for me and a few other nondrinkers—go to a bar and get drunk.

But before we arrived in Kobe, I got my chance to buy a camera from a fellow Detroiter on the ship. A Marine named Myers was selling a 35mm, American-made Argus C-3 for a low price. I asked him, "Is there anything wrong with it?"

"No, it takes good pictures," he answered, truthfully.

So I paid him the money and had the camera with me when I landed in Kobe. I soon found out that I could buy new, low-cost, excellent quality Japanese-made 35mm cameras. They were much better than my newly acquired, used, 35mm American-made (bargain-priced) Argus C-3. Naturally, the former owner of my camera bought a new Japanese camera.

My visit to the geisha house in Kobe was like the one I had the previous year. However, after this visit, it occurred to me that it was the fourth time I had engaged in sex with a woman. The first time was in Canada, the second in Kobe, the third in Wonju. Suddenly, I realized that after I got back to the United States, my sex life might end because it seemed that I had to leave America to have sex. Or maybe my luck would change. Ultimately, I might even have to get married; I hoped it would be in America. But how long would it take for me to meet the right woman? It would have to wait until I finished college, four years. But there might be an interim solution: Canada was a foreign country, but it was just across the river from Detroit. My sexual future might not be so bleak.

My next purchase was a bargain, and the satisfaction has lasted far longer than what I got from the camera or the geisha. It was a set of high-quality porcelain chinaware dishes and a tea set, manufactured by a famous company: Noritake. It would be a present for my dear mother.

There was a problem: the chinaware was packed in two heavy wooden crates, each about two-thirds the size of a Marine Corps locker box. But there was a solution. All I had to do was get a rickshaw to take me and the crates to the dockside.

I paid the merchant, using most of what money I had, and arrived at the dock, where I waited for the next Marine going aboard. I asked for his help, and we shlept the crates down to our compartment.

¶The *Gordon* pulled away from the dock and steamed out to sea. How smooth and peaceful the water was, for the first thirty minutes. That's when we passed the breakwater and entered the rough waters of the northern Pacific.

For the next two weeks, I was seriously seasick. This ship would not sink, like the one mentioned in Shakespeare's *The Tempest*. But the voyage lends itself naturally to a description in his Elizabethan English:

> *Now began the fortnight of my distress. 'Twas the affliction of the sea, a malady from which I had been spared when first I fared across that broad expanse, but now tormented me, most cruelly, day unto day, despite my repeated petitions to the Lord above, until lo, mine eyes beheld a glimpse of salvation, a blessed horizon, a welcome shore, an anchored land that offered deliverance from my affliction and upon which I would step forth, free of despair, sure of step and clear of vision. In that fair country, would I no longer spend my days and nights dizzy, hung over, and puking into the sea. I would joyously utter my gratitude to the Almighty; He had vouchsafed to deliver me from King Neptune's vile and turbulent grip and deposit me, weak but safe, into the embrace of my motherland.*

Fig. 32-3: USNS Gen. W.H. Gordon

All the while my mother was avidly searching the newspapers for any tidbit relating to me. After her death in 1967, my sister found a 1952 newspaper clipping among her belongings:

Transport Brings 1,890 From Korea

SAN FRANCISCO, March 29 — (AP) — The transport Gen. W.H. Gordon is due here Sunday with 1,890 Marine and Navy veterans of the Korean War. Among them are 1,556 men of the 1st Marine Division, 205 from the first Marine Air Wing, and 129 Naval medical personnel who were attached to Marine combat units in Korea. Most of the Marines are returning under the rotation plan.

¶An oceangoing ship is the perfect stage for exhibiting the highest level of human anticipation. That was the *Gordon* as we approached San Francisco on Sunday, 30 March 1952.

We were dressed in our green, woolen uniforms, with khaki-colored dress shirt and tie, and spit-shined dress shoes. Nearly all of us were on deck, looking eastward at the brightening dawn.

At first, we saw four layers of color on the horizon. Just above the massive sea's surface was a thin dark layer; that must be the land. Above that was a grey layer, twice as wide as the dark one; that must be the fog. Next above was a golden layer—sunshine; and topping them all was the blue sky. To my mind, all of it was "the Golden Land." My surging joy brought tears to my eyes, close to overflowing, but not enough to embarrass me among my fellow Marines, nor blur my sight of that fair land. It was America, my country, my home.

Our exuberance was suddenly curbed as the ship stopped, well before we could pass under the Golden Gate Bridge. But it was quite brief; a very small boat had come to meet us and deliver the pilot who would direct the ship along the safe passageway leading to the docks.

Too quickly we passed under the bridge, all heads gazing up at its height, realizing that we were crossing a friendly border. On each side of our ship came the welcoming honor guards: the fireboats, saluting us with powerful streams of water, arching high up from their sides. They stayed with us as we turned slowly to starboard,

249

Fig. 32-4: USS Gordon docking at San Francisco wharf

southward, and approached the dock. Then the little boats held back
to allow us to dock alone, in the place of honor, where a Marine band
played music and a vibrant crowd of people was waiting for us. The
starboard side of the *Gordon*'s hull tenderly touched against the pier;
the lines lashed her securely to the welcoming wharf. The people
were waving and calling out to us; now we could see their faces
more distinctly. None of my relatives or friends was among them;
but I was not dismayed. I was back in the land where I belonged.

Chapter 33
CALIFORNIA FAZE OUT

I STRODE DOWN THE GANGPLANK and walked past the crowd toward waiting buses. I envied those Marines who were getting hugged and kissed by friends and kinfolk. The young women look prettier than I remembered. But at least I was safely back in the States. In less than two weeks I would be back in Motor City.

The buses took us across the bridge to Treasure Island (TI). I thought of Robert Louis Stevenson's famous *Treasure Island*, an adventure story about pirates, but I saw no pirates. I guess the Marines had cleared them out ages ago, like they'd done on "the shores of Tripoli." I did see that TI was an active military installation and had a beautiful view of the city and its magnificent bay.

At the base, we filled out official forms and received our orders. Then they fed us a good meal, including fresh milk. My orders were to proceed to San Diego for further processing and release from active duty. I was soon aboard a bus going to the train station for the trip south. Our train route seemed more inland than necessary. I wondered why.

A railroad closer to the Pacific coast would provide more scenic views to passengers. Yet we were going to go thru the Mohave Desert. That made sense; we were Marines and not supposed to have a pleasant trip. At least my seasickness had fully disappeared, and the train's motion was soothing compared to the ship's.

In San Diego, buses took us to the Marine Corps Recruit Depot, the place where I had gotten my boot camp training. This time I would have a much higher status; I was now a combat veteran—and a sergeant. Also, I was authorized to wear the following ribbons on my jacket: Korean Service Medal, United Nations Service Medal, National Defense Service Medal, U.S. Presidential Unit Citation, Republic of Korea Presidential Unit Citation, and maybe a few more.

We got a thoro physical examination. It included a blood test, something I didn't recall ever having before, even when I joined the reserves in Detroit, twenty-seven months earlier. Unfortunately, it didn't reveal the congenital anemia trait (*thalessemia minor* or Mediterranean anemia) that had constantly bedeviled my exertions climbing around all those Korean hills, lugging those damn ammo cans.

When the hypodermic needle was stuck into my arm, I watched as the plunger pulled back, drawing out my blood. As I looked, I started getting dizzy and nauseated. By the time the needle was withdrawn, I was unsure whether I would faint first or vomit.

I told the Navy Corpsman my symptoms, and he steadied me. "Don't get up until you're over it," he said. I waited about fifteen minutes and told him, "I think I can walk now."

He said, "Just go back to your rack and rest. Don't do anything strenuous. Be sure to eat a full meal."

I walked slowly and not too steadily back to my quarters. Along the corridors, I stayed close to the bulkhead, in case I lost my balance.

Why had the sight of blood bothered me so? I'd seen enough of it on Hill 676 and certainly on Hill 749. Maybe the sick bay's odor of alcohol had caused my problem. I was sure it was nothing to worry about. My mind was unwilling to admit that it could harbor anything disturbing from the war, however deep it might be dwelling in my subconscious.

To collect a stool specimen for the laboratory, we were handed a container, which greatly resembled the thin cardboard containers used by Chinese restaurants for carryout foods, tho much smaller, In the head, I squatted over the toilet bowl, held the container under me, took careful aim, and dropped a few turds into it. Then I closed the container top and walked back to the lab. A Marine sarcastically referred to these specimens as "box lunches for the Navy." Maybe the Navy medical staff had their own quips about the Marines, like momentarily refusing to accept the container by saying, "Marine,

252

don't hand me that shit," which is slang for "don't lie to me" or greatly exaggerate what you are talking about.

When my specimen proved to be positive, I immediately suspected a serious disease. I asked the Corpsman, "What have I got?"

"Just worms. We can take care of it."

He gave me three large pills and told me to take one each day and come back on the fourth. "Don't drink any alcohol." On the fourth day, I came back to the sick bay and was given a small paper cup full of a thick clear liquid.

He told me, "Drink this in one fast gulp." It was vile tasting and potent. Right away I felt a fast-developing storm in my gut. I had swallowed an explosive; I wondered whether it contained *tetracol*. I sped to the head. If someone had been in my way, I would've knocked him down, lest a second's delay make me shit in my trousers.

I got to the head just as the internal storm was developing hurricane force. I dropped my trousers in record time and plopped down on the toilet seat as the noisy storm exploded out of my bottom.

The treatment worked but left me wondering how I had gotten worms in Korea. Was it from swimming in that nice stream near Hongch'ŏn? Or had I drunk contaminated water?

Fifty-six years later, my fellow Detroiter from the 17th Infantry Battalion, Bob Rhodes, explained,

> Most of our drinking water came from streams. The water-treatment tablets that we put into our canteens killed bacteria, etc. Unfortunately, they didn't touch the microscopic worm eggs, which later matured, inside of us.

On my first weekend liberty, I visited the two families in Los Angeles that had befriended me before I shipped out to Korea: the Nizibians and Balmases. The young adults asked me to join them for a recreational outing. They asked, "Do you want to go skiing in the San Bernardino Mountains or swimming at a beach on the Pacific?"

I had never been skiing before, so I chose that. As for the Pacific, I had had my fill of it coming back from Korea. I would rather break a leg as a new skier than get close enough to the ocean to get seasick again.

The San Diego zoo was well known for the variety of its wildlife and the landscape. Perhaps the same statement could be made about Korea. Nevertheless it was safer and I did not feel the need to be carrying a gun when I went to visit it with fellow-Marine, Charles C. Bachert. Charlie had been in the 2nd Battalion's H&S Company with me. I believe he was from New Jersey.

The zoo visit was a delightful experience. I doubted that I would ever come back to that part of the country but years later I visited the zoo two more times.

I shipped the Noritake chinaware to Detroit and hoped it would arrive undamaged. It did. My mother would treasure it for the rest of her life. After inheriting it from her in 1967, I kept it some thirty years and then passed it on to my son John and his new wife, Patti.

¶On Maundy Thursday, 10 April 1952, I was "honorably separated" from active duty. I had served 589 days (nineteen months and eleven days); my overseas service portion was 1 year, 1 month, and 16 days. I got paid the balance of my salary, received a *DD Form 214* (Report of Separation from the Armed Forces of the United States) plus a voucher to purchase airfare to Detroit and was given a certificate of service, small enough to carry in my wallet.

Both the form and the little certificate indicated that I had served "honorably" in "operations against enemy forces in South and Central Korea 5 March 1951 to 16 March 1952." My Military Specialty Number was 0335, Machine-Gun Unit Leader. As to my qualifications for civilian employment, the *DD Form 214* indicated a "Related Civilian Occupation" of "Proof Technician, Small Arms." But what did that mean? I guess it showed that the Marines had taught me how to shoot. Other than becoming a policeman, guard, robber or assassin for hire, I wasn't sure what kind of civilian job my military experience had prepared me for.

The next morning I hitchhiked to the Burbank Airport; it was no longer the main airport. So I hitchhiked to the LA Airport for the flight to Detroit. I wondered what kind of a life awaited me back in Motor City.

Chapter 34
SAFELY BACK IN MOTOR CITY

SPRING IS THE BEST TIME to return home from a long and dangerous journey. It is the season of new life, of infinite possibilities. Only in spring can there be an Easter to signify the promise of rebirth. On Easter 1952, when the minister proclaims that "Christ is risen," I will join the church's congregation to affirm: "Yes, verily risen!" And my true joy and spontaneous tears will announce that I believe that I too have obtained new life. Glory be to God!

It was not as a dead warrior being transported by a Valkyrie to Valhalla, but as a live warrior being flown in a Lockheed Constellation, that I landed at Detroit's Willow Run Airport on 11 April 1952. It was Good Friday, a very good Friday. And soon I was being hugged and kissed by my mother, sister Geri, Aunt Rose, and Dad. I was home.

They were all older. Mother had not gotten any grey hairs, but she had gained weight, the same with Aunt Rose. Geri was now sixteen years old and taller and prettier than I remembered. My father was a little greyer and balder. Only I was the one who had not changed.

We sat down in the airport lobby to chat before exiting to the parking lot. They had a lot of questions about my experiences, but I wanted to avoid talking about Korea. Their eyes seemed riveted on my face, and Baba asked me why I was "doing that" with my eyes. The others noticed it too; I was nervously blinking my eyelids. I don't know why or when I had developed this nervous habit. I assumed it was my reaction to stress during the war. It stayed with me for a few years, gradually diminishing.

To reach our house at 5111 French Road, we drove more than an hour. There were no freeways yet, so the neighborhoods were still intact. But "progress" was bearing down on us; Detroit would soon try to *Los Angelize* itself. Many things would be destroyed on

Detroit's misbegotten road to urban suicide. Even the naval armory would suffer neglect and eventual ruin.

We arrived at the house; I was surprised at how small it was. Between ours and the neighboring houses on each side was no more than eight feet. Its backyard had a car garage, accessible only from the alley that paralleled French Road. The backyard between the house and the garage was about twenty-five by twenty-five feet. That was enough for planting vegetables and flowers, including those runaway vines of morning glories that Mom often had to pester Augie into cutting away, because she found them too expansive to justify their pretty blossoms.

The house must've been at least thirty-five years old. Still it showed that we were in the middle class, albeit at the lowest rung. On reconsideration, I cannot say we were middle class. We were in the lower class but maybe at the highest rung.

But it was our house, a far cry from the cramped and dreary apartments and flats of Detroit's inner city that I had known for the first eighteen-and-a-half years of my life. And I would have a bedroom all to myself, no more sleeping on a couch. I had a dresser and a small closet and a window to look out. What more could I ask for?

The family all wanted me to do more talking about my experiences. But I spoke in generalities about Korea, how mountainous it was and how poor the people were. I emphasized how glad I was to be back home.

I was more interested in telling them my plans for the future: I wanted to go to college in September, but I needed money for it and planned to work at Hudson Motor Car Company where I had worked in the summer of 1950. "But first, I want to buy a car and just take time off for a couple weeks."

My mother's husband, Augie, was not at home; he worked on the late afternoon shift at the Grand Trunk Western Railway. We would have a chance to talk and become acquainted the next morning, if he was sober and not suffering from one of the hangovers that followed his weekend binges of drunkenness. This second marriage would be somewhat better for my mother, altho Augie's alcoholism was onerous. Still, Augie did not slap her when he was angry; my father had done so, one time too many, and that had led her to initiate the divorce in 1940.

When it was time to go, Dad asked me to come visit him, and I said I would, the next day. Aunt Rose offered to drive him home, and he accepted.

¶Around midday on Saturday, I rode the bus downtown to the Turkish coffeehouses around the intersection of St. Antoine and Lafayette streets on Detroit's lower east side. The immigrants socialized in the coffeehouses and ate at the Turkish and Greek restaurants in the neighborhood ("Greektown" was one block away from this "Turktown"). The immigrants were bachelors and lived in the tiny bedrooms of rooming houses nearby.

I was wearing my Marine uniform, so I got a lot of attention as I walked thru the area to meet Baba at the coffeehouse owned by the Red Crescent Society. It was good to see the many familiar faces and hear them welcome me back.

I opened the Society's door, stepped across the threshold, and began climbing the noisy wooden steps—something I had done many times since I was a young boy. As I climbed, I smelled familiar smells, usually cigar smoke and the odor of coffee and tea. When I reached the top, I saw the familiar scene: a potbellied cast-iron heating stove in the center; a large circular oak table; eight or nine white marble, square-top tables, about half of them with one or two persons seated, most of them having beverages. A few were playing cards and some avidly playing *tavla* (backgammon).

This time Baba saw me before I saw him. He came up quickly with smiles and hugged me. His big brown eyes were moist. *Why do men become more sentimental with age?* He asked me how I was, *nasılsın?* And I said *iyiyim*, I was fine.

258

We sat down, and I asked, "What kind of work are you doing now?" He had never been able to get a good or steady job following the end of Detroit's full-employment days of World War II. He told me he sold ice cream from a freezer box mounted on a rented commercial tricycle. He peddled thru neighborhoods on Detroit's lower east side, which was nearly all populated by African-Americans and where business was good during the hot weather. Unfortunately, black teenagers would hassle him and run off without paying for their ice cream. He couldn't chase them because that would leave his ice-cream box unguarded.

During the cold months, he used to go at night to the taverns or nightclubs downtown, toting a basket and selling little packages of nuts and yellow raisins to the patrons. He owned the basket and bought the nuts and raisins at wholesale prices.

My father eagerly told me about a ceremony he attended at the Veterans Memorial Building, early in 1952. The Department of Defense was conducting a public relations tour of major American cities and introducing personnel of the UN military units in Korea; among them were Turkish soldiers. Members of the Turkish American community were invited.

He proudly told the Turkish soldiers, "My son is serving in Korea." The Turkish soldiers said they hoped to meet me someday. It was probably the only time in his life that he felt so proud and important.

As I left him, I realized just how hopeless his English was. Yet I wanted to communicate with him. He was my father, but because he had been divorced by my mother, I had not spent enough time with him growing up and I felt cheated of the full bonding that a father and son should have. To strengthen the bonds, I would reach out to him. That, more than anything else, was what inspired me to learn Turkish.

¶After several days in Detroit, an uneasy feeling grew in me. I didn't feel safe without a weapon.

259

For twelve-and-a-half months in Korea, I had carried a weapon with me, night and day. In fact, I had even tried to get a second weapon, a pistol. I wrote to Henry Tazzia, my longtime best friend in Detroit, and asked him to buy one for me, preferably a P38. I told my mother that she should wait before sending me another package until Henry had purchased the pistol for me. I justified getting a pistol by saying, "That way I won't have to drag a rifle around all the time. We have to stay armed even in rear areas. You can put it in a big, metal coffee can, pack it tight and seal it. Be sure to insure the package, but don't mention the pistol inside to anyone."

Neither Henry nor my mother complied with my request. They were not going to get involved in violating U.S. postal laws just to let me have a second (and unnecessary) weapon.

Twice something happened to endanger my life soon after I got back; both were mishaps, and carrying a gun would not have helped me. I was walking in downtown Detroit when I heard a whooshing sound like an incoming mortar shell, followed by the sound of crashing glass. I plastered myself against the wall of the building next to the sidewalk. Then the sounds came again. A drunk was dropping beer bottles from a floor high above, and they were crashing onto the sidewalk. If one had hit my head, I would have surely died. I rushed into the hotel to tell the clerk, and he raced upstairs to stop it. After having survived Korea, I never dreamed that I might be killed by a senseless drunk flinging beer bottles out of a window.

A month later, I was going to a party at a summer cottage near Lake St. Clair. I was riding in the backseat of a convertible with its top down when the driver lost control on a gravelly road, and we crashed into a ditch. Fortunately, none of us was pitched out. I walked away from the scene wondering, *what's the next danger going to be?*

If having a pistol would not have protected me from the real threats of falling bottles and auto accidents, why did I have a compulsion to get one? By telefoning the police department, I learned that I had to be twenty-one years of age. On the phone, the cop sarcastically asked, "What do you want to do? Go out and shoot somebody?"

I would have to wait about eight months for my twenty-first birthday. I had been trained by the Marine Corps to use all sorts of weapons, and even tho I had been in a war, I was too young to purchase a weapon in civilian life.

While shopping for a car, I found that I had to be twenty-one years old to own one, unless my mother signed as a co-owner. The 1952 presidential election would take place in November, three months before my birthday; I was too young to cast a vote. Whether I wanted to purchase alcohol at a liquor store or be served in a bar, I had to be at least twenty-one years old. Since I was not a drinker, I could live with that.

Despite my young age, I was a responsible person. I had been in charge of about 120 Korean laborers; the Marine Corps had seen fit to promote me to sergeant. I felt that I was being discriminated against. I thought:

Too young for a gun,
Or even a car,
I'm only twenty,
Too young for a bar.

I fought for freedom,
That's something they note.
But I'm only twenty,
I can't even vote.

I was rehired to work on the assembly line again at the Hudson auto factory, but I didn't want to stay there because of the lousy labor-management relations. The workers went out on wildcat strikes too readily. I needed to make enough money to pay for college tuition, starting with the September 1952 semester. Being on strike would delay my plans.

I went to the Packard Motor Car Company. Labor relations there were as sedate as the styling of their cars. That allowed me to get three-and-a-half months' earnings until I quit in mid-August and used the final weeks of summer to pal around with my friends.

There was still no GI Bill for Korean War veterans when I began studying at Wayne State University in September, majoring in economics. Fortunately, Congress passed legislation before my first semester ended, and I received $110.00 per month while studying full time. After I got married in January 1954, I was entitled to $135.00 per month. My wife Frieda, also a college student, and I would have to work part-time jobs for us to get by.

Michigan's state legislature approved a bonus for all Korean War veterans, effective March 1955. It amounted to $10.00 for each month domestic military service and $15.00 for each month overseas service. I was thankful for the expression of their appreciation—a check for $270.00. It came when I really needed it.

Fig. 34-1: Grosse Ile NAS Marines; Sgt Tanner at right

We were in the midst of the Cold War against the Soviet Union and China, and I was definitely concerned about having to go into another "hot" war. I still had a Marine Corps Reserve obligation to serve until my original four-year enlistment was completed. That meant twenty-one more months of service in a reserve unit, ending 11 January 1954.

Fig. 34-2: Grosse Ile Naval Air Station; WEA front row, center

The old 17th Infantry Battalion had been disbanded and the Marine Corps had already directed me to report to the Marine Reserve unit at the Grosse Ile Naval Air Station, on the southern tip of an island in the Detroit River between Canada and the United States. They had cargo aircraft—the Douglas R4D (same as the Air Force's C-54)—and some Corsairs.

I couldn't imagine what my duties would be. There was no infantry unit there. When I reported for duty on 3 August 1952, they told me, "You're going to be an Air Intelligence NCO." It was officially "Aviation Intelligence Clerk," with an MOS of 7011. I would be on duty for one weekend each month and a full two weeks in the summer. At least I wouldn't have to lug any cans of .30 caliber machine-gun ammo up and down any hills. I wouldn't be shot at or run risks of stepping on enemy antipersonnel mines. I wouldn't even have to stand nightwatch. I couldn't have asked for anything better.

The Department of Defense informed Marine Corps Reservists that they would have their enlistment extended by one year. That extension was dubbed the "Truman year." And it made me even more convinced that I would wind up again on active duty in a dangerous location.

On 17 January 1955, six days after I was discharged from the Marine Corps Reserve, I took my discharge papers with me and went to nearby Self-ridge Air Force Base; it was at Mt. Clemens, just north of Detroit. I wanted to get into a unit where I would be less likely to be called up to active duty as an infantryman and more likely to be involved with airplanes. I harbored a secret desire to be a jet pilot and the Air Force had a lot more of them than did the Marine Corps.

Fig. 34-3: WEA in Argentia Newfoundland on return from trip to Turkiye

The 439th Fighter-Bomber Wing was based there. They were transitioning from Lockheed P-80 Shooting Stars to North American F-86D Sabers. I would love to fly any of those aircraft. Later they would move to transport aircraft, the Fair-child C-119, which could carry cargo, litter patients and mechanized equipment; they could even drop cargo and troops by parachute.

Fig. 34-4: SSgt WEA with TSgt and Major at Selfridge AFB

The Air Force Reserve accepted me for a four-year enlistment and even gave me an extra stripe. Now I was a staff sergeant. I was proud

264

that they equated a Marine buck sergeant (three stripes) with an air force staff sergeant (four stripes). Of course, they made me an air-intelligence NCO. Maybe that would help when I finished college and tried to join the Air Force to become a pilot. At least the pilots didn't have to lug ammunition to the plane's guns; that was the job of the ground crew. Meanwhile, I would have to attend reserve training one weekend a month and two full weeks every summer.

Nearly two years into my Air Force Reserve service, I took an examination to qualify for becoming an officer. I passed with "one of the highest scores we've ever seen," said the personnel officer.

On 22 March 1957 I was made a second lieutenant, meaning I was an officer—the same as the pilots. I was designated an Air-Intelligence Officer. I felt that was another step in ultimately becoming a pilot, but as one of my eyes began losing its acuity, I realized that a career as a military pilot was no longer possible. Unless Uncle Sam ordered me to active duty, my future career would be outside the military.

Fig. 34-5: Memphis TN - USAFR 2dLt WEA, Officer-of-the-Day during 1957 annual encampment

265

Chapter 35
A WIDER PERSPECTIVE

AMERICA'S KOREAN WAR VETERANS returned with neither a bang nor a whimper. Unlike their older brothers, the World War II veterans, they had no victory parades. And why should they? No one but an incurable chauvinist could proclaim the 27 July 1953 cease-fire to be a victory for America.

The cease-fire line was close to the original border between North and South Korea, the Thirty-eighth Parallel. Both countries were still their prewar size. The massive loss of life had lasted thirty-seven months, apparently ending in a draw. Death seemed to be the sole victor.

And what about free and democratic nations saving South Korea from Communist aggression, wasn't that a victory?

Only in hindsight do we realize that it was more a victory than a draw. But no passage of time was needed to understand that what we had saved in South Korea was a repressive dictatorship. And dictatorial rule would grind on until 1997! Freedom and democracy came hard and late to the South Koreans.

Even so, America and its allies were fully justified in defending South Korea. It was a key part of defending many nations against communist totalitarianism during the Cold War. After the 1991 collapse of the Soviet Union, our sacrifices in Korea seem even more worthy.

Actually, the world avoided World War III, partly because of the impact of the Korean War. That standoff war led to "rules of engagement," which guided the West and the Soviet Union for nearly forty years, ending with the Soviet collapse. Those powerful adversaries had decided that they would allow no regional conflict to set off a worldwide nuclear war between them.

The war in Vietnam is much harder to assess. Before we got heavily involved in Vietnam, retired Marine LtGen Puller said in an interview that, "saving the world for democracy" has never been acceptable as a vital interest by the American people. Chesty considered the Korean War "strategically necessary." He also predicted that the Communists would win a war in Vietnam. [WHD]

¶The history of the twentieth century was drenched with the blood of tens of millions of innocent people murdered by Marxist regimes described as Leninist, Stalinist, Maoist, Castroist, etc. North Korea is among that odious group. With its utopian promises of ending poverty and oppression, Communism deceived millions and followed up with totalitarian excesses that far overshadowed actual, but meager, increases in living standards for some of their populations.

As he begins volume one of *The Gulag Archipelago*, Aleksandr Solzhenitsyn conveys his awareness of the enormity of Lenin and Stalin's crimes:

> I dedicate this to all those who did not live to tell it. And may they please forgive me for not having seen it all nor remembered it all, for not having divined all of it. [AIS]

Communism's depredations dwarf the shortcomings, or even crimes, committed by "our side" during the Cold War, even tho we allied ourselves with a lot of bad people. We, the heirs of the Renaissance and the Enlightenment, must march to the beat of a different drummer. We have a tradition of nurturing the human spirit and advancing its potential. While utopias are unattainable and human perfection impossible, we are committed to human progress and the free inquiry that it embodies, indeed, requires. We can, and must, criticize our mistakes and learn from them. We can believe in and defend such rights as "life, liberty, and the pursuit of happiness." All this we can do while opposing the totalitarians.

¶Besides South Korea, twenty-one countries were in the UN coalition. How free and democratic were they? Denmark, India, Italy,

267

Norway, and Sweden provided medical units (but no combat troops). Of the five, India was, and still is the most flawed, due to its illegal occupation of Kashmir and oppressive social and economic treatment of millions of "untouchables" (*dalits* or *harijans*).

About half of the sixteen other countries were seriously flawed. Only in February 2008 did Australia's government own up to that nation's long history of mistreating aboriginal people. Since then, a new path seems to be opening for reconciliation, and Australia's attempts to redress past injustices deserves praise.

The U.S. government's official and massive mistreatment of aboriginal peoples was immoral. [HHJ] [HZ] However, for decades, many official U.S. and private efforts have sought to make amends. The most effective and unintended "reparations" seem to be the huge revenues going to Indian-owned gambling casinos out of the pockets of the gamblers who are mostly non-Indians.

In 1953, Ethiopia was still under the autocratic rule of Emperor Haile Selassie. France had an empire and soon engaged in a barbaric campaign against equally violent native Algerians seeking independence. South Africa was a racist society; the preponderant black majority were third-class citizens and Asian immigrants second-class. Minority whites held all the levers of power and privilege. Thailand was ruled by a military dictatorship.

The Kingdom of Greece and the Republic of Turkiye were just emerging from autocracy into democracy (both would have serious stumbles along the way). They were "rewarded" in 1952 for their Korean War involvement by membership in NATO.

Freedom and democracy *did* need to be defended during the 1950s, but it wasn't just overseas. One place was the United States of America. Howard University's Spingarn civil-rights collection contains a photograph of a tall African-American war veteran holding a picket sign outside of a Washington DC restaurant that denied service to African-Americans. His sign says, "I fought in Korea but I cannot eat here."

Not until 1965 did the U.S. government make a full commitment to freedom and democracy for all Americans; it was called the Civil Rights Act—and the struggle to implement it has taken decades. It's not finished yet. [HZ]

When they returned to the United States, many Korean War veterans were dismayed to find that America's major veterans organizations, while supporting the country's war effort, refused to call the conflict a "war." Wasn't it President Truman himself who labeled it a "police action"? Never mind that the "police" were United Nations military forces fighting an enemy who also had strong military forces.

So the first returning veterans were not eligible to join these veterans organizations. Eventually, the organizations' leaders recognized that it was a war and that there were advantages in replenishing their dues-paying membership rolls; the American Legion approved Korean War veterans for membership on 28 December 1950. Until then, Korean War veterans could ask, "Why would a World War II soldier, who worked Stateside in a military warehouse, be more entitled to membership than a soldier or Marine who had gone thru the fury at the Pusan Perimeter or the Inch'ŏn Invasion, etc.?

During the mid- and late 1950s, returned veterans from Korea were moving into the workforce directly or attending school under the GI Bill. The legislation wasn't as generous as the program given to the World War II veterans, but it went thru Congress pretty fast. This time university officials did not go to Washington DC to express fears of "socialism" or a federal government power grab, as they had done for the World War II legislation.

Not all Korean War veterans returned to civilian life; some stayed in the military. Many of those had easy duty in Germany, Japan, Okinawa, etc. A substantial number served in the Vietnam War. There are even veterans who have served in World War II, Korea, *and* Vietnam.

269

¶Americans were reminded of the Korean War when a prominent Republican presidential candidate lied about his wartime service and was publicly exposed during the 1988 presidential primary elections. The candidate was Pat Robertson, a well-known televangelist. The details are described in Paul N. McCloskey's 1992 Korean War memoir, *The Taking of Hill 610*.

Candidate Robertson's false claims to have been a *combat* veteran of the Korean War were exposed, after other Marine Corps veterans of the war disputed his claims about combat service.

When Robertson sued McCloskey in the U.S. District Court for the District of Columbia many incriminating documents and depositions were revealed. It seems that Robertson's influential father, a U.S. Senator, had gotten his son pulled off a Korea-bound troopship and given duty in Japan. Later duty was in Korea, but back in the safety of the 1st Marine Division's command headquarters.

As McCloskey describes it:

On March 4, 1988, Federal Judge Joyce Hens Green gave Robertson the Hobson's Choice of either going to trial on March 8 and hearing the parade of former Marines testify against him, or dismissing his libel suit with prejudice. Robertson chose to dismiss.

. . . on Monday morning, March 7, 1988, Robertson really had no choice. He agreed to accept the judge's condition, dismiss the lawsuit with prejudice and pay his opponent's court costs. He had chickened out in federal court as he had chickened out on the way to Korea thirty-seven years earlier. [PNM 116]

Pat Robertson's website does talk about his military service and candidacy for the presidency. Understandably, it contains a lot of God-talk but fails to mention any of the damning information revealed by McCloskey and the other Marines, under oath, at the trial.

¶The government of South Korea has been humane and generous in recognizing the sacrifices of America's armed forces in saving their country. For several decades, U.S. veterans (and those of our allies) have been hosted in South Korea under a yearly "revisit" program, which pays for five days of first-class lodging and sightseeing.

In June 2000 I went on one of these "revisits" and was overwhelmed by the official and unofficial expressions of Koreans' gratitude. All of us were astounded at the progress of that nation, which has risen from utter ruin to become a modern and prosperous democracy.

Fig. 35-1: Manert Kennedy and WEA,
Seoul Korea, June 2000

How fortunate I was to meet Manert Kennedy in Seoul on 25 June 2000, at a celebration of the 50th anniversary of the beginning of the Korean War. The event was a "Salute to Heroes," sponsored by the USO and took place in a luxury hotel.

Manert and I were both members of Charlie Company in the 17th Infantry Battalion back in Detroit, altho I have no memory of ever having met him before.

He was to be a marvelous source of information for me when I began writing this memoir. Being a sergeant, he knew much more than I did about what was going on during the different phases of the war. He helped me understand more keenly what he and the other Marines had experienced in the Chosin Campaign (to this day his feet bear the lingering pain that frostbite causes).

Manert opened my mind to understanding, and being more sensitive to the psychological distress of PTSD. He also inspired me by relating the struggles of those who have managed to gain dominance over—if not total freedom from—that affliction. Now I know there is hope for all of us veterans who still suffer.

I also met retired General Bowser. He was General O. P. Smith's officer responsible for operations, part of that brilliant staff that led the First Marine Division during the epic "Frozen Chosin" campaign. [USMKW]

In the capital city, Seoul, the Koreans have constructed their splendid War Memorial. It has a large war Museum that houses exhibits covering the periods of the ancient kingdoms, the Japanese colonial era, and the Korean War. A Memorial Hall provides a space for meditation, under its beautiful dome structure that displays sculptures, mural paintings, and reliefs dealing with military history.

On each side of the ceremonial grounds are colonnades that contain bronze tablets listing the names, by state, of each American who died during the Korean War. They also show the names of Turks, Brits, and other UN combatants who died.

These trips are filled with moments to treasure. And, like other treasures, it includes sadness and tears, along with joys and smiles. For those who have survived that war but are still burdened by it, the visit may bring a healthy dose of healing to the mind, as well as to the spirit.

Fig. 35-2: WEA with General Bowser

On these visits, Americans surprise themselves and their Korean hosts, when the music of a famous Korean folk song is played. After the passing of

272

so many years, most of the vets actually remember the tune and some of the words. The song is "Arirang."

Arirang, arirang, arariyo
Arirang kogærül nŏmŏganda;
Narŭl bŏrigo kasinŭn nimŭn—
Shimnido motgasŏ balbyŏng nanda.

Arirang, arirang, arariyo
Arirang kogærül nŏmŏganda;
Ch'ŏngch'ŏn Hanŭl en Janbyŏlda Manko—
Urine Kasŭmen Kŭnshimdo Manda.

¶Following the 27 July 1953 cease-fire, the public's memory of the War declined, especially in the 1960s, as the Vietnam War plus civil-rights struggles shredded the social and political fabric of our country. The Korean conflict was soon referred to as "the forgotten war." But efforts were afoot to remind Americans of the war. I would have a hand in those efforts.

CHAPTER 36
A DEEPER PERSPECTIVE

DESPITE DR. WATSON'S ASSISTANCE, a modern Sherlock Holmes would have difficulty measuring the effects of the Korean War on veterans. He could easily collect information about the veterans' activities. But he would have more trouble ascertaining the motives, state of mind, etc. These less tangible factors are difficult, as the great detective might say "to deduce, even tho they are elementary, Dr. Watson."

Thru the ages, veterans have agreed on one thing: combat is traumatic and can cause mental problems for some men. We read about "soldier's heart" in the Civil War, "shell shock" in World War I, and "battle fatigue" in World War II and Korea. Nowadays it is posttraumatic stress disorder (PTSD), a "severe and ongoing emotional reaction to an extreme psychological trauma." [DS&]

Some American psychiatrists have called for a change in the name; one recommendation is PTSI, for "posttraumatic stress injury." The Canadian military has coined the term "Operational Stress Injury," (OSI) which refers to "persistent psychological difficulty resulting from military service ... such as anxiety, depression and post-traumatic stress disorder." They also make their soldiers who have OSI eligible for the Sacrifice Medal -- the Canadian equivalent of the U.S. Purple Heart.

Perhaps all veterans experience some minor stress, such as anxiety, difficulty in concentrating, and sleeplessness. The wars in Iraq and Afghanistan have produced their share of PTSD. Most seem to "get over it," to some degree, some more than others.

However, for the veterans who have debilitating PTSD, the families, the medical community in particular, and society in general have their work cut out for them. [C&L] The experiences of the Korean War veterans, like those of other wars, may shed light on what to expect.

I contacted eight of my fellow veterans and asked them, "How was your life affected by having served in the Korean War?" This group's size is too small to be representative of all Korean War veterans. But it can, and did, yield fascinating insights.

They told me about their lives, added reflections about the war, and made interesting observations about people, politics, etc. Was I tracing causation, or merely the *sequence* of happenings in their lives?

Because these are real persons, I have fictionalized their names, altered geografic and other specifics, and switched the order of some sequences. I have kept most of their basic life stories intact, embellished only by a few inferences. The more I learned about them, the more I gained empathy and affection for them – and further insight about my own life story.

¶Wilhelm "Will" K. Barr said, "I have always wanted to be a "military guy." As a captain, he was wounded on Hill 749, temporarily going deaf. He wanted to stay in the Marines, but *only* as an aviator. After being rejected, he returned home to Illinois and enrolled in law school under the GI Bill. After two semesters, he enrolled in the graduate business administration program at the University of Colorado and earned an MBA. He married Ahnali in Colorado and accepted a job in Brazil, working for an American insurance company.

Several years later he returned with his family (now including a son and a daughter) and worked in New York City. He used the GI Bill to finance a mortgage on a new house. He moved on to new jobs and at retirement was living in St. Louis, by then divorced.

Will says,

"I have had no serious health problems, other than 'normal' arthritis in my late years. I have had one artificial knee and one artificial hip installed. Nothing really serious has happened to my sense of mental well-being, altho I used to have flashbacks. I saw no particular pattern and concluded that it was part of me

275

and I had to keep going on with my life."

Will avoided politics and usually voted, like most of his family, for what he considered "moderate Republicans." He says that after being so close to death in combat, his "Christian beliefs were reinforced and have not significantly changed since then."

As to war, his philosophy is that it will always be with us. "When man becomes part of a government, he allows negative impulses to come forth."

¶At eighty-three years of age, Vaughn Kinster has been working nearly ten years on a memoir about his time in Korea and previous Marine Corps experience. He says, "I have done a lot of thinking about those times and there have been numerous occasions when I broke down and sobbed while writing something that brought back certain experiences."

Returning from Korea about the time of the cease-fire, he earned a PhD degree. This led to appointment as assistant professor in philosophy at a Midwest college, a career lasting more than three decades.

For twenty-three years he was very active in the Marine Corps Reserve and retired as a colonel. He has been quite active in several veterans organizations.

Vaughn married Peggi before starting graduate study. After twenty-one years she died and he married a fellow faculty member. After nearly nineteen years of marriage, his second wife died and for the past fifteen years he has been married to a friend of his second wife. Now with a total of six children and eight grandchildren, and reflecting on his past, he says "My life has contained much grief and much happiness."

Vaughn has been an active churchman all his life. "My Korea experience only reinforced my faith. Korea left no physical, spiritual, or psychological damage. And I have enjoyed good health most of my life."

Since Korea he has been active in politics, "usually working for and voting for Democrats, but often for independents and even voting for Republicans a number of times." He was an independent city councilman for 12 years.

Vaughn Kinster has strong pride in his Marine Corps service and little patience for draft dodgers. He also has disdain for: "the flag-wavers who were so eager to send our young servicemen and women to war in Iraq, yet had never served in the military themselves." He says there's a good reason these chauvinists deserve to be called "chicken hawks."

¶Soon after returning to the U.S., Andru Prinston began working as a salesman with an insurance company in Boston. He married and fathered two children. He became active in veterans organizations and more conservative in his political views.

His traumatic experiences in Korea (wounded twice) made him more contemplative about religion. "I wondered why I had survived and whether some divine hand was guiding my fate." He left his sales job and became a Presbyterian minister for five years, continuing to experience a "closer relationship with God."

He became dissatisfied with the "political machinations" of church administrators, returned to the private business sector, and moved to North Carolina. Thru the GI Bill he got financial support for a college education and for purchase of a house.

His son and daughter each received college educations. His wife, Jeraldien, is a retired government employee.

Andru maintains pride in his military service and has great appreciation and respect for people in military service today, as well as those who served before him. He is not able to be active in veterans activities because of health problems; he is 85 percent disabled because of his service in Korea and has severe hearing loss.

"Andy" had serious symptoms of PTSD and benefitted greatly from several years of psychiatry at a Veterans Administration medical facility. He was inspired to help other veterans by encouraging them to deal with their PTSD thru medical care and support groups.

¶Jeymz "Jim" Dekmelerik is a considerate and steady-minded person. His values, behavior, and even survival during the Korean War, are based on his religious faith. He believes that his church, the United Avtoenkefali Orthodox Church, is the true church of Christ, but he feels that many Catholics and mainline Protestants can live moral lives too. He avoided using his rank, Sergeant, to seek converts to his religion. But he was resolved to live by the highest standards that he had been taught at church. By setting a good example he hoped to do good for humanity.

Jim survived the Chosin Campaign, Pohang Guerrilla Hunt, Operations Killer and Ripper, and Hill 749, where he got wounded. He was evacuated to a hospital ship for treatment, then to Japan for recuperation. He came home to Philadelphia in late autumn 1951.

Shortly after returning, he married Ethel, a former high-school classmate, and started working for a major construction company. Jim was obsessed with making up for the time he had spent on active duty. He wanted to quickly and totally submerge himself into a stable and secure family life and a civilian occupation.

Soon after his honeymoon, the nightmares began – just before midnight and about two or three times a week. He would leap out of bed, run to the window, look thru it, and yell "they've broken thru the lines! Shoot! Shoot!"

Jim had always prayed before going to bed. Now he dragged out his prayers, said them more beseechingly, and even threw in all sorts of expressions of deep regret for every sin he felt he had ever committed. His outbursts diminished over a three to four-year period. Then he went thru a period of feeling very tense in bed. He would open his eyes wide and stiffen his body, but stay in bed, without shouting, and silently say a prayer of thanks. Sleep would follow.

By the time of his seventh wedding anniversary, he had decisive-

278

ly subdued his mental demons. The demons were too weak to overcome the defenses of his mind; he had followed St. Paul's instruction: "Put on the whole armor of God."

Jim's pride in having served as a Marine was low-keyed during the first few years of civilian life. As his four children grew older, they asked questions and he would give general answers about having been in a war in Korea. His pride grew and he wondered how other veterans were relating to their war experiences as they approached middle-age.

He finally joined a veterans organization, "The Chosin Few." Then he got more involved in other veterans organizations. He displayed more Marine Corps memorabilia around his house.

In retirement, he and Ethel have traveled a lot around America, whenever he wasn't busy helping out with the grandchildren or visiting kinfolk and other friends.

He thinks he has maintained emotional steadiness and fidelity to his family as well as to his church. His motto is: "Count your blessings and try to live the Golden rule; God will take care of the rest."

¶Mort Lamont seems to have adjusted quite well to civilian life. He acknowledges having hearing problems, because he served with a heavy mortar unit. He is one of four brothers who performed military service in and around Korea; Mort and one other brother were Marines. He is proud of his family's military service but is skeptical of people, especially politicians, who exploit patriotism for specious reasons.

Mort used the GI Bill for two years of college and then worked in the aviation industry in Texas. He got GI Bill financing for the mortgage on a house and has had a good life there with his wife, Meyri Martha, and two children.

After retiring, he started a part-time business, repairing computers in his home workshop. He and Meyri enjoy traveling and he is an avid reader.

Mort attends a Protestant church and frequently reminds himself how lucky he was to have survived the war unscathed. He does not belong to any veterans organizations.

He considers himself a political moderate, and is registered as an Independent. Mort has strong feelings about ex-President George W. Bush: "I cannot stand the way that president ruined our country!"

¶Ned Harpur returned to his Cleveland home, physically un-scarred by the war. He worked briefly in a truck-manufacturing factory and began college, using the GI Bill. He married Khristie, a fellow college student; both graduated in 1956.

With Khristie working full time as a nurse and Ned part-time in various jobs, they lived in public housing until Ned finished his graduate studies. In 1958 he got a job in Washington DC as a statistician with the DOD; later he was a management planner. Except for a two-year assignment in Germany, they and their three children have lived in a Virginia suburb of DC; their house was purchased using GI Bill financing.

Ned avoided joining veterans organizations until he reached middle age. By then his offspring had finished college. He was active in the DOD's program of commemorating the fiftieth anniversary of World War II.

Ned's mental health history includes mild PTSD; he realized it only when he was seventy-five years old! Soon after returning from Korea he had experienced a sense of dread; these led to panic attacks. He acted remote from people, even in their presence. He found it easy to shut down his mind as he had done in Korea, to keep from dealing with problems.

A few years of psychiatric sessions helped diminish his panic attacks, but he never gave up the habit of shutting down his mind when under severe stress. Ned's frequent withdrawals seemed to have made his offspring think that he did not love them. One day he accidentally found his daughter's diary and read about her anguish at not being loved at home. Soon after her college graduation she left

280

home and had both her middle and last name officially changed.

Ned claims that, "My mental health returned when I quit organized religion, forty-four days after my sixtieth birthday. I became a born-again Tom Paine deist, like my father."

Nowadays he admits that he was premature in thinking his mental health had become fully satisfactory. Something new was needed in his mentality, and he became aware of it soon after his eightieth birthday.

A very savvy and caring physician at the Veterans Administration told him that he could gain further understanding and growth by reading stories of hope and healing in the lives of other veterans and their families. To encourage him, the doctor gave Ned a book containing such stories. Miraculously, the author had summed up, in just one short paragraph, what Ned had to deal with; he was ready to be born again and started to memorize the author's words:

> "Stoicism is important even essential, especially on a battlefield. It creates protection from untrustworthy influences. It's the relationship to stoicism that needs modification. Its overuse creates problems as serious as the problems it has been used to counteract. It can be used inappropriately to block energy and emotion from one's self or interfere with expressing love to others." [DLG 53]

Ned says "you're never too old to learn." He hopes it's never too late to prove his love to his estranged offspring.

¶Politics was something that Richard "Rik" Genscher had no opinion about, until after the war. "Then I became a right winger," he states. He came back with a Purple Heart, deeply grateful for having survived.

Rik stayed in the Corps a few years and was posted to Camp LeJeune. There he met Jeni, a woman Marine, whom he married. He thought about staying in the service, but returned to civilian life in his home state, Maine. Being the "outdoor type," he joined the

U.S. Border Patrol. He and Jeni divorced, ending an acrimonious marriage.

He liked his job and living in Maine. He was more than comfortable carrying a pistol, thinking he might never have to use it. As an avid hunter he enjoyed deer hunting. He expected to finish his work career without ever shooting anything, except deer.

However, he was in a gunfight with southbound Canadian fugitives, dropping both but getting badly wounded. After a long recuperation and an official award for courage, he was back on the job.

While recovering he thought about his good luck, both in Korea and in Maine, but felt anxious about the future. He says, "Then I realized I had some kind of PTSD, altho we didn't use that term in those days." He doesn't say what his symptoms were or whether he still has any. But a low level of tension seems to reside in him, he says. And he has never been able to quit smoking.

Rik was a local hero; many citizens praised him over the shooting incident. At a citizens group, he met an admirer and later married her. They had a son but the marriage ended in a divorce.

He considers himself a Catholic but does not go to church. His basic philosophy is: "If people obey the law and keep their minds out of other people's business, most of society's problems would be solved."

¶Max Buzman was tenacious and inspiring – a natural leader. He was a sergeant with the Marines at Chosin. Amazingly, he also survived the Pohang Guerrilla Hunt, Operations Killer and Ripper, and Hill 749. He returned to Wisconsin and "jumped back into civilian life."

Max says, "We came back naïve." He did not recognize how much he embodied the physical and mental trauma of his combat experiences. He does recognize that he returned determined to "justify my survival by leading a successful and worthy life."

His sister told him that he had "gone away as a teddy bear and

282

come back as an icicle." Others too noticed his "flat emotions."

Already married to Eymie, Max worked part-time using his GI Bill benefits to earn a PhD in environmental sciences. He got a teaching job at a local university. In the 1960s they moved to Arizona and Max taught at a state university.

He gained wide recognition for his ability to bring business, industry, education and political groups together to deal with problems in science education. He "fathered" the International Alliance for Science movement, a prime example of public and private partnership for promoting science education.

But Korea stayed with him. Frostbite had permanently impaired his feet. Extra layers of stockings did not fully assuage the pain, even in summer. A full-night's sleep became a rarity. It still is.

Panic attacks woke him up in a cold sweat. For several years he was out of control in using alcohol. Grief sometimes left him weepy, lethargic, or even agitated. A few times he mentioned his mental turbulence and anxiety, but other veterans told him, "Get over it." He didn't get over it; he clammed up.

Max joined the "The Chosin Few," later seeing it as the first step toward recovery. Slowly, with other vets' support, he began to understand his PTSD and start the healing process. He says, "It's a journey. You do not graduate, but you can get much better."

Korea affected him again when he traveled there to help develop materials and systems for science education. On his first trip back in 1960, he suffered barely controllable anxiety. His departure after just a few days was like fleeing from a combat zone.

On his second – and short – trip, Max was in the Andong/Wŏnju area, where he had been in combat. An anxiety attack overcame him and he jumped on a fast train to Pusan, immediately boarding a ferry boat to escape to Japan.

Despite it all, each succeeding trip to Korea lessened his distress. He came to know the Korean people and become their friend. He even brought his wife and other relatives on later trips. Psychologists told him he was benefitting from "exposure therapy."

His twenty-fifth time was a six-month stint as a visiting university professor. It coincided with the fiftieth anniversary of the start of the Korean War. How far he had come! The external road had been long; but the internal one – toward mental stability and wholesomeness – was much, much further.

¶In spite of discordant passages, the life symphonies of these, and other veterans, are still being performed; the music plays on and no one knows when or how they will end. Like those in Tchaikovsky's Sixth Symphony (the "Pathétique"), the themes of their lives range widely, from hopeless to hopeful, and from the unsettling to the soothing. Listeners may feel drained by the symphony's somber moods yet haunted by its melodious power. It can incline them to believe that life's dreams are not cancelled out by its nightmares, nor its beauty by its ugliness, nor its worth by its tragedies.

Chapter 37
AN HONORABLE PORTRAYAL

IN THE COLD SILENT PREDAWN of a January morning, the Marine was intently watching the dark figures in the snow ahead and getting ready to shoot. They were clear of the tree line behind them and seemed taller than normal men—almost giants—but then darkness plays tricks on the eyes. His own father, a former Marine, had wryly told him about nervously shooting at a tree one night during the battle of Hill 749, near the Punchbowl in North Korea.

There were more than twenty of them in a phalanx standing motionless. The point of the phalanx was aimed at him; if they were to charge, they would quickly overwhelm him. But he *knew* they had not seen him.

Altho well bundled in winter clothing, he was shivering. Racing thru his mind were thoughts of those other Marines who suffered so much back in the frigid Hell of the Chosin Reservoir Campaign in 1950. He thought, *If I am so chilled and uncomfortable in this temperature, how agonizing was it for those Marines in that brutal Siberian-like winter.* It humbled him immediately, and the cold became more bearable.

Now he knew it was time to act. The dawn was sneaking up on him, and them, without any transitional colors of red or gold. Because of a filter of thick clouds, he was now confronted with a dramatic scene, bathed in a soft morning light of blue, grey, and green.

He was confident that he had properly assessed what was on each of his flanks and could now focus on what was directly in front of him. He had confidence in his equipment. He took careful aim and then took his first shot.

The camera's shutter worked perfectly, and Captain John W. Alli decided to take more photographs of the Korean War Veterans Memorial (KWVM) on Washington DC's National Mall. He would

285

send off the roll of film the next day to the best foto lab for professional development of the negatives and printing. Next would come framing of the picture with his mother's collusion. It should make a fine gift to give to his father at the retirement party coming up soon.

¶On 28 February 1996, I went to the retirement luncheon that my office had organized for me at a hotel in Rosslyn VA, across the Potomac River from Washington DC. What a fine occasion. I was completing nearly forty years' service as an employee of the United States government. And so many friends had come, altho I did not see my wife Frieda there.

The food was good, but I don't remember what I ate. My supervisor's tribute to me was warm and upbeat; however, I cannot recall what she said. The gifts were nice but I don't remember what most of them were.

During the proceedings, I saw my wife Frieda and our son John enter the banquet room. John was carrying a large object; it looked like it might be a bulletin board wrapped in plain brown paper. I was surprised and curious. *What on earth can that be? I hope it's not a heavy thing that I'll have to lug back home this afternoon.*

The master of ceremonies ended the gift presentations by calling up my son and saying, "He also has a gift for you." John walked up and gave me the package.

All of us wondered what it was. He helped hold it as I removed the wrapping paper. Then I beheld the twenty-by-twenty-four-inch fotograf, professionally framed in sober, and proper, blue and grey mounting. My eyes filled with tears. I didn't know what to say, yet I had to say something. I know I thanked him. I don't remember his reply—no doubt something congratulatory.

I looked out at the audience. I knew that I was viewed as an outspoken person, a crusader against indoor air pollution (mainly secondhand tobacco smoke), and a union official who defended employees' rights but was critical of employees who were not trying

286

to be productive on the job. I didn't seem "the emotional type" to other employees of my agency.

I had to explain to the guests my obviously emotional state at seeing John's gift to me. So I decided to say, "You know, I am really a sensitive person. I even cry at weddings."

Despite my intention, everybody burst out in wild laughter. Apparently, what came out of my mouth was, "You know, I am really a sensitive person. I even cry at *funerals*."

Then John told me that the title of the photograph was "Real Life." For some people it may be thought of as: "first Snowfall on the Korean War Veterans Memorial in Washington DC." By any name, it is stunning.

Fig. 37-1: John Alli, 28 February 1996

Why would a picture of the Washington DC Korean War Veterans Memorial cause me to misspeak? Was it coming from something deep in my memory? Was it just a quirk? Was something else at work?

John was showing his respect and appreciation to me, one of the surviving veterans. He was saying what every Korean War veteran deserves to hear: that "the forgotten war" is not forgotten. Perhaps it might remind people that freedom is neither free nor cheap, and liberty for succeeding generations of men and women was bought at the price of blood shedded in Korea

The foto grabbed attention and admiration thru-out the veterans community and beyond. It appeared on the Internet and even the cover of a Korean War novel.[EHS] In April 1998, the Naval Institute awarded John first prize in its 36th Annual Photo Contest.

287

John fully deserved the honor; he had created an enduring reminder of the sacrifice of those who had served in a just war.

Chapter 38
DEDICATING A MEMORIAL

AMERICANS WERE ENCOURAGED ON 27 JULY 1995 to
remember the war as
President Clinton pre-
sided over the dedica-
tion of the KWVM.
The Memorial repre-
sented the culmination
of years of fundraising
by Korean War vete-
rans. Invitations went
out to all of the United
Nations members to
attend the dedication
and march in the
celebratory parade.

Fig. 38-1: KWVM 1995
Dedication patch

I was looking forward to seeing former Marine buddies of the
Second Battalion First Marines, and even the 17th Infantry Battalion.
Perhaps I would again see some of the Turkish Brigade veterans.

Beforehand a letter came to my house from one of the Turks,
Erdoğan Başaran. He was the guy who had hosted me at his home in
Ankara on my first visit to
Turkiye in the summer of 1953,
my first summer vacation from
Wayne State University after
finishing my freshman year of
study under the G.I. Bill. I
opened the letter expectantly, I
was hoping that he was inform-
ing me about his plans to see

Fig. 38-2: KWVA circular patch

289

me at the KWVM edication.

Erdoğan's letter dismayed and angered me. He revealed that the Turkish government's funding of Turkish veterans for attendance at the KWVM dedication was limited to two groups: (1) veterans who had been commissioned officers in the war and (2) young cadets in the military Academy who were members of the marching band. That's all! No NCOs and no privates!

Fig. 38-3: 2/1's logo

I sent a letter to the Turkish Prime Minister, Mrs.Çiller, expressing my dissatisfaction with the exclusion of the lower-ranked soldiers. I couldn't understand why a marching band of military cadets should get any preference. She never replied to my letter.

Ten years before the dedication of the KWVM, veterans had founded the Korean War Veterans Association (KWVA) and began to assiduously work to raise funds for building a national memorial. Surprisingly, the KWVA found substantial resistance to its attempt to obtain a federal charter, which would acknowledge that the group serves the public interest by providing member services and promoting community support. Only in June 2008 was the legislation enacted and signed into law by the President.

The crowds admired the new monument; it was

Fig. 38-4: MG-Unit, right side

unique. The 19 stainless steel statues were 10-foot tall and had such realistic-looking details. And the black granite Memorial Wall on the South side was shiny enough to reflect the figures back to the eyes of the people viewing them from the walkway along the North side. Added together the 19 statues and their reflections amounted to 38: the same number as found in the phrase "38th Parallel" which was the bloody boundary that divided North and South Korea.

The back left corner of the falanx grabbed my attention and I nearly gasped; the three statues were of Marines; they were even wearing the camouflaged helmet covers like we did, unlike Army personnel who usually wore bare helmets. And two of these Marines belonged to a machine-gun unit, just like mine. There was the gunner carrying the tripod and near him the assistant gunner carrying the 30 caliber Browning light machine-gun which we had. But the third statue was not part of the machine-gun unit; he was the Navy Corpsman. They were a godsend to Marines who had been wounded.

But there was no figure of an ammo carrier! That's what I had been! In fact, for each machine-gun there were four to six ammo carriers.

Had the architecture been faulty? Oh no!

When we read about the thinking behind the design by architect William Lecky, we must pause and enlighten our expectations:

> It is my feeling that memorials should be about the emotional impact related to the event being recognized. They should be a place [for a person] to be moved, to feel, to remember, to cry, or to celebrate. They should capture the essence of that which is being memorialized. They are there to touch our souls, not our minds. And their images, their messages, should resonate in our memory for all time. [WPL, 162]

Fig. 38-5: MG-Unit, left side

And so it happened; mixed memories started flowing thru my head—both good and bad—as I gazed at these statues and their surroundings. But the bad memories could not prevail. I had been thru the "valley of the shadow of death;" I had survived the war. And my cup had "runneth over," but more with wine than blood.

Chapter 39
AFTER 50 YEARS: A COMEMORATION

RENEWED PUBLIC INTEREST IN THE KOREAN WAR was stimulated, from 2000 to 2003, by the Department of Defense's sponsorship of a program to commemorate the fiftieth anniversary. The program's goal was this: "To ensure that every Korean War veteran and their families are properly thanked and honored for what they accomplished and know that our nation remembers their service fifty years ago."

Fig. 39-1: Logo, DOD 50th Anniversary of the KWCC

Thru-out the United States, the Republic of Korea, and the other allied countries a wide variety of events were sponsored by veterans organizations, civic associations, academic institutions, government agencies, and even business organizations. These included wreath-laying ceremonies, parades, media broadcasts, newspaper and magazine articles, history seminars, and many others.

Fig. 39-2: American & Turkish Veterans Association patch

¶In 2002, I led a group of American veterans on a tour of Turkiye, where we participated in a ceremony at a four-story pagoda-like building in Ankara, a gift from the government of Korea. Fittingly, it is Turkiye's war memorial in honor of their illustrious brigade's service and sacrifices.

On behalf of the American and Turkish Veterans Association of the USA (ATVA), I laid a wreath—somberly and respectfully—to honor the fallen Turkish soldiers. Tho not in military uniform, I was inspired to show my respect to the Turkish soldiers by rendering a military salute. In my heart, I knew that I was also honoring the entire legion of the dead and their comrades, from all the countries who saved South Korea. [WEA]

One specific focus of our trip was to find and thank a special Turkish veteran. At the time we did not know his real name. All we knew was his nickname: "Hakim," the equivalent of "Doc" in our language.

Hakim was one of 244 Turkish prisoners of war, nearly all of them wounded before capture. The special thing about Hakim was what he had done while a POW in a Chinese Communist prison camp. He had helped an American POW survive the brutality of that camp. Repatriated after the war, the American said,

> We didn't know how to look after ourselves, and the Turks took pity on us. . . My friend was Hakim. . . .When I was sick, he brought me food, and he looked after me as he would have another Turkish person. . . . When our sweaters and socks wore out, they picked the wool apart and reknitted it. Hakim made me a pair of socks. . . We had informers among us, and we knew who they were. I still know. The Turks did not have one single informer. . . When I was so sick I thought I was going to die, Hakim brought me soup and sat with me, and pulled me through it. I think he gave me courage; so many GIs just died because they gave up. . . I taught Hakim English, and he taught me Turkish. He studied it so well that he became a driver for an American officer in Turkey after the war. But I only remember one Turkish phrase. I have remembered it for nearly 40 years. It is *iyi arkadaşım*, my good friend. [MLS 232-33]

At the beginning of our arrival in Ankara, the Turkish Veterans Association introduced a Turkish brigade veteran whom they said was the "Hakim" we were looking for. He had been located a few hundred miles east of the capital. ATVA gave them some money to cover the expenses of bringing him to Ankara. One of our ATVA members asked the man whether he remembered his POW experiences with the American mentioned in Mary Lee Settle's book. He said he did not remember, alluding to the forgetfulness of old age.

After we returned to the US, we learned that the man who had been brought to Ankara was not the "Hakim" that we were searching for. Because the name Hakim is so common in Turkiye, it is easy to understand why the Turkish Veterans Organization had made an honest mistake in identity as they presented this man to us in their Ankara headquarters. A few months later we learned that the real Hakim was Adil Oral. He died in late 2002, shortly after our tour. He had been living in a town near Izmir in western Anadolu.

A year after the ATVA tour I got a letter from the wrong Hakim asking that our organization invite him, and his son, to America for a tour; obviously we were to pay for it. With the letter was a fotograf of the man showing him wearing the ATVA patch we had mistaken-ly given to him in Ankara. The size of the foto was similar to the ones that appear in passports.

Later the man even sent me a gift: a decorative walking cane. I was angry at this attempted swindle and never replied to him.

Fig. 39-3: U.S. postage stamp issued 27 July 2003, 50TH Anniver-sary of Korean War Armistice

¶War veterans from around the world came to Washington DC to commemorate the fiftieth anniver-sary of the cease-fire on 27 July 2003. Marine LtCol John W, Alli

295

was a special guest of honor at the Department of Defense ceremony on the National Mall. His fotograf of the Korean War Veterans

Memorial was appearing on 75-million first-class U.S. postage stamps that were being issued starting that day.

Being president of the American and Turkish Veterans Association (and an honorary member of Turkiye's national veterans association), I was one of

Fig. 39-4. John Alli autografing stamps for former 2/1 Marine Ray Gramkow

the planners for a ceremony to be held in the Turkish embassy. I had two functions during the ceremony. The easy one was handing out a special gift to each of the attending Turkish Brigade veterans: an eight-by-ten-inch copy of John's iconic foto of the Korean War Memorial. That would come near the close of the program.

The second function would not be easy. I was to read, in English, the poem I had copied in 2000 at the UN Memorial Cemetery in Pusan; it was etched on a bronze

Fig. 39-5: Turkish Brigade veterans with Gen. Orhan Uğurluoğlu

plaque in the Turkish section. I rendered its stark Turkish title—*Pusan'da Yatıyorum* (I am lying [recumbent] in Pusan)—as "Ode to the Turkish Soldiers Fallen in the Korean War, 1950–53."

I had attended a similar ceremony at the Turkish Embassy on January 25, 2001. The occasion was a commemoration of the 50th anniversary of the award of the United States Presidential Unit Citation to the Turkish Brigade in Korea. The brigade was cited for "exceptionally outstanding performance of duty in combat in the area of Kumyangjang-ni, from 25 to 27 January 1951." Even the government of Korea awarded its PUC to the Brigade, noting that the enemy force (Chinese) was three times the size of the Turkish force. [CD, NDS]

In preparation for the 27 July 2003 Armistice Day commemoration activities involving American veterans and visiting Turkish veterans, I worked with the Turkish Armed Forces Defense Attaché, General Orhan Uğurluoğlu of the Turkish Embassy. In fact, thru-out the 3-year 50th Commemoration period (2000-2003) both the civilian and military staff members there gave unstinted support to the American and Turkish Veterans Association. They were very understanding when I explained to them the importance of bringing a representative group of Turkish veterans to Washington DC. I did not want to see a repetition of the 1995 situation where only officer veterans and non-veteran cadets of a military band came.

At the ceremony in the embassy's large reception hall, all eyes were on me as I walked to the podium. I had promised myself that I would control my emotions as I read each line of the poem. It would be hard because, as a veteran mindful of the loss of fellow Marines, I knew I could not keep my eyes dry as the words came off my tongue.

Oh God, don't let me choke up or even have my voice crack, I prayed and slowly kept reading until I had finished the text and then pulled out my handkerchief to dry my eyes, as did others around the room.

For the reading in Turkish, six of the Brigade veterans read, one stanza each. They too and their compatriots thru-out the hall were teary-eyed and were trying to maintain their composure.

I found that by the time of hearing the final stanza—those words linking the Turkish homeland with its fallen sons in Pusan—we Americans are moved to think of our own fallen sons (and daughters), realizing the bond between all the fallen and the shared mourning that all families have endured in all of history's wars.

297

ODE TO THE TURKISH SOLDIERS
FALLEN IN THE KOREAN WAR, 1950–'53

Beyond frontiers and faiths
Our rights now in a rendezvous;
Enabled thus to sense and caress
The hugging warmth of all that is past.

How precious were times before Pusan
When sharing the glory of unified thought,
And of battling hand-to-hand
Over vast valleys and hills.

Brief was this advent for soon I parted
In much mysterious a way,
My life-blood drained away one night
In flag-like waves and flutters.

Now enwrapped in Pusan's soil,
My senses reaching death's infinity;
And "Fatherland" grown to such dimensions
Conversant I am, in all tongues there are.

We martyrs are actually alive;
With our hands joined, reaching for the skies,
We have embraced each other
On this thriving land which belongs to us.

I salute you, oh Turkish martyr!
You in Anadolu and I in Pusan;
You have fallen for my Turkiye
And I, for our world.

Chapter 40
FORGETTING AND REMEMBERING

THE FORGETTING OF THE KOREAN WAR QUICKLY RESUMED, quite understandably. Interest in current wars crowds out thoughts about previous wars, despite the attempts of current commentators to draw analogies. At the time of the Korean War armistice's fiftieth anniversary, America was involved in two wars: since 7 October 2001, the pursuit of the 11 September 2001 terrorists (mainly al-Qaida's leaders and their Taliban hosts) in Afghanistan and, since 19 March 2003, the misbegotten Iraq War.

In 2007, the final book by one of America's most distinguished journalists and historians, David Halberstam, was published: *THE COLDEST WINTER, America and the Korean War*. The author revealed his acuity as a historian by showing some similarities between wars involving Korea, Vietnam and Iraq. He starts by describing how MacArthur and his staff began a dire pattern by doctoring intelligence during the Korean War, in order to permit MacArthur's forces to go where they wanted to go militarily.

Halberstam writes:

> In the process they were setting the most dangerous of precedents for those who would follow them in office. In this first instance it was the military that had played with the intelligence . . . Deliberately manipulating the intelligence it sent to the senior military men and civilians back in Washington. The process was to be repeated twice manipulating the military, with the senior military men reacting poorly in their own defense and thereby placing the men under their command in unacceptable combat situations . . . In 1965, the government of Lyndon Johnson manipulated the rationale for sending combat troops to Vietnam, exaggerating the threat posed to America by Hanoi, deliberately diminishing any serious intelligence warning of what the consequences of American intervention in Vietnam would be . . . Thereby committing the United States to a hopeless, unwinnable post-colonial war in Vietnam . . . In 2003, the administration of George W. Bush . . . Completely miscalculating the likely response of the indige-

299

nous people; and ignoring the warnings of the most able member of the George H.W. Bush national security team, Brent Scowcroft; and badly wanting for its own reasons to take down the government of Saddam Hussein—manipulated the Congress, the media, and most dangerously of all, itself, with seriously flawed and doctored intelligence, and sent troops into the heart of Iraqi cities with disastrous results. [DH 390-91]

¶Like the rest of society, we veterans must deal with a rapidly changing world. But the future does not look very promising. In our final years, our planet is confronted with the threats of global warming and climate change, Jihadi terrorism, and famine and epidemics around the world.

America's political system is broken. The U.S. Supreme Court has declared that money is "free speech," thereby opening the floodgates to money's corrupting influence on politics at all levels. The Court has even bestowed personhood on corporations on top of government's original legislative grants of limited liability and perpetuity of business operations. America has indeed become a corporatocracy.

How can we maintain the resolve that President Lincoln entreated us to do in his speech at Gettysburg in 1863? He called for a permanent realization of the great sacrifices made by our fallen military combatants, along with tying it in with a moral/spiritual commitment to producing a new birth of freedom. He saw its potential for enabling us to maintain government of the people by the people and for the people. But we certainly won't do it with so many Tea Party and other Americans condemning moderation and compromise as immoral, asserting that government is a natural enemy of the people, and even rejecting scientific evidence (as with global warming trends).

Economic distress and political frustrations have agitated many Americans. It is easy for me to sympathize with dissatisfactions, and even aspirations, expressed by demonstrators in the Occupy Wall Street movement and other protesting groups.

Will the current worldwide recession become a worldwide depression, like the one in the 1930s, when every Korean War veteran experienced his early childhood? Will our offspring be fortunate enough to find a leader like the great President Franklin Delano Roosevelt and a government as committed to helping our people as was his New Deal administration? [HWB]

Fig. 40-1: President Franklin Delano Roosevelt

There is much to speculate about, but one thing seems sure: violent conflicts will occur, whether conventional war or unconventional and whether by accident or by contrivance. All of them will cause suffering and both spiritual and material loss. Fatalism seems to be the best attitude for keeping one's sanity in such times; war veterans learned that a long time ago.

¶I found fatalism among veterans Bob Davis and Jack Underwood. Before the Korean War, seventeen-year-old Davis was a Marine in northern China and was appalled at the unimaginable poverty and cruelty. He witnessed:

. . . infants being discarded, babies thrown on frozen ponds to die. Young children digging in garbage dumps for anything edible . . . Chinese men shot in the head at close range because they tried to steal clothes to keep warm. So this killing and dying [I] witnessed in Korea was not new to me.

Davis describes his faith:

I believe, as do many, the Lord has a purpose for each of us. Simply, I believe we should accept that when He believes we have satisfied our purpose in life He will call us home. I can't change that so I

301

accept its entirety. . . I no longer believe that each man's death diminishes me. We look at enemy dead, not as someone's son, father, husband or betrothed, only as a terminated enemy. We look at our dead or wounded troops with sympathy and thankfulness that it was not us . . . death to me is impersonal and war changed me that way. I know that the demise of some of my family would devastate me and I certainly sympathize with survivors.

He concludes that "the Korean War may have changed me in another way. . . rarely before would anything bring me to tears. Things do now. Man's inhumanity to man brings tears. Kind acts and happy endings bring tears. I am no longer ashamed nor feel unmanly about those responses."

Jack Underwood has reflected a great deal upon his Korean War experience and vividly recalls:

Right after the first young soldier I killed, my first thought was of his mother, whom I had never seen. I momentarily bowed my head and spoke to her as if I were praying. "I'm sorry. Forgive me." But this type of innocence soon fades as the carnage of war progresses and men become hardened to killing for the sake of survival and not by choice. I thought of what pain friends and families have to endure on both sides of a conflict, no matter the political or religious reasoning.

With this analysis, and in the twilight of my life, I conclude that the impact of the Korean War on me is to emphasize a continuing message of never-ending tragedies inflicted by wars, regardless of the glories proclaimed by the states . . . That warring is [due to] the framing of the mind and the innocent can be caught up in the melee. True wars are sometimes necessary and are inevitable, but peace is the bliss of life in whatever stage of life one might be . . . I have realized that not a single individual had a choice of being, genetically, who they are in the time frame of their existence and we all have to play out our role on the stage of world events.

¶Now I am ending my journey of memory. A memoir is evidence of my travel. But I realize that words on paper cannot fully convey what I have seen and done, nor what my fellow veterans experienced. Literature both explores the human condition and is limited by it.

Fig. 40-2: USMC
Eagle, Globe, & Anchor

The Marine Corps' motto is *Semper fidelis* (Always Faithful). For all, I pray that I have done my duty faithfully. My hope is that my family and friends will find worth in what I've done and that the veterans will feel that I have been respectful in describing our experiences and thoughts, thru the ups and downs of war and its aftermath. I have already received expressions of gratitude from Randy's daughter (for saving his life) and Punte's family members for my describing the laudable service Gene rendered during the war. Just doing my duty does not make me any kind of hero.

As to any larger purpose or context for this book, I must ask this: Isn't every story about war a cautionary tale? Does it not proclaim that war should be only a last resort?

I guess I could have wrestled more with moral questions and explicitly indict self-righteousness, whether religious or secular. Some readers might have looked for expressions of my religious beliefs. I still accept a Christian teaching that I learned as a boy that "if we say we are without sin, we deceive ourselves and the truth is not in us. For all have sinned and fallen short of the glory of God."

Likewise, nothing has diminished my appreciation for the moral teachings of Rabbi Yeshua (Jesus), especially the Golden Rule, tho I now realize that it is found in ethical belief systems around the world. Like Thomas Paine, I believe in one god—and no more—and I hope for happiness beyond this life. So I believe that God created

Man and Man created religion. I see no further need to comment on faith.

So have I settled anything in my journey? Perhaps I have satisfied something deep inside me. I'm not sure. But I do feel a sense of accomplishment and an awareness that now is the time to explore some new vistas—if there *is* time. Amen.

AFTERWORD

IN GOOD FAITH, I began my memoir with a visit to "The Steel Temple" (Chapter 1). It was my sincere attempt to describe a moving experience aboard the USS *Missouri*. But I was under a misapprehension when I described that visit as closing "a ring of memory and letting me depart, thankful to have survived the war and make the pilgrimage."

Soon after finishing my final chapter, at the beginning of July 2008, truth—or at least historical accuracy intruded, and I learned that the Missouri had left the East Coast of Korea on 19 March 1951, bound for its new assignment as flagship for Rear Adm. J. L. Holloway, Jr., Commander, Cruiser Force US Atlantic Fleet. [DANFS]

Actually, what I had seen in May 1951 was one of the *Missouri's* identical sisters, the USS *New Jersey*, whose first shore bombardment of her Korean career was at Wonsan on 20 May 1951. Most of her duty was along North Korea's east coast. I apologize to all readers.

But an apology would not be enough. I needed to make another pilgrimage.

¶America's mighty battleship, the USS *New Jersey,* was peacefully docked on the Delaware River at Camden New Jersey, beneath a clear sky as I prepared to go aboard her late in the afternoon of 8 July 2008. To me it was not an act of tourism; it was my second act of pilgrimage to a big temple, made of steel. My thoughts and actions would be appropriate—a feeling of awe and respect and an awareness that in some way my life had been affected, for the good, and I needed to offer up my thankfulness to something far more powerful than I.

I would not be boarding her as a crew member because neither the *New Jersey* nor I were on active duty. Rather she was open to visitors as a floating museum. But I was more than a mere visitor; I

305

was a pilgrim seeking to relive a memory anchored in 1951, when I was in a "forgotten" war and too young to understand much about what was going on around me.

Reverence cannot be rushed. So before going up her gangplank, I needed to behold the *New Jersey*'s towering presence, from bow to stern, from waterline to top of the main mast. But most of my attention was on her huge gun turrets because these had displayed her awesome power, when I looked down at her from my foxhole, high in the North Korean mountains that overlook the shores of the "Eastern Sea."

An obeisance was in order. It required that I go somewhere port side amidship. There, I stood, facing the bow, with my legs spread out slightly, as one does for stability at sea—part of having "sea legs."

Then I slowly tilted my head up about forty-five degrees as I turned it to look over my left shoulder. In a worshipful mood, I thought, *If a crew member had been doing this, one brightening morning in May 1951, he would be looking up at the mountains where I was looking down.*

That act finally closed the ring of memory, and I departed, thankful to have survived the war and make the pilgrimage to the true temple.

BACK MATTER

* * * * *

APPENDIX GRAFIX LIST

A-3-1: Right side of wide-angle foto; WEA is in third row, 8th man from the right

A-3-2: Middle section of wide-angle foto

A-3-3: Left side of wide-angle foto

B-1-1: WEA next to top row, 6TH from the left. In top row: 2ND from left, Bob Roeszler; 5TH from left, Bill Searles; 5th from right, Ted Bergren. Bottom row, 4th from right, Barnes. The three Drill Instructors are in the center of the 2ND row from the bottom.

B-2-1: Members of the machine-gun unit in a jovial mood. Top row (left to right): Larry Moore (?), Randy Lohr, Don Newell, WEA, Henry Thompson, Dick Whitten, Gene Punte. Bottom row (left to right): Felix Mancha, Myles Jackman, Vic Knabel

B-2-2: L-R, back row – Les, W. J. Novak, front row – "Frib", WEA, Mancha

B-3-1: Yüzbaşı (Captain) Nazım Dündar Sayılan

B-3-2: Three Lieutenants; Süleyman Yakın is in middle

B-3-3: Ergün Kırtaş

B-3-4: Orhan Fırat in the Midland Sea, before Korea

B-3-5: Unidentified. In Turkish camp before leaving for Korea

B-3-6: Hilmi Korugan

B-3-7: Fikret Erzinlioğlu (?)

B-3-8: Kemal Talay & friends

B-3-9: Hasan Atakan

B-3-10: Nurettin Yıldız & friend

C-1-1: Korean War Service (USA)

C-1-2: Korean War Service (United Nations)

C-1-3: US Presidential Unit Citation

C-1-4: Presidential Unit Citation (ROK)

C-1-5: National Defense (USA)

C-1-6: ROK Medal of Appreciation; Commemorations 2010-13

C-1-7: ROK Medal of Appreciation, reverse side

C-2-1: KW veteran's hat patch

C-2-2: Korean War Marine Veteran

C-2-3: Flag of DOD 50th Anniversary of the KW Commemoration Committee. The circular object is a 3-lobe Tæguk. The
Tæguk is a traditional symbol used (with two lobes) on the flag
of the Republic of South Korea (ROK). The KW50 Tæguk's red
and white striped lobe represents the United States; the dark blue
lobe represents South Korea; the light blue lobe with 22 gold
stars represents these UN countries involved in defending South
Korea: Australia, Belgium, Canada, Colombia, Denmark*, Ethiopia, France, Greece, India*, Italy* (UN membership – 1955),
Luxembourg, Netherlands, New Zealand, Norway*, Philippines,
South Africa, South Korea (UN membership-1991), Sweden*,
Thailand, Turkiye, United Kingdom, United States.

Note: An asterisk (*) indicates medical personnel only; no combat
forces were provided.

C-2-4: Logo of DOD 60TH Anniversary of the KWCC

309

C-3-1: L-R, WEA and George T. Coyle at KWVM, October 2011

C-3-2: Graveside commemoration ceremony for "Chesty" Puller at Christ Church in Saluda Virginia, October 2011. At far left, saluting – Col(ret) George Van Sant; near him is Rev. Paul Anderson, Rector. Color Guard is from Detachment 1062, Marine Corps League

C-3-3: October 2011, USMC Museum bookstore; WEA at left, signing book (TYFW, first edition). From right: John Broujos, Elden Koon, George Van Sant.

C-3-4: Reunion Coordinators with wives: seated, George & Arline Coyle; standing, WEA & Frieda. Quantico VA, 2011

C-3-5: USMC Museum. Left to Rt, Gene & Audrey Punte, Frieda & Bill Alli, 2010

C-3-6: Memorial Park, North Upper Crucible: Alli Family's Memorial Brick No. 2877

C-3-7: USMC Museum. Gene Punte at Chosin Exhibit, 2010

C-3-8: First 2/1 memoir author Burton F. Anderson. Palm Springs CA 2009.

C-3-9: 2/1 memoir author George Van Sant at Authors Forum. Palm Springs CA 2009

C-3-10: 2/1 memoir author WEA at Authors Forum. Palm Springs CA 2009

C-3-11: 2/1 memoir author Carl V. Lamb at Authors Forum. Palm Springs CA, 2009

C-4-1: Ankara. US & Turkish vets after wreath-laying at the Korean War Veterans Monument

C-4-2: Turkish veterans welcoming American vets in Ankara. Numbered left to right: Front row – (2) Gen. Dir. Alpuğan, (4) WEA, (5) James Hooper; Back row – (1) Joseph Pirrello, (5) John Delaney, 6) Carl Collier, (7) John Murray. At far right, behind automobile, close to far wall: Col. Martin Rollinson, US Military Attache in Ankara.

C-4-3: John Sinnicki & WEA with welcome bouqet

C-4-4: Military Academy Commandant Gen. Hulusi Akar presenting souvenir plaq to WEA. At right, M. Gültekin Alpuğan, Gen.-Dir.Turkish War Veterans Association. (30 October 2002)

C-4-5: Selimiye Barracks, Üsküdar. Gen. Çetin Doğan returning salute from KWVA members (L-R): Paul Kim, Yong Kouh and Hosurl Pak

C-4-6: Gen.Doğan presenting to WEA a ceramic souvenir of ATVA's visit to Selimiye; at left is Admiral Işık Biren

C-4-8: Selimiye. WEA & Lee Turcotte in the Florence Nightingale Clinic museum

C-4-9: Efesus, L-R, John Murray and Carl Collier with Turkish vets

C-4-10: Efesus. ATVA tour group in front of the Celsus Library

C-4-11: Gallipoli, L-R, John Sinnicki, John Delaney, Harry Clark saluting monument displaying Atatürk's "Golden Words. [see footnote on the next page in Appendix C-4]

C-5-1: 80th Birthday: Left to Rt. – Daughter Cindy, son Rob, wife Frieda, WEA, Daughter-in-law Patti, son John with atografer: Dan Lee.

C-5-2: 2004 Wedding: Left to Rt. – Daughter-in-law Patti with Danny, niece Nancie, son John with Luke, sister-in-law

311

Angie, bride Jennifer; groom/son, Rob, wife Frieda, WEA, daughter Mary, son-in-law Simon, daughter Cindy, son-in-law Gary, sister-in-law Vicky and husband Jim.

C-5-3: 2004 Wedding Guests: Sister Geraldine & husband Gerald Wooldridge

C-5-4: 1954: WEA, Baba, sister Geraldine (before her wedding), Mother

C-5-5: 1954: First Xmas of married life; WEA & Frieda

C-5-6: Mother,1953

C-5-7: Baba, 1950

C-5-8: WEA high school graduation, June 1950

C-5-9: WEA in ROTC at Cass Technical High School; third row, fourth from left

C-5-10: WEA & sister Geraldine Yvonne Alli, 1936

C-5-11: WEA with father and mother, 1934

APPENDIX A-1
The 17th Infantry Battalion USMCR
Copy of Orders to Extended Active Duty

HEADQUARTERS
SEVENTEENTH INFANTRY BATTALION
U.S. NAVAL AND MARINE CORPS RESERVE TRAINING CENTER
7600 E. JEFFERSON ST., DETROIT 14, MICHIGAN

1990/JMM-wjf

FIRST ENDORSEMENT on CMC Ser MC-1212649 of 4AUG50

From: Commanding Officer AUG 30 1950 *[hand-stamped date]*
TO: Private William E. ALLI 1118655/9900/USMCR, 1414 Pine,
       Detroit, Michigan

Subj: Orders to Extended Active Duty

1. Countersigned and delivered. This will constitute your
original orders.

2. Effective at 0800 on the above date you are hereby ordered
to report to the Commanding Officer, 17th Infantry Battalion,
U.S. Marine Corps Reserve(O) at the U.S. naval and Marine Corps
Reserve Training Center, 7600 E. Jefferson, Detroit 14, Michigan
for extended active duty for a period in excess of thirty
(30)days.

3. Upon reporting you will be examined physically to determine
your physical fitness for assignment to extended active duty.

4. There are no Government quarters or messing facilities
available for assignment at this station.

5. You will comply with the basic orders.

[signed]
JOHN M. MURPHY
By direction

- -

_____
(Date)

SECOND ENDORSEMENT

1. Received these orders at Headquarters, 17th Infantry Bat-
alion, USMCR(0), Detroit, Michigan, at _____ this date.
                                          (Time)

_____ USMCR
   (Name)   (Rank)

313

APPENDIX A-2
The 17th Infantry Battalion USMCR
Activated Duty Rosters

The Marines of the 17th Infantry Battalion reported for active duty on 31Aug1950 at the Brodhead Naval Armory, 7600 East Jefferson Avenue, Detroit Michigan. It was the site of the U.S. Naval and Marine Corps Reserve Training Center. The rosters for the personnel in the four Companies add up to:

Rank/Service	HQ	A	"B	"C	Total
Officers	9	6	6	4	25
USMC Enlisted	114	108	103	134	459
USN Enlisted *	10	–	–	–	10
Total	133	114	109	138	494

* Medical personnel.

Marines reported as dead 1/ are:

Ranks 2/	HQ	"A"	"B	"C"	Total
Officers	–	–	–	1	1
Marine Enlisted	4	3	–	3	10
Total	4	3	–	4	11

1/ "Dead" includes killed in action, died of wounds, captured and died, missing in action and presumed dead.

2/ No Naval personnel were reported dead.

My estimate of wounded is: 66. I derive it by using the *total* Korean War casualties of the Marine Corps. These are: dead and wounded (4,267 and 23,744), producing a ratio of 1 to 5.56, rounded to 6, hence 6x11=66. The full rosters are shown on the pages that follow, with (N) meaning no middle name.

314

(KIA Casualties in ***BOLD ITALICS***)

OFFICERS

Bradbeer, John D.	Capt.
Eade, George N., Jr.	Capt.
Flaten, Glen L.	CWO
Mullen, Donald (N)	1st.Lt.
Murphy, John M.	Major
Pierce, James H.	Capt.
Stapleton, James (N)	1st.Lt.
Wallace, William L.	1st.Lt.
Wilson, Walter A.	1st.Lt.

ENLISTED

Abaldo, Gino (N)	PFC.
Adair, Edward H.	PFC.
Baker, Girdley (N)	Pvt.
Bancroft, William F.	Cpl.
Barton, Ferman L.	PFC.
Bean, William H.	Sgt.
Bentley, Larry V.	Cpl.
Bergamo, Vircent M.	SSgt.
Bida, Joseph J.	Sgt.
Brady, Justin W.	SSgt.
Braidwood, Milton R.A.	TSgt.
Briggs, Merton E.	*PFC.*
Britt, Edwin (N)	Sgt.
Brown, Earnest E.	Pvt.
Bryant, Raoul J.	Pvt.
Buckley, William H.	*Cpl.*
Coleman, Ford L., Jr.	PFC.
Cornwell, Claude R.	Pvt.

Crisman, Richard L.	Pvt.
Crooks, Jack K.	Sgt.
Cromwell, John V.	PFC.
DeMeulenaere, Wayne A.	Pvt.
Diabo, James G.	PFC.
Dickson, David R.	SSgt.
Dudas, Leo J.	Sgt.
Dudek, Paul B.	Pvt.
Fallon, Chester	Cpl.
Fischer, Robert G.	Sgt.
Flanigan, William J.	MSgt.
Frank, Donald F.	Sgt.
Gawlas, Robert J.	Pvt.
George, Lawrence W.	PFC.
Gibbs, Burdette C.	Sgt.
Gillis, James W.	PFC.
Goszczynski, Ignatius C.	SSgt.
Hacker, Ora (N)	PFC.
Hale, Douglas L.	PFC.
Henry, Vaughan C.	PFC.
Herjo, Arthur J.	Sgt.
Hill, Rowland W.	Sgt.
Hill, William B.	Cpl.
Hindman, Lester E.	Cpl.
Hollifield, James M.	TSgt.
Hommel, Joseph C.	PFC.
Howard, William J.	Cpl.
Huffman, Edward M.	Sgt.

Hyba, Raymond T.	Sgt.	Orenstein, Hyman M.	MSgt.
Ireland, George S.	PFC.	Patterson, Allen J.	Sgt.
Jablonski, Donald J.	Cpl.	Pelto, Andrew B.	PFC.
Johnson, Jack W.	*Cpl.*	Poduska, Harold W.	Cpl.
Jones, James C., Jr.	TSgt.	Purgatori, Donald (N)	Cpl.
Jones, Joady (N)	PFC.	Quinn, Joseph J.	PFC.
Klingensmith, Dale L.	Cpl.	Robinson, Paul E.	Cpl.
Knasiak, Frank B.	Cpl.	Rocovich, Daniel M.	PFC.
Koeppen, Elliott F.	PFC.	Rodriguez, Charles J.	SSgt.
Kott, Donald A.	Sgt.	Sanders, Delmar A.	Cpl.
Kovach, Joe S.	Pvt.	Schrein, Melvin R.	SSgt.
Kosniewski, Edward A.	Cpl.	Sherry, John L.	PFC.
Kozlowski, Jerome C.	Cpl.	Shimanoff, Morris "B"	SSgt.
Kramer, Russell G., Jr.	PFC.	Skorupski, Gerald F.	PFC.
Kroepel, Richard J.	Sgt.	Slowiak, Leonard J.	Cpl.
Kumka, Russell L.	PFC.	Steele, Frank S.	PFC.
Lilla, Donald E.	PFC.	Strange, Robert E.	SSgt.
Lilla, Robert F.	PFC.	Style, Walter F.	Sgt.
Maccaroni, Alfio J.	Cpl.	Suarez, Vincent (N)	PFC.
MacDonald, Neil A., Jr.	Cpl.	Suigiar, Walter F.	PFC.
Maglocci, Pete A.	Sgt.	*Templeton, Douglas E.*	*PFC.*
Mattes, William R.	SSgt.	Tomlinson, William H.	SSgt.
Maula, Robert (N)	Cpl.	Toutant, Joseph H.	Cpl.
McGowan, Richard W.	Cpl.	Turner, Jack W.	Sgt.
McSloy, James H.	Cpl.	Updike, Robert A.	PFC.
Miller, Claude P.	SSgt.	Vandenberg, Wallace E.	Pvt.
Moir, Alec J.	Cpl.	Vavia, Edward (N)	PFC.
Mudge, Glen R.	Sgt.	Vavia, Peter S.	PFC.
Myers, Charles L.	Pvt.	Verardi, Robert (N)	PFC.
Myers, John W., Jr.	Pvt.	Warren, Oadies (N)	Sgt.
Myers, William C.	Cpl.	Welter, Woodrow L.	Cpl.

Weitlauf, Alpheous H.	Sgt.	Clapper, Mark I.	HN
White, Herbert L., Jr.	SSgt.	Dragus, Stephen (N)	HM1
		Molony, Donald P.	HM2
White, Robert M.	PFC.	Newell, Ralph J.	HM1
Williams, Howard S.	Cpl.	Pennell, John G.	HN
Zick, William (N)	Sgt.	Platt, Duane L.	HN
		Sharp, Joseph G.	HM1
		Weaver, Stanley M.	HM3
NAVAL (ENLISTED)		Wycoff, Herman G.	HMC
Baro, Marte J.	HM3		

317

"A" COMPANY 1SEP1950
(KIA Casualties in *BOLD ITALICS)*

OFFICERS

Beauparlant, John C. 1st.Lt.
Brackett, John J.   1st.Lt.
Clarke, Thomas W.   1st.Lt.
Kohler, Louis B   1st.Lt.
Koster, Edward A.   1st.Lt.
Tozer, Forrest L.   1st.Lt.

ENLISTED

Alcala, Alfred H.   Pvt.
Aldrich, Gerald E.   Pvt.
Alexander, Philip E.   Pvt.
Amo, Francis A.   PFC.
Armstrong, Donald L. Cpl.
Balmes, Donald C.   Cpl.
Barnes, Claude L.   Sgt.
Barnes, Howard J.   PFC.
Baro, Robert G.   Cpl.
Beaudrie, George A.   Cpl.
Bowles, Joseph E.   PFC.
Brodzinski, George T. Sgt.
Burgess, Edward B.   PFC.
Burns, Christopher J.   Pvt.
Carpenter, Bill L.   PFC.
Cavanaugh, James L. PFC.
Cervini, Adrian A.   PFC.
Cieplak, Mitchell J.   PFC.
Collins, Harold D.   PFC.

Coy, Charles R.   Cpl.
Crabbe, James E.   Pvt.
Crilly, Charles F.   Pvt.
Crossen, Lawrence J. Cpl.
Czeponis, Bernard F. Cpl.
Da Silva, Richard C.   Pvt.
Dawber, John L.   PFC.
Deanovich, Milan (N) Cpl.
De Pew, Thomas A.   PFC.
Ellis, Ronald A.   Pvt.
Emery, Robert D.   Pvt.
Ford, Charles P.   Pvt.
Garvin, Patrick H.   Pvt.
Georgia, Barry J.   Cpl.
German, Paul (N)   TSgt.
Godwin, Robert R.   PFC.
Gough, Joseph G.   Cpl.
Guilloz, Edward W.   PFC.
Hackney, Norman R.   Pvt.
Haines, Richard L.   SSgt.
Hanchin, John R.   Pvt.
Harris, Charles H.   Pvt.
Head, Robert (N)   Sgt.
Hegyan, John (N)   SSgt.
Hintzke, Herbert C.   Cpl.
Holsbeke, Robert J.   PFC.
Hylko, James J.   PFC.
Ignagni, Alex D. Jr.   Pvt.

318

Jankowski, Richard C. PFC.

Jenkins, Lawrence T.   Cpl.

Jensen, Louis L., Jr.   Cpl

Jentzen, Bernard W.   Pvt.

Kahanek, Frank F. Jr. PFC.

Kalanquin, Richard J.   Cpl.

Kane, Francis J.   SSgt.

Kane, Thomas P.   Sgt.

Kattleman, George H. PFC.

Kennedy, Jack M.   Sgt.

Klepetsanis, George (N)   Cpl.

Laura, Malcolm B.   Pvt.

Lauth, Richard R.   PFC.

Lins, Lawrence L.   PFC.

Maiorana, Frank (N)   Cpl.

Maniaci, Charles (N) PFC.

Matice, Warren R.   Cpl.

Maynard, Johnnie M.   Cpl.

Mc Arthur, Morris E. PFC.

Mc Queen, Robert P., Sr. Sgt.

Meyer, Henry J.   Cpl.

Michalak, Jerome J.   PFC.

Migala, Gabriel P.   PFC.

Migala, Jerome P.   Pvt.

Mitchell, Philip T.E.   Pvt.

Morris, Earl J.   Sgt.

Okerblom, Haldor E.   Pvt.

O'Neill, Thomas C.   PFC.

Peplinski, Benjamin (N)Cpl.

Petrak, Donn R.   PFC.

Pickman, George (N)   Sgt.

Polak, Walter (N)   SSgt.

Prior, Edward A.   Pvt.

Provonche, Duane G. PFC.

Pryor, Ronald A.   Pvt.

Ready, Wayne M.   TSgt.

Reilly, John E.   Pvt.

Richter, Calvin E.   PFC.

Robinson, Russell P., Jr. Cpl.

Rundel, Earl M.   Sgt.

Serra, Philip F.   PFC.

Sharpe, Terrill R.   Cpl.

Silversides, Frederick R. Cpl.

Smiley, Sheldon A., Jr. SSgt.

Smith, Frederick E.   Pvt.

Smouter, Donald R.   PFC.

Sobocinski, Thomas E. Pvt.

Styles, Harry S.   Cpl.

Tlalka, Arnold J.   PFC.

Tolson, Gerald L.   Pvt.

Tomlinson, Thomas L. Sgt.

Tredinnick, Douglas L.   Cpl.

Van De Putte, Frank G.   Pvt.

Westfall, Robert M.   Cpl.

White, Dwight L.   Cpl.

Whitehead, Benjamin T. PFC.

Wieda, John F.   PFC.

Wiencek, Joseph L., Jr. Sgt.

Wilcox, Warner L.   Cpl.

Woods, Robert B.   TSgt.

Zobrovitz, Morris R.   Pvt.

319

"B" COMPANY 1SEP1950

OFFICERS

Callens, George U.   1st.Lt.
Clapper, Owen E.   1st.Lt.
Cresswell, Hugh E.   1st.Lt.
Hoffman, Wilbert J., Jr.1st.Lt.
Schrader, Lavern R.   1st.Lt
Thompson, Melvin J.1st.Lt.

ENLISTED

Amlotte, William R.   Sgt.
Amlosch, Richard D.   Pvt.
Baleczak, Stanley W.   Cpl.
Bederka, Albert P.   Cpl.
Benson, Robert F.   PFC.
Berry, Chester D.   PFC.
Berryman, Elwood C.   Pvt.
Blaszkowski, Thomas R.   Pvt.
Boyd, Harold B.   Pvt.
Branch, Duane E.   PFC.
Branch, Keith J.   Cpl.
Brancheau, Richard J.   PFC.
Brown, Edward H.   Cpl.
Brown, James E.   Sgt.
Buckner, Lewis L.   Pvt.
Clapper, Paul A.   Cpl.
Cooley, Morris B.   Cpl.
Corey, James F.   Pvt.
Cortez, John G.   Cpl.
Cutler, Harold W.   Sgt.

Dale, Thaddeus J.   Cpl.
Daniels, Donald W.   SSgt.
Davis, Clark (N) Jr.   PFC.
Davis, Glenn C.   Sgt.
Decker, Edward A.   Cpl.
Domman, Robert P.   PFC.
Donnelly, Russell W.   Pvt.
Doyle, Dave E.   Pvt.
Drummond, John F.   Cpl.
Ederer, Richard C.   Sgt.
Farrar, Donald F.   PFC.
Finley, John A.   PFC.
Fisher, John W.   PFC.
Garcia, John A.   PFC.
Hajduk, Walter R.   PFC.
Halle, Robert A.   Pvt.
Hein, Robert R.   Cpl.
Hegerich, Alfred F.   PFC.
Henry, Thomas R.   PFC.
Henry, William J.   Sgt.
Hinsch, Carl D.   PFC.
Hodson, Thomas E.   Pvt.
Hopkins, Orren W.   Cpl.
Hravatic, Rudolph (N)   MSgt.
Hughes, Frederick W.   PFC.
Hughes, James A., Jr.   PFC.
Januszkowski, Edwin J.Pvt.
Jedlowski, Steven A.   PFC.
Jenette, Charles F. Jr.   SSgt.

320

Johnson, Franklin J.   Cpl.
Jones, Charles N., Jr.   PFC.
Jones, Robert W.   Sgt.
Juiel, Isaac M.   PFC.
Kaiser, Kenneth L.   PFC.
Kanclerz, Ronald H.   PFC.
Kish, William J.   Pvt.
Klecha, Stanley R.   Sgt.
Kolehmainen, Henry M.   Sgt.
Kolehmainen, Theodore A. PFC.
Korona, Walter L.   Cpl.
Lamontagne, Joseph E.   Cpl.
Laybourn, John P.   Cpl.
Lesinski, Clarence M.   PFC.
Little, William J., Jr. PFC.
Loyd, Donald R.   Pvt.
MacDonald, James A.   Sgt.
McAfee, Leonard B.   PFC.
McCombs, Donald F.   PFC.
Metivier, Bernard E.   Pvt.
Mitchell, Charles D.   Cpl.
Morrin, James L.   PFC.
Nieman, Gerald L.   PFC.
Norrix, Arron J.   Pvt.
Norton, Gernett B.   PFC.
Nygard, Gerald O.   PFC.
O'Connell, Cecil D.   Sgt.

Polaczyk, Frank E.   Cpl.
Preiskorn, Neil I.   Cpl.
Pugh, Billie F.   PFC.
Reid, Jack L.   Pvt.
Reilly, James J.   PFC.
Scott, Charles P.   Cpl.
Sharkey, David F.   Pvt.
Sharkey, John P.   PFC.
Sholund, Neil E.   Pvt.
Short, Robert J.   PFC.
Siana, Richard T.   SSgt.
Simmons, Perry S.   Sgt.
Smith, Frank C.   Cpl.
Spencer, William S.   PFC.
Stork, Stanley C.   Sgt.
Tejada, Raymond.J.   PFC.
Thomas, Henry L.   Cpl.
Tillman, Edwin A.   Sgt.
Tomaszczyk, Andrew P.   Sgt.
Turbin, Dennis D.   PFC.
Vincent, John E.   Pvt.
Warring, John B.   Sgt.
Willette, Gordon L.   Cpl.
Williamson, John W. Jr. Sgt.
Wilson, Robert G.   Pvt.
Wrobbel, Harvey G., Jr. PFC.
Yeager, Wayne W.   Pvt.

"C" COMPANY 1SEP1950
(KIA Casualties in *BOLD ITALICS)*

OFFICERS

Crockett, David M. 1st.Lt.

Esmann, William H. 1st.Lt.

Sidor, Joseph (N) Jr. 1st.Lt.

Thomson, Thomas L. 1st.Lt.

ENLISTED

Aguanno, Dante (N) PFC.

Alli, William E. Pvt.

Anderson, John C. Pvt.

Augustine, Gerald E. Cpl.

Baker, Lawrence B. Pvt.

Baumgartner, Gordon D. PFC.

Bednarz, Richard E. Cpl.

Bielski, Joseph B. PFC.

Bielski, Joseph J. PFC.

Boes, Thomas G. Pvt.

Bolchi, Marvin J. Pvt.

Brandt, Bruce G. Pvt.

Brennan, Joseph P. Pvt.

Brennan, Robert E. Cpl.

Brokenshire, Arthur M. PFC.

Brown, James E. Sgt.

Browne, Robert W. PFC.

Burns, George H. Pvt.

Camillo, Ronald W. PFC.

Chedister, Norman J. Cpl.

Chojnowski, Kenneth S. Pvt.

Cima, John A. Sgt.

Clark, Joseph P., Jr. Cpl.

Clark, Neale R. PFC.

Cornett, Leonard E. Pvt.

Cox, Eugene J. Pvt.

Crittenden, Sheldon T. Cpl.

Curle, Fred G. Pvt.

Daniels, Robert A. Pvt.

Dave, John S. PFC.

Day, Harold M. SSgt

Dietrick, Frank M. PFC.

Dinger, Fred C. PFC.

Dornan, John E. PFC.

Duval, Ronald R. PFC.

Feger, Laurence A. Cpl.

Fields, Thomas F. PFC.

Finn, William D. Pvt.

Gamble, Frank R. , Jr. Pvt.

Gartner, John J. Pvt.

Geldhof, Julius C. PFC.

Goodbred, Robert L. Cpl.

Grimble, James F. PFC.

Griswold, Ralph H. PFC.

Guindon, George J. Sgt.

Hale, Richard J.S. Cpl.

Hanna, Dean A. PFC.

Hays, Jacky E. PFC.

Heffernan, Harold J., Jr. PFC.

322

Hitchcock, Ted R. PFC.
Holmes, Roy J. Pvt.
Hutek, Fred A. Pvt.
Jackowski, Edward J. Cpl.
Janiski, Daniel B. Pvt.
Janisse, Andre D. PFC.
Jeavons, Bernard T. Cpl.
Johnson, Donald R. Cpl.
Jones, Robert W. Pvt.
Kalaput, Ronald T. Pvt.
Keenan, Peter F. PFC.
Keenan, Thomas J. Cpl.
Kelley, Frank E. PFC.
Kennedy, Manert H. Sgt.
Kregoski, Donald V. PFC.
Kuczynski, Leo C. PFC.
Kwiet, Edward E. Pvt.
Le Faive, Claude (N) Cpl.
Leonard, Thomas M. Pvt.
Lockwood, Kenneth R. PFC.
MacInnis, Lawrence E.L. Pvt.
Mallett, Robert A. PFC.
Manglos, Clarence K. PFC.
Marcus, Fred A. PFC.
Maxwell, James A. Pvt.
McGuire, James N. PFC.
McLeod, John A. Pvt.
McIntyre, Angus J. TSgt.
Middleditch, Murray "J" Jr. Sgt.
Miller, David F., Jr. Pvt.
Mitchell, George R. Cpl.

Moorcroft, James L. Pvt.
Morkowski, Richard J. Pvt.
Mumford, Frank L., Jr. Sgt.
Munger, Parker H. PFC.
Murphy, Thomas J. Pvt.
Nadeau, Robert S. SSgt.
Nielsen, Niele R. Cpl.
Pappert, Elmer J. TSgt.
Papuga, Arthur F. Pvt.
Pentacoff, Donald G. Pvt.
Piasecki, Robert T. Cpl.
Piesz, Joseph J., Jr. Cpl.
Poe, Robert L. Pvt.
Popa, Samuel G. Sgt.
Poulos, James N. PFC.
Pradragovich, John (N) Pvt.
Puskar, Robert W. Pvt.
Q'kon, Harvey J. Pvt.
Rapaski, Clarence C. PFC.
Rappold, Harold J. SSgt.
Rattray, Charles D. Pvt.
Reardon, John C. PFC.
Reid, Willis A. Sgt.
Rembacz, Bill C. PFC.
Rhodes, Robert J. Sgt.
Robertson, William C. Cpl.
Rodger, Bernard J. Pvt.
Rupp, Waldemar F. Cpl.
Saunders, Thomas J. SSgt.
Scheuer, Edward W. Cpl.
Seitz, Martin F. Pvt.

323

Shefpo, Leon M.	PFC.	Thomas, Anthony J.	Pvt.
Shimer, Paul F.	PFC.	Thomas, Jack W.	Pvt.
Sidor, Henry H.	Cpl.	Timlin, James E., Jr.	PFC.
Skerske, Donald (N)	SSgt.	Timlin, Joseph R.	PFC.
Sobodash, Robert P.	PFC.	Tombros, Aristides G.	PFC.
Stein, James S.	Pvt.	Tompkins, Thomas H.	Pvt.
Stephens, John L.	Pvt.	Topolski, Walter (N)	PFC.
Stevens, Earl R.	Cpl.	Trupiano, Anthony (N)	Sgt.
Stevens, Victor A.R.	PFC.	Williams, Robert E.	PFC.
Strom, Alvin L.	Pvt.	Zimmerla, Norman R.	PFC.
Sulesky, Walter J.	PFC.	Zuck, Norman F. (Pletz)	Pvt.
Terwilliger, Marion D.	Sgt.		

APPENDIX A-3, page 1
"C" Company Fotos at Pendleton, 6 September 1950

*Fig. A-3-1: Right side of wide-angle foto;
WEA is in third row, 8TH man from the right*

Fig. A-3-2: Middle section of wide-angle foto

"C" Company Fotos at Pendleton, 6 September 1950

Fig. A-3-3: Left side of wide-angle foto

Boot Camp Graduation Foto

Fig. B-1-1: WEA next-to-top row, 6TH from the left. In top row: 2ND from left, Bob Roeszler; 5TH from left, Gaylen Searles; 5TH from right, Ted Bergren. Bottom row: 4TH from right, Earl Barnes. The three Drill Instructors are in the center of the 2ND row from the bottom.

Fig. B-2-1: Members of the machine-gun unit in a jovial mood. Top row (left to right): Larry Moore (?), Randy Lohr, Don Newell, WEA, Henry Thompson, Dick Whitten, Gene Punte. Bottom row (left to right): Felix Mancha, Myles Jackman, Vic Knabel

Fig. B-2-2: L-R, back row – Les, W. J. Novak, front row – "Frib", WEA, Mancha

APPENDIX B-3, page 1
APPENDIX B-3, page 1
Members of the Turkish Brigade

Capt. Sayılan was born in Bursa in 1920, during the Greek occupation. He graduated from the Turkish Military Academy in 1941. He was a captain and volunteered to serve in Korea, serving in reconnaissance and intelligence until being wounded in 1951. He was evacuated to Japan for treatment and after recovery returned to front-line service in Korea.

Fig. B-3-1: Yüzbaşı (Captain) Nazım Dündar Sayılan

After discharge he worked in several government and private jobs and was a researcher, a book author, a playwright and a poet. In his support for President Atatürk's principles of modernization and

Fig. B-3-2: Three Lieutenants; Süleyman Yakın is in middle

world peace, he was industrious and unflinching – a true patriot.

Members of the Turkish Brigade

Fig. B-3-3: Ergün Kırtaş

Fig. B-3-4: Orhan Fırat in the
Midland Sea, before Korea

Fig. B-3-5:: Unidentified, In camp
before leaving for Korea

Fig. B-3-6: Hilmi
Korugan

Members of the Turkish Brigade

Fig. B-3-7: At right,
Fikret Erzinlioğlu (?)

Fig. B-3-8: Kemal Talay &
friends

Fig. B-3-9: Hasan Atakan

Fig. B-3-10: Nurettin Yıldız
and friend

APPENDIX B-4
Chronicle - Regimental Memo 40-51

Headquarters, First Marines,
First Marine Division, Fleet Marine Force,
c/o Fleet Post Office, San Francisco, California
14 June 1951

REGIMENTAL MEMO:
: Operations of this regiment since June
1
NUMBER   40-51:

1. The regimental commander wishes to express to all hands of the regiment and to attached and supporting elements, his boundless admiration and heartfelt congratulations for their conduct of the operations of the past two weeks.

2. The missions you have been called upon to accomplish during that period have been very difficult. Added to the rugged terrain has been a dogged and fanatic resistance from a competent, resourceful and heavily-armed enemy estimated to have been, at the very least, three regiments in strength. You have attacked him in his prepared positions in very rugged terrain and you have never been stopped. Even considerable losses have not turned you from your objectives, nor shaken your morale. And the losses you have inflicted on the enemy have been tremendous. You have counted many hundreds of dead in the various positions taken in spite of the enemy propensity for burying his own dead, so that is most probably only a small part of his casualties. His wounded will probably die, ours won't.

3. In accomplishing this you have demonstrated professional skill of the highest order. You have used ground and cover with consummate skill, as I have personally observed; you have used your organic supporting arms very intelligently; you have used your attached supporting arms, including air, tanks and artillery, to their maximum potential; you have used patience, common sense, and good judgment in regulating the speed of your advances; and, when time was of the essence, you have used sheer guts and determination to close with the enemy and destroy or rout him with grenades, bayonets,

332

clubbed rifles and even with bare hands on at least one occasion.

4. I have never in my life been so proud as I am to be permitted to command this regiment. I have been here less than a month to date, so can take no credit for your professional ability. That was taught to you and learned by you through bitter experience long ago. I have served in infantry with the 5th Marines as an enlisted man in the First World War, and as a junior officer in the Nicaraguan Campaign. I have supported a lot of infantry regiments while I was an artilleryman before and during the Second World War. It is my carefully considered opinion that this is the best regiment of infantry that I have ever seen. I'm glad to be allowed to join your club.

5. A lot of comrades, officers and men, have died or been injured in this "police action". I fear that more, very probably, will be before it is over. But you are making traditions of valor and professional skill that will rank alongside of, or outrank, the achievements of Marines in the First World War, the Second World War and all our minor campaigns. And I urge you all to believe, whether or not you are or have been, religiously in-clined, that in this struggle for decency among men, we are fighting on the side of the Lord. The Communists who oppose us are fighting to deny his existence.

6. There are those, of course, who hardly can be called friends of the Marine Corps. The well-earned fame of our Division has been such a byword at home and abroad that some people would like nothing better than to see us drop the ball just once. As long as you carry on the way you have done the past nine months, particu-larly the last two weeks, they never will.

7. This memorandum is written to tell you how one old Marine, who isn't about to fade away as long as he can serve with men like you, feels about you young Marines.

8. I think you are grand. Thank you for all your most gallant and effective work.

[*signed*]
W. S. Brown
Colonel, U. S. Marine Corps
Commanding

333

Subject: Historical Diary for June 1951, Excerpt, KWP USMC-04300102

9 June 1951

Enemy Probing Attack on FOX positions at 0530. Attack repulsed after brief firefight. At 0730 received short 4.2 inch mortar barrage which caused approximately 40 casualties. Lt. Col. MCCLELLAND, Battalion Commander, wounded and evacuated. Major MAYBURY in command.

Battalion jumped off at 0830. FOX moved along ridge toward Hill 399 TA 1426 (sheet 6828) followed by EASY. DOG to move up right flank when ordered. OY reported scattered enemy on ridgeline to the front at 1100. FOX heavily engaged with the enemy to the front at 1130. DOG ordered up right flank at that time and engaged with the enemy at 1215. Hill 399 secured at 1645.

Heavily engaged with the enemy on Hill 339 until 1715. Enemy resistance was determined and heavy. Mortars especially were used to good advantage.

Consolidated front line positions at 1730, TA 1426 UVWXY, 1526 PQ. CP established TA 1425 C-4. Continue to receive sporadic enemy mortar fire throughout the night. DOG Company repelled an enemy probing attack of approximately 20 enemy at 0030.

Received six (6) Officers and fifty-six (56) Marines as replacements.

Casualties suffered: KIA   6; WIA 81

Enemy casualties: Counted killed 5, Est Add casualties 25, POWs 2

10 June 1951

Battalion jumped off at 0800. DOG to move down ridge to Hill 339 then across road and a prominent nose to objective BAKER, hill 676, TA 1427. EASY to follow until arriving at the lateral road, at which point it would move up nose to left of DOG. FOX to remain in reserve at Hill 399. One platoon of ABLE Company tanks to support attack from road on the left.

DOG engaged enemy on forward slopes of Hill 676 at 1030. DOG received heavy artillery and mortar fire at 1045. EASY Company commenced moving up the left slope of 676 at 1155. Heavily engaged with the enemy at 1230. The enemy defending this Hill in Battalion strength. Both companies received continuous mortar barrage.

The enemy were well entrenched in heavily covered log bunkers emplaced part way down the slopes. When the companies approached within 35 yards of the enemy positions, they were fired upon from the front and flank noses, several of which ran up to the Hill. The enemy used large quantities of grenades and satchel charges and expended extreme quantities of MG ammunition, all the while pouring in mortar fire.

Air had been requested the previous night to be on station during the day, and the request renewed at 1030. Air support was not received until 1930.

The tanks supported the advance of EASY but cannot be placed so as to destroy the bunkers to the right. Practically continuous artillery and mortar fire was called on the bunkers, the crest of the hill and the reverse slope position; but the nature of these positions was such that effective artillery was minimized. The most effective supporting arm would have been air, for some inexplicable reason this was not received until late.

The 75 mm RG very effectively supported the advance of DOG until 1515, at which time its ammunition was expended. Resupply was impossible because of the long distance and difficult terrain.

EASY attained the left portion of the objective and 1730, but a deep saddle held up its advance along the ridge line. FOX was committed at 1730 in order to pass through DOG and continue to advance up the nose to the right. FOX was heavily engaged with the enemy at 1845. An airstrike, utilizing napalm, was finally called on the peak at 2000 and effectively broke the back of the resistance. EASY crossed the saddle at 2030. The hill was secured at 2220, at which time the front lines were consolidated.

FOX repulsed an enemy counterattack at 2345. The assault described above proved to be the most difficult made by this battalion since the landing at Inchon.

Numerous enemy officers, including the battalion commander, were killed on the crest of the hill. POW interrogation indicated that the battalion was ordered to remain at all costs, which it did. Resistance was brutally determined and the defending forces were so skillfully employed that escape of personnel would have been impossible, even if desired. This necessitated remaining in position until the end.

Without air support it was necessary to have hand-to-hand fighting all the way up the slopes which were exceedingly steep and rocky, being cliff-like immediately below the crest. The hill is taken only because of the determination of the Marine carrying the rifle.

USMC Casualties suffered: KIA 9; WIA 201.

Enemy casualties: Counted killed 97; Estimated Additional casualties 310; POW's 8. Ordnance destroyed: 22 burp guns, 5 Russian rifles,

10 M-1 Rifles, Many grenades, satchel charges, and assorted ammunition.

Subject: Historical Diary for September 1951, Excerpt, KWP AND USMC-04300154, SUMMARY

At the opening of this period, the battalion, with other elements of the 1st Marines was in X Corps reserve bivouacked in the HONGCHON area, in KOREA. The battalion, having been alerted for possible employment on short notice, continued its training of replacement personnel on a day-to-day basis until 11 September when it moved by motor to a forward assembly area in the vicinity DT 3140.

On 12 September the battalion moved out by foot with the mission of relieving elements of the 1st Battalion, 7th Marines and elements of the 2nd Battalion, 7th Marines and proceeding into the attack phase. The relief of elements of 1/7 in the vicinity of Hill 673 (DT 298442) was effected during the night of 12 September with no incident other than heavy enemy "H" and "I" fire on the approaches to Hill 673. Due to the late hour [that] such relief was effected, the battalion was directed to tie-in with elements of 2/7 for the remainder of the night and to effect relief and passage of lines of 2/7 on 13 September.

On 13 September, inasmuch as all elements of 2/7 were not in physical contact, it was directed that the battalion move forward maintaining physical contact with Co "F" 2/7, made contact with other elements of 2/7 reported to be on the high ground vicinity DT 298462.

Co "F" was moving north toward Hill 749 (DT 297456) and became heavily engaged with enemy forces and the battalion was ordered to pass through Co "F", continue the attack to destroy what appeared to be a small pocket of enemy resistance on Hill 749, and effect the relief of remaining elements of 2/7, reported to be on the high ground vicinity DT 298462.

The situation presented the following problem - that of strong enemy resistance on key terrain separating known positions of elements of 2/1 and reported positions of elements of 2/7, with forward movement of elements of 2/1 being denied the full use of supporting arms in view of the reported close proximity of elements of the two friendly battalions.

Elements of the battalion effected relief and passage of lines of Co "F" and proceeded into the attack. This attack was resisted fiercely by a well-emplaced and supported enemy. The enemy employed such tactics as taking cover in his prepared bunkers and calling down his own mortars on attacking elements when they came within range of hand-to-hand combat.

After two attempts an extremely heavy casualties, Co "E" secured Hill 749 (DT 297456) and Co "D" was passed through with the mission of attacking North along the ridge line from Hill 749 to effect a linkup with friendly elements of 2/7, still reported to be in the vicinity of DT 298462. The progress of Co "D" was slow and costly, however [it] continued until late in the afternoon when elements of 2/7 made contact with the left rear of Co "D".

It was now apparent that in fact no elements of 2/7 were on the high ground in the vicinity of DT 298462, but had occupied ground in the vicinity of DT 295455, approximately 400 yards to the Southwest of the crest of Hill 749. With the situation, as it now presented itself, clear, Co "D" was ordered to hold and immediately steps were taken to effect defense for the night. Elements of 2/7 were subsequently relieved of responsibility in the sector and moved to the rear.

On 14 September, Co "F" was passed through Co "D" in the continuation of the attack with the mission of securing that part of Division objective "BAKER", DT 297462 to DT 304463. This attack was stopped approximately 200 yards short of the left flank of the objective by extremely heavy small arms and automatic weapons crossfire supported by accurately placed mortar and artillery fire taking advantage of the intricate and deceptive configuration of rugged mountainous terrain. A defensive perimeter was then established holding the ground gained for the night.

On 15 September, the attack was resumed late in the afternoon after extreme efforts were made to neutralize the enemy resistance by artillery and air, although air was in no sense adequate in numbers. This attack was again stopped and the battalion withdrew to its positions held the previous night.

During the night of 15-16 September, the battalion was counterattacked by the 91st NK regiment. The attack lasted for a period of 3 hours and 55 minutes and was repulsed with great loss to the enemy. At no time during the counterattack was the integrity of the battalion's perimeter defense endangered. Although the enemy attempted to encircle the left flank of the defense, his efforts were thwarted by the time that the shifting of the 4.2 inch mortar barrage was allotted [to] the battalion.

On 16 September, elements of 1/1 executed a relief and passage of lines of 2/1 and continued the attack securing the objective. The battalion now had the mission of providing security for an extended man-pack supply route to elements of 1/1 until 1640, 19 September, when it reverted to Division Reserve and withdrew to an assembly area vicinity DT 3040.

Throughout the operation, the evacuation of the high number of casualties was expeditiously accomplished by the tireless and coordinated efforts of VMO-6 and HMR-161. Helicopters of HMR-161 proved exceedingly useful in the delivery of critically needed ammunition of all types and medical supplies, and the evacuation of wounded on the return trips.

From 19 September to the end of the current reporting period, the battalion remained in Division Reserve. This latter period was highlighted by the practice lift of a reinforced company and the forward command group of the battalion by units of HMR-161 both in a day and a night lift. "Copter" assignment teams, prepared and based on tactical considerations were in the same manner as boat assignment teams which proved to be the key to expeditious embarkation and disembarkation with minimum time and without loss of control. Throughout the period, the morale and fighting spirit of the battalion, even in the face of very heavy casualties, proved to be excellent.

Summary Statistics are:

Item	13Sep	14Sep	15Sep	16Sep
US Forces				
-KIA	4	17	-	10
-WIA	224	109	70	50
NKPA				
-POW	-	6	2	2
-Counted KIA	15	66	25	187
-Estimated KIA	20	70	40	300
-Estimated WIA	40	90	100	90
NK Asset Losses				
.60 cal AT gun	-	1	-	1
Pistols	-	3	-	5
Russian HMGs	-	2	-	2
Russian LMGs	-	2	-	5
Russian rifles	-	24	-	42
"Burp" guns	-	14	-	11
82 mm mortar [1]	-	1	-	1
Grenades	-	numerous	-	800
Bullets [2]	-	numerous	-	numerous

Footnote: [1] From air strike. [2] Loose rounds, small arms.

339

APPENDIX B-5
Chronicle - Col. Nihart's Recollections of Hill 749

This paper is from Col. Nihart's original notes and has been slightly edited with a few insertions [in brackets] and minor punctuation changes to facilitate both print and speech presentations. This is *eyewitness* testimony (2007Apr01, rev. 2012Apr25) and must be considered by any person who reads James Brady's book, *"THE SCARIEST PLACE IN THE WORLD: A Marine Returns to North Korea."* **Brady's book fails to acknowledge the central role of the 2nd Bn/1st Marines in the capture of Hill 749.**

A fuller account of the battle is in the official USMC publication: *"U.S. Marine Operations in Korea 1950-53, Vol. IV, The East-Central Front."* pages 190-94. *W.E.A.*

Prepared Remarks to Be Delivered at Korean War 50th Anniversary, 2002Nov04, US Marine Corps Base, Camp Lejeune, North Carolina, by Colonel Brooke Nihart, U.S. Marine Corps (Retired)

1951: Main Events thru Summer. The history of the second year of the war is the forgotten year. The year saw allied forces drive North to regain ground lost to the Chinese offensives of early 1951. Peace talks at Panmunjom dragged on through the summer. An offensive on the East front was mounted to drive into a mountainous area of Korea, north of the 38th parallel. The 1st Marine Division attacked from the Hwachon Reservoir to the mountainous Kansas Line from June to August and then into X Corps reserve.

Taking Command of 2/1. It was in August that I, as a member of the second team, arrived for the second year of the war. Assuming command of [the] 2d Battalion, 1st Marines I enjoyed the welcome opportunity of several weeks of small unit training, battalion exercises, and getting to know the outfit. That respite and renewal of the battalion paid off in the coming fight.

Moving toward the Attack. The division moved out in early September with the 5th and 7th Marines in the attack, leaving the 1st for a few more days in reserve. The 5th and 7th took high ground on the east rim of the Punch Bowl and Yoke Ridge. And then to Hills 673-749 [on the] south-north ridge line of Kanmubong Ridge.

The plan for the 1st Marines was to pass through the 7th on the 12 September and for 3/1 to take Hill 854 on the east of the Soyang Gang river and Kanmubong Ridge.

My battalion, 2/1, after passing through Marines on Hill 673 and on Hill 749, was to take Hill 812 to the west on Kanmubong Ridge.

Hill 749 was to be our line of departure for further attack to Hill 812. [However], we had been misinformed: Hill 749 had not been taken by another unit as claimed.

As we approached the crest of 749 to pass through supposedly friendly lines, our lead elements were hit with a storm of fire. Moreover, Hill 749 was not a North Korean outpost line, as we had been informed by intelligence, but their main line of resistance, heavily bunkered with permanent log-covered machine-gun emplacements, deep trenches, and well-organized defensive fires.

So much for the background. I must speak of the human factor.

The Leadership and Bravery of My Marines. Company commander Bill Rockey and lead platoon leader Jack Freese, instead of being pinned down, immediately attacked from their approach march formation. Units to the rear, without hesitation, delivered covering overhead fire.

That is leadership, initiative and tactical savvy – typical of Marines. This level of leadership was exhibited throughout the operation.

There was ample bravery:

-- On this first day, Corporal Ed Gomez was posthumously awarded a Medal of Honor for his heroism. His two machine guns

341

had to be sited close together because of the narrow ridge. A grenade landed between them. Gomez fell on the grenade, thereby saving his guns, which enabled them to continue to support the attack;

-- Sergeant Matthew Dukes received a Navy Cross that day for his bravery as did Marine Jim Southall;

-- Marines George Baker, Charles Dunne, Dick Matheney, and Tom Marter all got Silver Stars on September 14th.

On the 15th we had to attack a slightly lower crest about 300 yards beyond the main crest of 749. Again there was need for heroes and they stepped forward.

Lieutenant Birney Adams received a Silver Star for his leadership, followed by Marines Al Barnes, Leroy Corbett, Oscar England, Dick Mason, Tom Riccardi, and Max Stein.

Heroism wasn't confined to the infantry. That night we had a serious casualty. He would not have survived the long trip down the hill on a stretcher followed by a rough jeep ride to the field hospital.

We called on VMO-6 -Marine Observation Squadron Six - attached to the 1st Division. VMO-6 flew advanced Piper Cub type fixed wing observation aircraft and two-man Bell helicopters. You will remember these helicopters from the M.A.S.H. TV show.

[Also] We called VMO-6 for a helicopter casualty evacuation. It would be difficult and dangerous. The pilot would fly at night, up a valley, then up a draw, to a sloping area where my cooks had cut down trees and leveled off a spot where helicopters could land. This mission would be the first one into this spot.

Major Dave McFarland, skipper of VMO-6 called for volunteers. EVERY PILOT in his squadron volunteered. Dave told me later, "What could I do; this mission was mine." He skillfully got to us, guided by my cooks [with their] flashlights, loaded the badly wounded Marine, and got him to a field hospital. The Marine survived. I recommended McFarland for a Silver Star which he got.

With Hill 749 in our hands, we had breached the North Korean main line of resistance. It was a hill they wanted back badly. We knew they could counterattack that night. I went forward and personally sited machine guns and riflemen's foxholes.

A full September moon rose late – an ominous pale yellow moon. Yellow, not as a harvest moon, but from the dust in the air from days of battle. By midnight it was high enough in the sky to cast some light on the ridge.

Then they came. First, a heavy bombardment by artillery and mortars, then flares and bugles. By first light they gave up the attack leaving several hundred dead scattered in front of our position.

My Marines hadn't given up a yard of their defense; our position held through heroic efforts of all. As casualties were suffered, they were quickly replaced by Marines moving up the ridge from the rear and manning their positions.

Three Marines especially stood out that night:

-- Corporal Joe Vittori (from Beverly Massachusetts), with his Browning Automatic Rifle, roamed from hot spot to hot spot – protecting the machine guns from close in grenade attack and manning guns when the gunners fell. He finally fell himself from multiple wounds. His Medal of Honor was posthumous;

-- Marine Lyle Conaway armed with an M1 rifle and Thompson Sub-Machine Gun accompanied Vittori, adding to his fire and protecting him as he reloaded. Conaway received a Navy Cross.

-- Another Navy Cross went to Corporal Bill Blasongame who led a section of two heavy water-cooled Browning Machine-Guns and kept them in action all night long as backbone of our defense.

All did their part those days; I must mention:

-- the staunch support of my Exec., Major Jack Lannigan, and my operations officer, Major Carl Walker;

343

-- my supply officer, Lieutenant George Stavridis, [who] kept the ammunition, C-rations, and water coming up the mountain on the backs of 400 Korean Service Corps (KSC) bearers;

-- Sergeant Richardson, in charge of one company's Korean bearers, who insisted on wearing a field hat – instead of a helmet – and carried a heavier load than any Korean, thus motivating them (as they would lose oriental face if they could not keep up);

-- my mess sergeant and cooks with nothing to cook and never having worked with helicopters before carved out a landing spot on the hillside and operated a landing zone;

-- Marine Helicopter Squadron HMR-161 pilots and crews [who], on their first mission in Korea, delivered essential water and ammunition (when the Korean bearers couldn't keep up with [our] expenditure) and evacuated our numerous casualties;

-- our doctors and hospital corpsmen [who], with their hands more than full, performed magnificently;

-- our communicators, who nursed fading radios and kept repairing wire lines frequently cut by enemy fire;

-- our artillery and mortar observers, who shared the same dangers as the riflemen and kept the defensive [support] fire coming.

It was a typical Marine team in violent action. I salute their courage and their memory.

Later that day (the 16th), 1/1 passed through and continued the attack to the next hill on Kanmubong Ridge.

Aftermath

The offensive was called off by Eighth Army commander, General Van Fleet. The peace talks at Panmunjom were seemingly making progress. However, they lingered on for another year and a half. Meanwhile, the fighting continued across the front with raids and attacks on outpost positions.

The division, in March 1952, moved by truck and helicopter to the west front – astride the road to Panmunjom and protecting Seoul, the Capital. But that is another story.

Fig. C-1-1: Korean War
Service (United States)

Fig. C-1-2: Korean War
Service (United Nations)

Fig, C-1-3: US Presidential
Unit Citation

Fig. C-1-4: ROK Presidential
Unit Citation

Fig. C-1-5: US
National Defense
Medal

*Fig. C-1-6: ROK Medal of
Appreciation; Commem-
orations 2010-13*

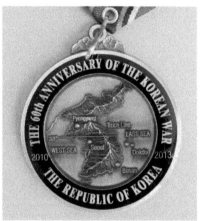

*Fig. C-1-7: ROK Medal of Appreciation,
reverse side*

KW veteran's hat patch

*Fig. C-2-2: Korean War
Marine Veteran*

*Fig. C-2-4: Logo of DOD 60TH
Anniversary of the KWCC*

*Fig. C-2-3: Flag of DOD 50th
Anniversary of the KWCC*

APPENDIX C-3, page 1
2/1 Korea Marines Organization

Fig.C-3-1: L-r, WEA and George T. Coyle at KWVM,

Fig. C-3-2: Graveside commemoration ceremony for "Chesty" Puller at Christ Church in Saluda Virginia, October 2011. At far left, saluting – Col(ret) George Van Sant; near him is Rev. Paul Anderson, Rector. Color Guard is from Detachment 1062, Marine Corps League

Fig. C-3-3: October 2011, USMC Museum bookstore; WEA at left, signing book (TYFW, first edition). From right: John Broujos, Elden Koon, George Van Sant.

Fig. C-3-4: Quantico VA, 2011: George & Arline Coyle; standing, WEA & Frieda.

Fig. C-3-5: USMC Museum. Left to Rt, Gene & Audrey
Punte, Frieda & Bill Alli, 2010

Fi.C-3-6: Memorial Park: Alli Family's
Memorial Brick No. 2877

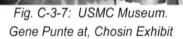

Fig. C-3-7: USMC Museum.
Gene Punte at, Chosin Exhibit

Fig. C-4-9: 2/1 memoir author George Van Sant at Authors Forum. Palm Springs CA 2009

Fig. C-4-8: First 2/1 memoir author Burton F. Anderson. Palm Springs CA 2009

Fig. C-4-11: 2/1 memoir author Carl V. Lamb at Authors Forum. Palm Springs CA 2009

Fig. C-4-10: 2/1 memoir author WEA at Authors Forum. Palm Springs CA 2009

ATVA 2002 Friendship Tour of Turkiye

*Fig. C-4-1: Ankara. US & Turkish vets after
wreath-laying at the
Korean War Veterans Monument*

*Fig. C-4-2: Turkish veterans welcoming American
vets in Ankara*

Fig.C-4-3: John Sinnicki & WEA with welcome bouqet

Fig. C-4-4: Academy Commandant Gen. Hulusi Akar presenting plaq to WEA. At rt., M. Gültekin Alpuğan, Gen.-Dir. Turkish War Vets Assn. (30 October 2002)

Fig. C-4-5: Selimiye Barracks, Üsküdar. Gen. Çetin Doğan returning salute from KWVA members (L-R): Paul Kim, Yong Kouh and Hosurl Pak

Fig. C-4-6: Gen.Doğan presenting to WEA a ceramic souvenir of ATVA's visit to Selimiye; at left is Admiral Işık Biren

Fig. C-4-8: Selimiye: WEA & Lee Turcotte in the Florence Nightingale Clinic museum

Fig. C-4-9: Efesus, L-R, John Murray and Carl Collier with Turkish vets

Fig. C-4-10: Efesus. ATVA tour group in front of the Celsus Library

*Fig. C-4-11: Gallipoli, L-R, John Sinnicki, John Delaney, Harry Clark
saluting monument displaying Atatürk's "Golden Words"*

Footnote for *Fig. C-4-11, Ataturk's "Golden Words"*

April 25, 1934: The first official memorial ceremony was conducted at Gelibolu (Gallipoli) for families who lost their sons in the Allies' invasion of the peninsula. Most of the attendees came from Australia, Great Britain, and New Zealand.

The visitors received an official message from the former Commander of the Osmanli forces who had fought against their sons. He, Atatürk, was now the President of Turkiye. He wrote:

To the Fallen Allied Soldiers:

THOSE HEROES THAT SHED THEIR BLOOD
AND LOST THEIR LIVES
YOU ARE NOW LYING IN THE SOIL
OF A FRIENDLY COUNTRY.
THEREFORE, REST IN PEACE.
THERE IS NO DIFFERENCE BETWEEN
THE JOHNNYS AND THE MEHMETS TO US,
WHERE THEY LIE SIDE-BY-SIDE,
HERE IN THIS COUNTRY OF OURS.

To the Mothers of the Fallen:

YOU THE MOTHERS WHO SENT THEIR SONS
FROM FARAWAY COUNTRIES,
WIPE AWAY YOUR TEARS.
YOUR SONS ARE NOW LYING IN OUR BOSOM,
AND ARE IN PEACE.
HAVING LOST THEIR LIVES ON THIS LAND,
THEY HAVE BECOME OUR SONS AS WELL.

The Bounty of Long Life & the Blessing of Family

Fig. C-5-1: 80th Birthday: Left to Rt. – Daughter Cindy, son Rob, wife Frieda, WEA, Daughter-in-law Patti, son John with grandsons Luke & Daniel; not shown, daughter Mary.

Fig. C-5-2: 2004 Wedding at Coronado: Left to Rt. – Daughter-in-law Patti with Danny, niece Nancie, son John with Luke, sister-in-law Angie, bride Jennifer; groom/son, Rob, wife Frieda, WEA, daughter Mary, son-in-law Simon, daughter Cindy, son-in-law Gary, sister-in-law Vicky and husband Jim.

Fig. C-5-3: 2004 Wedding Guests: Sister Geraldine & husband Gerald Wooldridge

Fig. C-5-4: 1954: WEA, Baba, sister Geraldine (before her wedding), Mother

Fig. C-5-5: 1954: First Xmas of married life;
WEA & Frieda

Fig. C-5-6: Mother,1953

Fig. C-5-7: Baba, 1950

Fig. C-5-8: WEA high school graduation, June 1950

Fig. C-5-9: WEA in ROTC at Cass Technical High School; third
row, fourth from left

Fig. C-5-10: WEA & sister Geraldine
Yvonne Alli, 1936

Fig. C-5-11: WEA with father and mother, 1934

APPENDIX D -1
Korean War Casualties of United Nations Forces, 1950 - 53

Country	Killed	Wounded	MIA	POW	Total
South Korea	137,899	450,742	24,495	8,343	621,479
United States	36,940	92,134	3,737	4,439	137,250
United Kingdom	1,078	2,674	179	977	4,908
Turkiye	741	2,068	163	244	3,216
Australia	339	1,216	43	26	1,624
Canada	312	1,212	1	32	1,557
France	262	1,008	7	12	1,289
Thailand	129	1,139	5	-	1,273
Netherlands	120	645	-	-	765
Greece	192	543	-	12	747
Ethiopia	121	536	-	-	657
Colombia	163	448	-	28	639
Belgium	99	336	4	1	440
Philippines	112	229	16	41	398
New Zealand	23	79	1	-	103
South Africa	34	-	-	9	43
Luxembourg	2	13	-	-	15
Norway	3	-	-	-	3
TOTAL	178,569	555,022	28,651	14,164	776,406

APPENDIX D–2, Korean War Casualties:
Major U.S. Combat Units, 1950 - 53

Unit	KIA	WIA
2nd Infantry Division	7,094	16,575
First Marine Division	4,004	25,864
7th Infantry Division	3,905	10,858
1st Cavalry Division	3,811	12,086
24th Infantry Division	3,735	7,395
25th Infantry Division	3,048	10,186
3rd Infantry Division	2,160	7,939
Fifth Air Force	1,200	368
Fifth Regimental Combat Team	867	3,188
45th Infantry Division	834	3,170
Seventh Fleet	458	1,576
187th Airborne Regimental Combat Team	442	1,656
40th Infantry Division	376	1,457
1st Marine Aircraft Wing	258	174
Total		
	32,192	102,492

Notes: Of the Americans killed by hostile action in Korea, 96% were in the units listed above. The 29th RCT was attached to the 24th ID and later assigned to the 27th and 35th Inf. Regiments of the 25th ID. It lost 313 men KIA on July 25 – 26, 1950 alone. Figures are included above.   In addition to the units listed, 1,432 Army personnel assigned to units independent of the Divisions and RCT's were also KIA.

Source: Battle Casualties of the Army, 30 September 1954 (Office of the Assistant Chief of Staff, G-1, Dept. of the Army) and other sources.

APPENDIX D-3
Marines and the POW Code of Conduct

After the war some American POWs were accused of having collaborated with their Communist captors. On May 18, 1955 the Secretary of the Department of Defense established an Advisory Committee on Prisoners of War to review the issues and determine a code of conduct for U.S. prisoners of war.

The Committee found that Marine Corps POWs performed far better than Army POWs. This was attributed to Marine Corps discipline, training and higher morale. Among our allies, Turkish POWs were found to have performed best.

One of the military officers on the committee's support staff was F. Brooke Nihart, who was commanding officer of the Second Battalion First Marines during the September 1951 combat at the Punchbowl in North Korea. He writes:

By the summer of 1955, American prisoners of war in Korea had been returned by the Chinese and North Koreans. Debriefing of POWs revealed that many, even a few Marines, succumbed to the cruelty and brainwashing techniques of their captors. What to do to avoid such conduct in the future?

I was a young officer serving in HQMC at this time when I was summoned to report to the Commandant. Apprehensively, I stood before Gen Lemuel C. Shepherd in his second-floor corner office in the Navy Annex, which overlooked the Pentagon. Shepherd told me that the Secretary of Defense had convened an advisory committee on prisoners of war in an endeavor to study the failure of some

366

of our POWs to resist their captors and to seek a solution to avoid such occurrences in the future. Retired general and flag officers were to constitute the committee, and Marine MajGen Merritt A. "Mike" Edson would represent the Marine Corps. "You," he said, "will represent the Corps on the committee staff."

The Commandant then issued his brief guidance. He explained that Air Force and Navy aviation wanted to protect their pilots by allowing them to tell their captors anything they wanted to hear to avoid mistreatment. We Marines, he emphasized, couldn't allow such laxness. We were to stick by the Geneva Convention and give the enemy only name, rank, and serial number, period. "Your job and General Edson's to see that we hold the line," he said. With an "Aye aye, sir" I departed for the Pentagon, and an interesting summer.

The committee heard the testimony of former prisoners from World War II and Korea and the views of senior military officers, religious leaders, educators, psychologists, heads of veterans' organizations, lawyers, and politicians. Deliberations of the committee members followed with staff members sitting in. The task of drafting a report with the recommended POW code of conduct fell to me. I conceived of the code as a catechism in the first person: "I am, I will," etc. A draft was submitted and then returned with further instructions. A second draft was accepted and turned over to professional wordsmiths for fine-tuning.

APPENDIX D-4, The POW Code of Conduct

Article I   I am an American, fighting in the forces which guard my country and our way of life. I am prepared to give my life in their defense.

Article II   I will never surrender of my own free will. If in command, I will never surrender the members of my command while they still have the means to resist.

Article III   If I am captured I will continue to resist by all means available. I will make every effort to escape and to aid others to escape. I will accept neither parole nor special favors from the enemy.

Article IV   If I become a prisoner of war, I will keep faith with my fellow prisoners. I will give no information or take part in any action which might be harmful to my comrades. If I am senior, I will take command. If not, I will obey the lawful orders of those appointed over me and will back them up in every way.

Article V   When questioned, should I become a prisoner of war, I am required to give name, rank, service number, and date of birth. I will evade answering further questions to the utmost of my ability. I will make no oral or written statements disloyal to my country and its allies or harmful to their cause.

Article VI   I will never forget that I am an American, fighting for free-dom, responsible for my actions, and dedicated to the principles which made my country free. I will trust in my God and in the United States of America.

NOTE: See *Bibliografy* for citations.

ACKNOWLEDGMENTS (First Edition)

I am grateful to all the people who assisted my journey of memory and its publication. My fellow Marines and I contributed to the tapestry of the narrative – all of us provided the threads; I then did the weaving. I appreciate their recounting stories of war and peace, despite the risks of opening up old wounds. Whether I used their names in the text or not, they contributed to my endeavors and I feel a deep gratitude and brotherly affection toward them.

From my 2nd Battalion, 1st Marines, they are: Burt Anderson, Galen Anderson, Ernie Brydon, George Coyle, Bob Davis, John Gearhart, Bob Hortie, Manert Kennedy, Vic Knabel, Steve Lacki, Paul Lamanteer, Randy Lohr, George McGarity, Dick Payne, Gene Punte, Bob Rhodes, Jack Underwood, and George Van Zant.

My thanks go to other Marines who provided suggestions, gave me materials or otherwise helped me in researching and networking. They include: Adrian Cervini, John Cummings, Stan Marangi, Phil Smith, and Tommy Tompkins.

At the United States Marine Corps' History Division in Quantico Virginia, Annette Amerman thoughtfully and positively introduced me to their archives and guided me along my researches. I thank her, and her fellow workers, for the valuable materials they supplied to me.

I thank the Nihart family, Mary Helen and Cathy, the widow and daughter of our valiant 2/1 Commander on Hill 749, LtCol Nihart. They generously gave me copies of some of his notes plus fotos of Hongch'ŏn and Hill 749.

Sonya Lee and Paul Dukyong Park of the Korean Section at the Library of Congress took extra steps to provide useful information and help me avoid feeling lost in dealing with Korean materials. They have my sincere gratitude. *Kamsahamnida* (thank you).

I finally got the North Star Brigade's shoulder patch, as a digital image, thru the efforts of Brigadier General Taner Düvenci of the Turkish Army. *Minnetarım* (I am grateful).

My family deserves recognition for their support over the past two years. My wife, Frieda, showed great forbearance toward my commitment of time to writing the memoir. She also provided many suggestions that clarified and enriched my narrative.

Our beloved offspring were solidly supportive of my undertaking and I marvel at my good fortune in having such a family. My eldest daughter, Cynthia, helped propel me into the project by urging me not to wait. That advice was based on her experience as a physician at the Veterans Hospital in Sacramento where she knows about the urgency of time for elderly war veterans.

My eldest son and his wife, John and Patti, inspired me with a Christmas gift, structured according to times and topics, and providing space for handwriting descriptions of my life, something like a diary. That book was ideal for stimulating memories and evaluations of my past – good materials for a memoir. A truly thoughtful gift.

With his permission, I used John's iconic photograph of the Korean War Veterans Memorial as part of the front cover of this book. Like the Memorial, his foto and my book are also intended to remind people of the Korean War.

My son Robert provided a sympathetic ear whenever I wanted to discuss my Korean War era Marine experiences in comparison with his Marine experiences. Like his brother John, he served both in peacetime and the Persian Gulf War.

My sister, Geri Wooldridge, helped fill in gaps in my recollections about times in Detroit. Also, she faithfully preserved, for forty years, a gold mine of information: my mother's collection of my letters from Korea. Her husband, Gerald, conscientiously read my drafts and gave me valuable suggestions for improvement.

I appreciate the staff at Xlibris for assisting me in getting the first edition of my book into print. Much credit goes to Jill Marie Duero, for her conscientious and assiduous editing of the text.

ACKNOWLEDGMENTS (Second Edition)

This edition benefits from my access to the unit diaries of the 2nd Battalion 1st Marines, which were not open to me in 2007, when I started writing the first edition of my memoir. I am grateful to Richard Payne of our 2nd Battalion 1st Marines Korean War veterans organization, who sent me the full collection by email in 2011.

The diaries covered the entire war and were fascinating. Based on my new knowledge I was able to make corrections and add some useful information, especially about the battle for Hill 676.

I have been heartened by the reaction to the first edition by my fellow Marines as well as Korean War veterans of the other armed services. Fellow Americans in general have shown me their appreciation for my honest presentation of the war and its aftermath.

In addition to those mentioned above, other 2/1 Marines who have been helpful are George Coyle, Carl Lamb, and Charles Lundeen. Army veterans include Carl Collier and Ernest Sohns. Two Air Force veterans deserve special mention: USAF Maj (Ret) Daniel G. Lee, a valuable advisor for my many forays into word processing and other aspects of computer technology. He served in Vietnam during that war. Dr. John H. O'Hara, was a B-47 crewmember during the Cold War; his thoughtful publicity initiatives have helped promote my book from early on.

JoanAnne Dubbs applied her valuable computer graphics skills to improve my photo gallery as well as enable me to format my manuscript with a minimum of travail. Her approach was not only to "supply me with fish, but also to teach me how to fish." Bill Curtis's intensive efforts, applying abundant computer knowledge, helpt salvage my manuscript at a crucial time. The Dubbs & Curtis team was a Godsend.

Dr. Cynthia Rosemary Alli also provided me with additional information about PTSD and other issues related to Korean War veterans. I am grateful to her because she helped me expand my understanding of the syndrome, disorder, or mental injury and inspired me to work on recognizing and overcoming whatever vestiges might be lurking in my subconscious. Other family members have been reservoirs of positive encouragement. During the book-writing process my daughter Mary, tho physically distant, was a consideration in my seeking to fully understand PTSD and other experiences which may have affected my personal relationships with family members.

From my late friend, Frank Ahmed, I learned more about the lives of the Ottoman Turkish immigrants, including details about their journeying to America. His book deserves to be updated and expanded.

I have learned much from Professor Justin McCarthy's prodigious output of scholarly studies on the history of the Ottoman Empire. His efforts are opening up great opportunities for repudiating distortions of history that underlie long-standing ethnic hatreds which, to this day, continue to poison the minds of so many people.

The Turkish-American community has shown me their respect and gratitude for my service. They embody these sentiments when they call me *Kore Gazisi*, meaning a veteran of the Korean War. Sevin Elekdağ of the Turkish Coalition of America has encouraged me to explore possibilities for using my book to promote good relations between the people of America and the Republic of Turkiye. Zafer Yakın gave me some useful photos of his father and other soldiers of the Turkish brigade.

In all my visits with veterans of the Turkish Brigade, as well as with both retired and active duty personnel of the Turkish Armed Forces, I have found hospitality beyond measure for me and other American veterans. They are precious *silahdaşlar* (comrades-in-arms). They include: Gen. Hulusi Akar (Turkish Army), Adm. Işık Biren (Turkish Navy), Gen. Çetin Doğan (Turkish Army), Adm. Özer Karabulut (Turkish Navy), Gen. Gürbüz Kaya (Turkish Army), Col. İbrahim Keskin (Turkish Army), and Gen. Orhan Uğurluoğlu (Turkish Air Force).

If I have overlooked anybody, then I apologize. My capacity for appreciation of the support I have gotten exceeds my capacity for name recollection. Mine is the responsibility for any errors or oversights. *WEA*

BIBLIOGRAFY

Notes:
1. Footnotes in the text refer to items below by the CAPITALIZED initials shown in brackets [...] f.ex., [WEA]. Any Arabic numbers in brackets, following the initials, designate pages.

2. Five veterans of the 2nd Battalion / 1st Marines have written memoirs of the Korean War. Except for mine (the first edition of *Too Young for a Forgettable War*), the authors are: Burton F. Anderson [BFA], Carl V. Lamb [CVL], John Schneider [JS], Clyde H. Queen, Sr. [CHQ], and George M. VanSant [GVS]. One 2/1 vet, Edward Franklin, has written a novel: *It's Cold in Pongo-Ni.*

Ahmed, Frank. *TURKS IN AMERICA, The Ottoman Turk's Immigrant Experience.* Washington DC: Columbia International, 1986. [FA]

Alli, William (E.) "Americans Join Turks in Wreath-Laying," *The Graybeards,* Official Publication of the Korean War Veterans Assn. Vol. 17, No. 1; January-February 2003. [WEA]

Anderson, Burton F. *WE CLAIM THE TITLE, Korean War Marines.* Aptos CA: Tracy Publishing, 2000 (Second Edition). ISBN: 0-9643110-1-1. [BFA]

Biderman, Albert. *MARCH TO CALUMNY.* New York: The Macmillan Company, 1963. [AB]

Blair, Clay. *THE FORGOTTEN WAR, America in Korea 1950-53.* New York NY: Doubleday, 1989. ISBN: 0-385-26033-4. [CB]

Brands, H. W. *TRAITOR TO HIS CLASS: The Privileged Life and Radical Presidency of Franklin Delano Roosevelt.* New York NY: Doubleday, 2008. ISBN 978-0-385-51958-8. [HWB]

Brown, Wilburt S. *Operations of this regiment since June 1.* Regimental Memo No. 40-51, 14 June 1951. Headquarters, First Marines, First Marine Division, Fleet Marine Force, c/o Fleet Post Office, San Francisco, California. [WSB]

Callaghan, Marty; Executive Producer. *THE ARMENIAN REVOLT, 1894 to 1920.* Documentary DVD by Third Coast Films; P.O. Box 664, Clarion PA 16214; ©2006. [MC]

Charette, Melissa M. & Lanham, Stephanie Laite. *VETERANS AND FAMILIES' GUIDE TO RECOVERING FROM PTSD.* Purple Heart Service Foundation. Annandale VA, 2004. [C&L]

Chenoweth, H. Avery with Brooke Nihart. *SEMPER FI : The Definitive Illustrated History of the U.S. Marine Corps.* New York, NY: Main Street, 2005. ISBN: 1402730993. LC Call No.: VE23 .C46 2005. [C&N]

Code of Conduct for Members of the Armed Forces of the United States. Executive Order [EO] 10631, Aug. 17, 1955; 20 FR 6057, 3 CFR, 1954-1958 Comp., p. 266. EO 11382, Nov. 28, 1967, 32 FR 16247, 3 CFR 1966-1970 Comp., p. 691. EO 12017, Nov. 3, 1977, 42 FR 57941, 3 CFR, 1977 Comp., p. 152. EO 12633, Mar. 28, 1988, 53 FR 10355, 3 CFR, 1988 Comp., p. 561.

Dabney, William H. "The Next Stop is Saigon," *Marine Corps Gazette*, June 1998. [WHD]

Dawson, A. K. "The Turkish Brigade," *Military History Magazine*, December 1997. [AKD]

Dictionary of American Naval Fighting Ships / edited by James L. Mooney. Naval Historical Center, Department of the Navy, Washington DC. 1970. [DANFS]

Dora, Celal. *KORE SAVAŞINDA TÜRKLER, 1950 – 1951,* [THE TURKS IN THE KOREAN WAR]. İstanbul: İsmail Akgün Matbaası, 1963. [CD]

Ehlioğlu, Zeki. *YEMEN'DE TÜRKLER, Tarihimizin İbret Levhası,* [THE TURKS IN YEMEN, A Warning Sign in Our History]. İstanbul: Kitabevi, 2001. [ZE]

Giusti, Ernest H. *MOBILIZATION OF THE MARINE CORPS RESERVE IN THE KOREAN CONFLICT, 1950-1951.* Marine

374

Corps Historical Reference Pamphlet. Headquarters, U.S. Marine Corps. Washington DC, 1951; reprinted 1967. [EHG]

Grassman, Deborah L. *PEACE AT LAST, Stories of Hope and Healing for Veterans and their Families.* St Petersburg FL: Vandamere Press, 2009. ISBN: 978-0-918339-72-0. [DLG]

Halberstam, David. *THE COLDEST WINTER, America and the Korean War.* New York NY: Hyperion, 2007. ISBN: 978-1-4013-0052-4. [DH]

Hughes, Charles. *ACCORDION WAR: KOREA 1951, Life and Death in a Marine Rifle Company.* CreateSpace [Amazon], 2006. ISBN: 978-1452827605. [CH]

Jackson, Helen Hunt. *A CENTURY OF DISHONOR, The Classic Expose of the Plight of the Native Americans.* Mineola NY: Dover Publications, 2003. ISBN: 048642698X (pbk.) [HHJ]

Johnstone, Major John H., USMC. *A BRIEF HISTORY OF THE FIRST MARINES.* Headquarters, U.S. Marine Corps: Washington DC: Historical Branch, G-3 Division, 1962 (revised 1968). [JHJ]

Kinkead, Eugene. *IN EVERY WAR BUT ONE.* New York: W.W. Norton & Company, 1959. [EK]

Krepps, Vincent A., *ONE CAME HOME.* Heritage Special Edition, American Literary Press, 200t. ISBN: 978-156167-988-1. [VAK]

Lamb, Carl V. *THE LAST PARADE, A True American War Story.* Teays WV: M. Anderson Publishing, 1999. ISBN 0-9673335-0-4. [CVL]

Lech, Raymond. *BROKEN SOLDIERS.* Urbana and Chicago: University of Illinois Press, 2000. [RL]

Lecky, William P. *DESIGNING FOR REMEMBRANCE: An Archetectural Memoir.* LDS Publishing: 2012. ISBN 978-1-4675-2748-4. [WPL]

Lewy, Guenter. *THE ARMENIAN MASSACRES IN OTTOMAN*

TURKEY, A Disputed Genocide. Salt Lake City UT: Univ. of
Utah Press, 2005. ISBN 13: 978-0-87480-849-0 ISBN 10: 0-
87480-849-9. [GL]

Mango, Andrew. ATATÜRK, The Biography of the Founder of
Modern Turkey. Woodstock NY: The Overlook Press, 1999.
ISBN 1-58567-334-X. [AM]

McCarthy, Justin. DEATH AND EXILE, The Ethnic Cleansing of
Ottoman Muslims, 1821 to 1922. Princeton NJ: The Darwin
Press Inc., 1995. ISBN 0-87850-094-4. [JMd&e]

McCarthy, Justin. THE OTTOMAN TURKS, An Introductory History
to 1923. New York NY: Addison, Wesley Longman Inc., 1997.
ISBN 0-582-25656-9. [JMot]

McCarthy, Justin. THE TURK IN AMERICA, The Creation of an
Enduring Prejudice. Salt Lake City UT: University of Utah
Press, 2005. ISBN 978-1-60781-013-1. [JMtia]

McCarthy, Justin [& Esat Arslan, Cemalettin Taşkıran, Ömer Turan].
THE ARMENIAN REBELLION AT VAN. Salt Lake City UT:
Univ. of Utah Press, 2006. ISBN 9780874808704. [JMvan]

McCloskey, Paul N. "Pete," Jr. THE TAKING OF HILL 610.
Woodside CA: Eaglet Books, 1992. [PNM]

Nalbandian, Louise. THE ARMENIAN REVOLUTIONARY
MOVEMENT, The Development of Armenian Political Parties
through the Nineteenth Century. Berkeley and Los Angeles:
Univ. of California Press, 1967. [LN]

Nihart, F. Brooke. Prepared Remarks to Be Delivered at Korean
War 50th Anniversary. November 4, 2002. U.S. Marine Corps
Base, Camp Lejeune NC. [FBN]

Öke, Mim Kemal. A CHRONOLOGY OF THE "FORGOTTEN
WAR," Korea, 1950-53. İstanbul: Atölye Burak Matbaacılık,
1991. [MKÖ]

Queen, Clyde H. Sr., THE ROADS I TRAVELLED, WERE NOT ALL
PAVED, [Philadelphia PA], ©Xlibris Corp., 2009. ISBN: 1-
4415-8034-4; ISBN13: 978-4415-8034-4. [CHQ]

Ridgway, Matthew B. *THE KOREAN WAR.* Garden City NY: Doubleday, 1967. L.C. Catalog No.: 67-11172. [MBR]

Satcher, David &others. *MENTAL HEALTH: A Report from the Surgeon General.* Rockville MD: Dept. of Health and Human Services, U.S. Public Health Service. 1999. L.C. Call No. RA790.6 .M385 [DS&]

Sayılan, Nazım Dündar. *KORE HARBİNDE TÜRKLERLE,* [WITH THE TURKS IN THE KOREAN WAR]. Ankara: Milli Eğitim Bakanlığı Yayınları (2935); Bilim & Kültür Eserleri (848), 2003. ISBN 975.11.0987.6. [NDS]

Schneider, John. *PURPLE HEARTS–BATTLE SCARS, Memories from the Forgotten War.* Charleston SC: Book Surge Publishing, 2008. ISBN 13:9781419689727. [JS]

Settle, Mary Lee. *TURKISH REFLECTIONS, A Biography of a Place.* New York NY: Touchstone, 1991. ISBN: 0-671-77997-4. [MLS]

Shaw, Stanford J. & Ezel Kural. *HISTORY OF THE OTTOMAN EMPIRE AND MODERN TURKEY.* Vol II. Binghamton NY: Cambridge University Press, 1978. ISBN 0-521-214491. [S&K]

Simmons, Edwin Howard. *DOG COMPANY SIX.* Annapolis MD: Naval Institute Press, 2000. ISBN: 1-55750-898-4. [EHS]

Solzhenitsyn, Aleksandr I. *THE GULAG ARCHIPELAGO, 1918-1956.* Boulder CO: Westview Press, 1998. ISBN: 0-8133-3289-3. [AIS]

U.S. Marine Operations in Korea, 1950-1953. Vol. IV, "The East-Central Front." Headquarters, U.S. Marine Corps. Washington DC: Government Printing Office, 1962. L.C. Catalog No.: 55-60727. [USMOK]

U.S. Marines in the Korean War / edited by Charles R. Smith. Washington DC: History Div., USMC, 2007. LC Classification: DS919 .U56 2007 ISBN: 9780160795596-0160795591. [USMKW]

ERRORS : In Chapter 6, near the top of page 420 (second column), lines 7 thru 9 erroneously state: "In January 1951, Jack Davis and his comrades of the 6th Replacement Draft boarded the Army transport *Randolph* for the trip to Korea."

Actually the Sixth Replacement Draft boarded the USNS *Randall* in February 1951, *not* "the Army transport *Randolph*" in "January 1951".

The error is repeated on p. 438, in the first sentence of the two-column-formatted article "Private First Class Jack Davis: Combat Marine". It states that, ". . . the Marines of the 6th Replacement Draft joined the 1st Marine Division in late January 1951."

The Marines of the 6th Replacement Draft joined the 1st Marine Division in early March 1951, *not* "late January 1951." Burton F. Anderson and I (William Edward Alli) were in the 6th Replacement Draft and have described it in our books. See Anderson (listed above), pp. 14, 72, and 412; see my book, Chapter 11. Altho both of our books use 5 March as the date for our arrival in Pusan, the 2nd Battalion 1st Marines unit diary shows that 2 Officers and 5 Marines arrived as replacements on 3 March 1951!

The above errors in Chapter 6 are also contradicted by information in Chapter 5 page 360, near the bottom of column number one. It states: "That much-longed-for transportation arrived when the troopship USS *General J.C. Breckenridge* (AP 176) delivered 71

378

officers and 1,717 enlisted men of the *5th* (emphasis added) Replacement Draft to Pohang on 16 February." Obviously the 6th Replacement Draft would have had to arrive *after* the 5th Replacement Draft's arrival on 16 February.

U.S. Prisoners of War in the Korean War: Their Treatment and Handling by the North Korean Army and the Chinese Communist forces / compiled and edited by Arden A. Rowley. Paducah KY: Turner Pub. Co., ©2002. ISBN: 1563118319. [USP]

Van Sant, George. *TAKING ON THE BURDEN OF HISTORY, Presuming to be a United States Marine.* Philadelphia PA: Xlibris, 2008. ISBN: 978-1-4363-2925-5. [GVS]

Varhola, Michael J. *FIRE AND ICE, The Korean War.* Mason City IA: Savas Publishing Co., 2000. ISBN: 1-882810-4-9 [MJV]

Witty, Robert M. and Neil Morgan. *MARINES OF THE MARGARITA, The story of Camp Pendleton and the Leathernecks who train on a famous California Rancho.* San Diego CA: Frye & Smith, 1970. [RMW]

Zinn, Howard. *A PEOPLE'S HISTORY OF THE UNITED STATES, 1492-present.* New York NY: Perennial (HarperCollins publishers Inc.), 2001. ISBN: 0-06-052837-0. [HZ]

INDEX

A

Abney (boxer Marine) 65-66, 76
aboriginal people 268
Advanced Infantry Training 60-61, 68
Afghanistan 274, 299
Afilani, Angelo 243
A-frame 219
African-American 177, 259, 268
Ahmed, Frank 372
air mattress 145-46, 186
Akar, Gen. Hulusi 354, 373
alcohol 59-60, 120, 169, 193, 232, 240, 252-53, 261, 283
Ali, Ahmet (Uncle) 37
Alli, Cynthia Rosemary 370-72
Alli, Daniel 359
Alli, Frieda 262, 286, 310-12, 359, 370
Alli, Geraldine (Geri) Yvonne 34, 63, 76, 126, 256, 312, 359-60, 363, 370
Alli, John 36, 254, 285-88, 295-96, 359, 370
Alli, Luke 359
Alli, Patti 254, 359, 371
Alli, Robert (Rob) 36, 370
Alli, Sam 74-75
Almond, Gen Edward (Ned) 92-95, 99
American & Turkish Veterans Assn. 294-97
ammo carrier 99, 111, 121-22, 129, 144, 155, 164, 166-67, 171, 196, 198, 206, 220, 291
Anadolu 35, 37, 74, 81, 179, 183, 186, 295, 298
Anadoluan 74, 183
Anderson, Burton F. 121, 171, 198, 369
Anderson, Galen P. 67, 369
anemia 252
Ankara 184, 187, 289, 293-95, 224, 228, App. C-4

Ari San 218, 221, 224, 228
Arirang 273
Armenian 73-75, 81
Armenian Revolutionary Federation 81
Armenian Revolutionary Party 81
armory 31-33, 37, 257
artillery 29, 38, 93, 98, 124, 127-28, 141-42, 150, 154, 158-59, 161, 185, 192, 194, 196, 200, 203-204, 206-207, 209, 216, 234-35, 243, 332-33, 335, 338, 343-44
Atatürk, Mustafa Kemal 75, 222, 311, 358
Augie 240, 257-258
Aunt Rose 34, 38, 63, 256, 258
Australia 82, 268, 358
Azeri 179

B

B-29: 158
Baba 60, 74-76, 81, 240, 245, 256, 258
Bachert, Charlie 254
Balmas (family) 73, 253
Baptist 62, 122
barber 45, 193
Barkley, Alben 49
Barr, Wilhelm 275
Battalion Aid Station 121
beef 46, 135, 238
beer 139, 170, 260
Beijing 30, 146
Bekir Çavuş 35, 63
Belgium 309
belt 117, 132, 145, 150-51, 159, 175-76, 182, 196-97, 232
Benskin, George Jr. 200-201
Bergren, Ted 45, 327
Big Dipper 57
Biren, Işık 311, 355, 372
bizner 169-70
bless 44-45, 130, 222

381

Curtis, William 371

D

Dad 34-35, 37, 41, 59, 61, 63, 74-76, 82, 118, 173, 175, 193, 256, 258
dagger 59, 188
Daunie, Frank 236-37
Davenport, Jack 213
Davis, Robert (Bob) 87, 96, 102, 126, 149, 204, 301, 369
DD Form-214: 254
deadly three 238
Defense, Department of 39, 181, 251, 259, 263, 280, 293, 296, 348 , 366
deist 281
Dekmelerik, Jim 278
Denmark 267, 309
Depression 32, 145, 245-46, 301
Detroit 31-33, 35, 37-38, 48, 52-53, 56, 60-61, 63, 66, 73-74, 100, 165, 187, 219, 240, 245, 247, Ch. 34, 271, 314, 370
Detroit Times 138, 173
Diamond Mountain 225-26
diarrhea 52, 83, 100, 107, 120-21, 147
dingleberry 79, 100
divorce 35, 37, 258-59, 275, 282
Doğan, Gen Çetin 355, 372
Dong, Lt. 219, 221-22, 225-28, 231
Donne, John 194
Drill Instructor 44, 55, 220, 308
Dubbs, JoanAnne 371
Düvenci, Gen Taner 369

E

Easter 122, 256
Eastern Sea 96, 104, 226, 241, 306
Edwards, Drew 109
Eighth Army 345
Elâzığ 173-74, 246
Elekdağ, Sevin 372

England 85, 194
English 10-13, 35, 66, 74-75, 165, 173-74, 176, 178-180, 183, 189, 219, 221-23, 232, 248, 259, 294, 296
Enver Pasha 63
Ethiopia/Ethiopian 177, 268, 309

F

Farquhar (Sgt) 233
Father 34-37, 42, 59-60, 73-76, 80-81, 173, 179, 183, 245-46, 256, 258-59, 281, 312
fire brigade 39
fire team 68
First Marine Aircraft Wing 127, 249
First Provisional Marine Brigade 40
Ford, Charlie 171
forest 143, 225
Forward Air Controller 29
Forward Artillery Observer 29
Four Deuces 125
four-holer 147-48, 186
foxhole 22, 24, 27-28, 114, 120, 124, 128, 131, 139, 145, 147, 161, 192, 195, 199, 208, 210, 216, 306, 343
France 68, 268, 309
fury 85, 115, 195, 198, 205-206, 269

G

galley 46-48, 52, 84
garlic 183-84, 216
Gearhart, John 200, 214, 217, 369
geisha 88-89, 119, 246-47
German 35, 53, 62-63, 132, 164
Germany 246, 269, 280
GI Bill 262, 269, 275, 277, 279-80, 283
God 11, 31, 35, 41, 44, 55, 57, 73, 84, 107, 129-30, 148, 155, 159, 189, 193, 216, 222, 236, 256, 270, 277, 279, 297, 303, 368
Gomez, Edward 208, 213, 341-42

382

384

mortar 67, 87, 124-25, 155, 161, 198-202, 204, 206-207, 210, 243, 260, 279, 334-35, 337-39, 343-44
Mother 34-35, 41-42, 48, 61-62, 66, 68, 78, 138, 164, 173, 181, 225, 232, 240, 245, 247-48, 254, 256-261
Mother Nature 191
music 38, 131, 169-70, 186-87, 226, 250, 272, 284
musicians 138, 171, 187, 234
Muslim 59, 62, 74-75
Myers 246
Myung Ha 231

N

National Mall 285, 296
Navy 11, 64, 91, 99, 104, 249, 252, 291, 366-367
Navy Cross 78, 96, 208, 342, 343
Nazi 31, 45
Neninsky, Ben 236-37
New Deal 301
New Jersey 65-66, 242, 254
Newell, Don 165, 328
Nihart, Col Franklin Brooke 195, 197, 201, 206-209, 211, 214, 220, 340, 366, 369, 376
Nizibian (family) 73-75, 253
Niziblian 74
North Atlantic Treaty Organization 181, 184, 268
North Korean People's Army 39, 85, 87, 108, 115, 141, 150, 201, 206-209, 212-13, 242
North Star 57, 187-88, 369
Norway 268, 309

O

O In Tæ 219, 221, 227, 231-32
Oberg, Augustine (Chief) 113
ocean 25, 45, 80, 84-85, 88, 105, 254
Ode 298

O'Hara, John 371
Ojibwa (Osage) 113
Okinawa 269
Operation Chromite 86-87
Operation Killer 4, 109, 115, 278, 282
Operation Mixmaster 94-95
Operation Rathunt 108
Operation Ripper 4, 115, 149, 278, 282
Oral, Adil 295
Osaka 88, 119

P

P'yongyang 167
P38 Walther pistol 132, 260
P-51 Mustang 203
Pacific 32, 65, 68, 73, 93, 248, 251, 253-54
Packard Motor Car Co. 262
Paine, Thomas 281, 303
Payne, Richard 369, 371
People's Liberation Army 91
pistol 51, 76-77, 97, 109, 132-33, 165, 175-77, 180, 182, 187, 196-97, 210, 260, 282, 339
pogey bait 55
Pohang Guerrilla Hunt 4, 108, 278, 282
porter 38, 110, 133, 198, 215, 219, 221, 224, 228, 235-36
Post-Traumatic Stress Disorder 272, 274, 277-78, 280, 282-83, 371-72
pounding 128, 195, 204, 207
POW 98, 109-10, 149, 151, 292, 294-95, 336, App. D-3 & D-4
Powers, Lt Pierce 213
prawns 58
Presidential Unit Citation 39, 87, 103, 186, 251, 296-97, 346
Providence 60, 74-75
Pukhan River 127-29
Puller, Gen Lewis (Chesty) 78, 96, 101, 104, 266
Punchbowl 4, 40, 124, 191-93, 214,

386

Stevenson, Robert Louis 251
Sweden 268, 309
swimming 37, 49, 54, 162-63, 253

T

Tæbæk Coastal Range 25
Tæguk 20, 309
Taliban 299
Tashnaks (see Armenian Revolu-
tionary Federation)
Tazzia, Henry 62, 240, 260
Tchaikovsky 284
Tennessee 34-35, 62, 66
Tent Camp 65, 67, 70, 76-77
Tetracol 216, 253
Tex/Texas 59, 135-36, 175-77, 180,
182, 236, 279
Thailand 268, 309
Thirty-eighth Parallel 64, 80, 108,
125, 130, 191, 231, 266, 291,
340
Thiwman, Lester 129
Thompson, Henry 165, 202, 204,
213, 328
Thompson submachine guns 150
Tokarev (pistol) 197
Toraji 226
Trabzon 60
train 33-34, 38-40, 88, 90-91, 104,
106-108, 110, 119, 146, 251,
283
Treasure Island 251
tree 41, 131, 136, 143, 145, 196,
203, 210, 220, 285, 342
Truman, Pres. Harry 125, 138, 167,
186, 246, 263, 269
Tsushima Strait 90
Turkish Army 187, 245, 369, 372
Turkish Brigade 173-76, 180, 183,
185-86 244, 289, 294, 296,
App. B-3, 373
Turkish soldiers 181, 183, 186, 244,
259, 294, 296, 298
Turks 30, 59-61, 73-75, 81, 173-76,
179-80, 182, 184-86, 189-90,
245, 272, 289, 294

Turktown 258
Twain, Mark 62
Twenty-fifth Infantry Division 173,
179, 365
Tyfoon 11, 85

U

Uğurluoğlu, Gen Orhan 296
U.S. Border Patrol 282
Underwood, Jack 86-87, 102, 113,
214, 301-302, 369
United Auto Workers 219
United Nations Memorial Cemetery
244-45
University of Colorado 275
US Air Force 10, 62, 217, 263-265,
365, 367, 371
US Air Force Reserve 264-265
US Marine Corps Reserve/Reservist
31-32, 40, 44, 65, 219, 262-64,
276, App. A
USNS Gordon 243-44, 248-50
USNS Randall 80-82, 84, 90, 379
USS Consolation 204
USS Missouri 22, 25-26, 28, 305
USS New Jersey 305-306
USS Texas 108
USSR 64

V

Van Fleet, Gen James 345
Van Sant, George 369
venereal disease 88, 232
Veterans Memorial Building 259
veterans organizations 269, 276-77,
279-80, 293, 295, 371
Vic (see Knabel)
Vietnam 61, 144, 266-67, 269, 273,
299
Vittori, Joseph 208, 213, 343

W

Wŏn 229-30
Wŏnju 166, 231-33, 283

387

CPSIA information can be obtained
at www.ICGtesting.com
Printed in the USA
LVHW111738310119
605945LV00004B/801/P